Joseph Edkins

Religion in China

Containing a Brief Account of the Three Religions of the Chinese, with Observations

on the Prospects of Christian Conversion Amongst that People

Joseph Edkins

Religion in China
Containing a Brief Account of the Three Religions of the Chinese, with Observations on the Prospects of Christian Conversion Amongst that People

ISBN/EAN: 9783337168612

Printed in Europe, USA, Canada, Australia, Japan

Cover: Foto ©Lupo / pixelio.de

More available books at **www.hansebooks.com**

RELIGION IN CHINA;

CONTAINING

A BRIEF ACCOUNT OF THE THREE RELIGIONS OF THE CHINESE:

WITH

OBSERVATIONS ON THE PROSPECTS OF CHRISTIAN CONVERSION AMONGST THAT PEOPLE.

BY

JOSEPH EDKINS, D.D.

AUTHOR OF "A GRAMMAR OF THE SHANGHAI DIALECT," "OF THE CHINESE COLLOQUIAL LANGUAGE, COMMONLY CALLED MANDARIN," "CHINA'S PLACE IN PHILOLOGY," "THE CHINESE CHARACTERS," ETC.

Second Edition.

BOSTON:
JAMES R. OSGOOD AND COMPANY,
(*Late Ticknor & Fields, and Fields, Osgood, & Co.*)
1878.

PREFACE TO SECOND EDITION.

THE history of the Chinese religions is replete with instruction. They have developed themselves from bases which are entirely Asiatic. Partly of native origin, and partly Indian, they have grown up quite independently of Judaism and of Christianity.

The nomenclature and fundamental ideas of Confucianism and of early Taouism are purely native, and bear testimony to the fact of clear moral distinctions, a strong appetite for legend, and a deep love of traditional religion. The Buddhism of India transplanted into a colder climate and adapted to the habits of a practical and unimaginative people, yet bears traces through all its immense ramifications of Aryan origin.

To show how the tree of religion in China has gradually attained its present size and shape is the object of this little book. Its root is native, and its principal branch has always continued so. But a mighty branch of foreign origin has been grafted in the old stock. The metaphysical religion of Shakyamuni was added to the moral doctrines of Confucius. Another process may then be witnessed. A native twig was grafted in the Indian branch. Modern Taouism has grown up on the model supplied by Buddhism. That it is possible to observe the *modus operandi* of this repeated grafting, and to estimate the amount of gain and loss to the people of China, resulting from the varied religious teaching which they have thus received, is a circumstance of the greatest interest to the investigator of the world's religions. This little book contains a brief sketch of a very wide subject. Only the main features could be embraced. It is hoped, however, that no very important points have been entirely omitted.

If Professor Max Müller succeeds in making the study of religions as popular as he has done that of Comparative Philology, the field for research presented by China may soon be worked by many new investigators. Meantime this book may continue to serve as a brief manual to the subject it treats for some years to come.

Those interested in the progress of the Christian missionary enterprise have here the means of judging what sort of work has to be done in China.

Ancestral worship is seen taking very much the place of a religion, and duty to parents needs, therefore, to be placed on the Christian footing. Reverence to heaven and earth is commonly inculcated, and instead of it has to be substituted the worship of the Supreme, Eternal God by every human being. The duty of man to man is very fully laid down. It is requisite for the Christian teacher to class all human duties in subordination to the love of God. The future life as presented to the eye of the popular religious consciousness does not command intelligent faith, because Buddhism has no confidence in its own teaching on this point. The Chinese will find in the Christian doctrine of the future life that which will help them to change vagueness and uncertainty for assured hope. So also with redemption as taught by Buddhists. There is no solidity in it. It reduces itself to abstractions and fine distinctions in words. Its indefiniteness is in strong contrast to the Christian redemption, which finding man beset with evil, holds out to him the strong hand of a divine deliverer, and makes him both virtuous and happy.

Thirty-five years have gone by since China was opened. Missionary progress was at first very slow. In some cities many summers and winters passed before the occurrence of a single baptism. After fifteen years a thousand converts rewarded the labours of the missionaries. Another fifteen years saw this number increased to ten thousand. The growth of the Christian element is now seen steadily advancing.

The number of points at which the work of the Protestant missions is carried forward is rapidly increasing, and the same is true of those of the Romish Church, which count their adherents by hundreds of thousands.

Among the causes of the more frequent baptisms that we hear of in most of the districts where missionaries are labouring at the present time, are the greater peace of the country during the last few years, and the fact that the local authorities and persons of influence understand better than before that the acceptance of Christianity is not a crime against the law. Wrongs inflicted on Christians have in several instances been rectified, and there is not so much fear felt as there was that baptism must involve very much suffering.

One of the concessions secured by Sir Thomas Wade in the negotiations of 1876, with Le-hung-chang, Governor-General of Chile, was the posting in all public places through the country of an imperial proclamation respecting the murdering of Mr. Margary. This is found to have a beneficial effect on the people, as making it their duty to look on foreigners as friends. Several instances have lately occurred of persons asking for baptism being led to think of it through this proclamation.

We can judge best of the prospect of the spread of Christianity in China by casting an eye on those districts where Christian communities have been gathered. They are extending themselves in many places with no small rapidity. In some parts the village population has during recent years shown a tendency to adopt new religious ideas, combined with the prohibition of opium and tobacco smoking, worship without images, and obedience in regard of doctrine to some spiritual guide. In the neighbourhood of Peking there are several such associations, all of modern origin. In some the abandonment of opium-smoking is rigidly enforced. Many persons follow the practice of these sects for a few months or years, and then, on being urged by the Christians to join them, they yield without much difficulty, saying that they did not in the new association they had entered realise the good they had expected.

There is a better prospect of progress in the village population than in the cities, because the influence of the literary class is little felt in country places. The attitude of the cultured class for the present is not favourable towards Christianity, and their policy is to say nothing about it. Most of the educated will read books on Western science, geography, and politics with much more willingness than on our religion. Illustrations on this subject will be found in the following chapters.

The first edition of this work was published in 1859, and has been long out of print. Four chapters are now added. One of these chapters contains a description of imperial worship. The other three are an account of a journey to Woo-tai-shan, a celebrated seat of Buddhist worship, and very popular place of pilgrimage. The book has been revised throughout.

PEKING, *October* 1877.

CONTENTS.

CHAPTER I.
INTRODUCTORY.

Interest of the subject—Confucius: what he did and aimed at—Laou-tsoo, the founder of Taouism—Buddhism: distinguished from Brahmanism and Lamaism—Early introduction of Christianity into China—Prospects of Christian missions in China—Opium   1

CHAPTER II.
IMPERIAL WORSHIP.

Prayer by Shun-che at the altar of Heaven and Earth at the establishment of the Manchoo dynasty—Three annual sacrifices at the altar of Heaven—Temple and altar of Heaven described—Burnt sacrifice offerings and libations—Burning of the prayer—Sacrifice to Earth—Burning of offerings—Notions on sacrifices—Worship of ancestors—Temple of ancestors—Offerings—Sacrifices to the gods of grain and land   18

CHAPTER III.
TEMPLES.

Confucian temple—Sacrifices to Confucius—Idea of these temples funereal—Temples to virtuous women—Temple to agricultural divinities—Buddhist monasteries: their idea: placed amidst fine scenery—Teen-tae—Monasticism—Taouist temples: idea of their construction—Temples of state gods—Imperial lectures   39

CHAPTER IV.

CONFLICT OF RELIGIOUS PARTIES IN CHINA.

Controversy between the followers of Confucius and those of Buddha and Taou—Government protests against idolatry—Feeling of the Confucianists respecting idolatry—Controversies among the Confucianists themselves . . 50

CHAPTER V.

HOW THREE NATIONAL RELIGIONS COEXIST IN CHINA.

China a field for observing the conflict of moral and religious ideas—The Chinese readily conform to three religions, which are all national, although based on different principles. The three religions are distinguished—Confucianism as moral—Taouism as materialistic—Buddhism as metaphysical—Scene in a Taouist temple—All three religions are supported by authority 55

CHAPTER VI.

INFLUENCE OF BUDDHISM ON CHINESE LITERATURE, PHILOSOPHY, AND SOCIAL LIFE.

Praise of Buddhism by the poets—Monastery of Teen-tso described by Taou-han—Influence on the philosophy of Choo-foo-tsze—Doctrine of Tae-keih—Mr. Cooke and Commissioner Yeh—Denial of Divine personality the effect of Buddhism—The Chinese really believe in a personal God—Name for God—Asserted identity of Buddhism with Confucianism—Chinese latitudinarianism—Influence on the worship of ancestors—A funeral procession—Faith in a future state 67

CHAPTER VII.

INFLUENCE OF BUDDHISM ON CHINESE LITERATURE AND SOCIAL LIFE CONTINUED.

A modern Hangchow author commenting on European astronomy, compares the European astronomers with the inventors of the Buddhist cosmogony—A Soochow author criticises Matthew Ricci and Copernicus: his views on the future state: denies the Buddhist and Taouist doctrine—Suitableness of Christianity to his mental condition—The Buddhism of private life at Soochow—Interior of a mandarin's dwelling—Common belief in a former life, and in incarnations—Buddhist phrases adopted into the language—Terms for heaven and hell, charity, retribution, &c. . 79

CHAPTER VIII.

CONFUCIAN AND BUDDHIST NOTIONS OF GOD.

Primitive Chinese conceptions of God and of spirits—Worship of heaven and earth—Their ideas on Divine attributes and on creation—Buddhist notions of God—Fuh and Poosa take the place of God—Buddhism is atheistic . . . 91

CHAPTER IX.

TAOUIST NOTIONS OF GOD.

Gods of the sea and the tides—Star-gods—Sublimated essences of matter transformed into planets and into divinities—connection of alchemy and astrology—Incarnations of star-gods—Wen-chang, Tow-moo, Kwei-sing, Pole-star, stated to be identical with God—Materialistic theory of creation—Taouist genii, Sien-jin—Buddhist element in Taouist mythology—Buddhist and Taouist trinity—Intellectual divinities—Yuh-hwang-Shangte, god of riches—San-kwan—Liturgical works—State gods . . . 105

CHAPTER X.

MORALITY OF THE CHINESE.

Fame of the Chinese moralists—What is the Confucian morality?—Controversy on the universal obligation to love—View of Mih-tsze—Controversy on human nature—Chinese education moral—Present moral condition of China—Moral influence of Buddhism—Klaproth praises Buddhism—Preservation of animal life—Denial of God and of Divine law—Buddhist almsgiving—Taouist doctrine of moral retribution in this life . . . 117

CHAPTER XI.

NOTIONS ON SIN AND REDEMPTION.

An old man's confession—Confucius admitted defect in every man—Buddhist consciousness of sin—Bodily calamities retribution for sin—Confucian notion of honour—Forgiveness on repentance—Buddhist notion of redemption through monastic discipline—Redemption consummated in the Nirvana—The ten vices—Forgiveness on prayer and fasting—The mute priest—Buddha as the redeemer—Taouist notions of sin 129

CHAPTER XII.

NOTIONS ON IMMORTALITY AND FUTURE JUDGMENT.

Silence of Confucius on immortality—Taouist conceptions of the soul as material tend to the denial of immortality—Buddhism advocates strongly the immateriality and immortality of the soul—Chinese word for soul, Shin, means invisible substance—What does ancestral worship show?—Three phases in the Buddhist view of the future state—Transmigration—The six states of the metempsychosis—Yen-lo-wang, the Hindoo Yama, god of death—The Nirvana: corresponds to our doctrine of immortality, and yet amounts to annihilation—The paradise of the Western heaven—The Taouist heaven of the genii—Star palaces—Terrestrial paradises 142

CHAPTER XIII.

CHINESE OPINIONS ON CHRISTIANITY.

Objections to Christianity—Its prohibition of ancestral worship—Its facts denied—Use of Syrian and Jewish monuments in defence of them—The morality of the Bible—Exclusiveness of Christianity — National prejudice—Charge of borrowing from Buddhism 153

CHAPTER XIV.

ROMAN CATHOLIC MISSIONS.

Numerous converts—Their ideas of Protestantism—Village communities—Schools—Seminaries for native priests—Life of the European priests—Discussion with one of them—They give little attention to literature . . 166

CHAPTER XV.

MOHAMMEDANS, JEWS, AND WOO-WEI BUDDHISTS.

Chinese Mohammedans numerous in the north—Charged by the Chinese with borrowing from Buddhism—Criticisms on Mohammed—Jews at Kai-fung-foo near to extinction—Woo-wei Buddhists: use no images: their sincerity . 178

CHAPTER XVI.

THE TAIPING INSURRECTION.

Began in a religious movement—Intermingling of fanaticism—Not impostors—Their opposition to idolatry—Their mixed character—Unpopularity—Results of this movement—An interview with one of them—Hope for the Protestant missions—Prospects of Christian conversion 189

CHAPTER XVII.

JOURNEY TO WOO-TAI-SHAN COMMENCED.

Left Peking on day of imperial marriage—Bales of cotton—Paved roads—Monumental gateway—Chinese inn—Loess formation—Cho-chow—Deification of Kwan-te—Slow spread of knowledge—Pau-ting-foo—Pilgrim Lamas—A fair—Tricks of mules—Plank bridges—Manufacture of earthenware jars—Vaccination—Native politeness—Exchange of money—Lung-tsiuen-kwan—Village combination against robbery 201

CHAPTER XVIII.

JOURNEY TO WOO-TAI-SHAN CONTINUED.

Lung-tsiuen-kwan passed — Monastery of Arshan-bolog—Another, Tai-loo-sze—A reader of the Bible—Threshing oats—Overshot mill—Woo-tai on a cold frosty morning—Dara-ehe—Manjoosere seated on a lion—Worship of Chi-chay, an ancient Chinese Buddhist—Readers of Mongol—Monastery of the Seven Buddhas—Image of Ochirwani—Poo-sa-ting—Present from the chief Lama—Old relics of Buddha—Temple of Ubegun Manjoosere—Legends—View of the valley—Temple of Dara-ehe—Sacred dance—Number of Lamas at Woo-tai—Soles of Buddha's feet—Mongol women as pilgrims—Rich temples—Daily life of Lamas 223

CHAPTER XIX.

JOURNEY FROM WOO-TAI-SHAN TO PEKING.

Splendid view from top of Pei-tai—Extent of the Woo-tai mountains—Ten thousand feet high—Kanghe's panegyric—Thoughts of pilgrims—Heng-shan, the sacred mountain of the Confucianists—Asked for our passports—Selling Christian books—Deep clefts in the loess formation—The Great Wall at Ping-hing-kwan — Numerous beasts of burden—State of the people—Wages—Temple to Laou-kiun in a pass—Temple to Kwan-te—A Buddhist advertisement—Great Wall towers of A.D. 1576—Tsze-king-kwan—A beautiful valley—The fruits of good and bad actions are not hidden—A Buddhist doctrine capable of being applied to Christian teaching . . 242

RELIGION IN CHINA.

CHAPTER I.

INTRODUCTORY.

No richer field for examination is presented to inquiring men at the present time than China. The barriers of that exclusiveness that have so long hindered the investigations of travellers, and checked the progress of Christian missions and of lawful commerce, are now broken down. The Chinese national spirit deliberately placed itself in direct hostility to the introduction of foreign customs and ideas. The great wall that forms the northern boundary of the Empire is the emphatic emblem of this national exclusiveness. It is so as much in its failure to attain its object as in the idea of its original construction. Several times has a Tartar race broken through that ineffectual barrier, and conquered the country it was intended to defend. The law against the entrance of foreigners and freedom of trade has proved equally useless; and China is now, through its whole extent, with its vast outlying dependencies, open to Europeans.

The richness of the Chinese field for inquiry is increased by the centuries of isolation in which the sons of Han have preferred to live. It is this circumstance that renders its contributions to the history of philosophy, literature, politics, and religion likely to prove full of freshness and instruction. If the opening of Japan is highly promising to Western enterprise because of the intelligence and civilisation of its inhabitants, that of China ought to be considered much more so, because the civilisation of Japan is based upon that of China. There is something that fascinates the foreign eye in the more cleanly habitations of the Japanese, and their more efficient police. They please by the quickness with which they learn to speak foreign languages, and the desire they have to acquire Western knowledge. But it should always be remembered that they can boast of no remarkable inventions and discoveries, such as printing, papermaking, the properties of the loadstone, and the composition of gunpowder. They study the books and reverence the sages and great authors of China as we do those of Greece and Rome. They derived their politics, religion, and educational system from the countrymen of Confucius, as they are now obtaining from us a knowledge of mathematics and mechanics. They must not be compared, then, with the Chinese for those things that constitute a great nation. In Eastern Asia it is only the race that spoke the Sanscrit language that can compete with China in the extent and depth of its influence.

If the Chinese are not so profound in philosophy or so acute in philology as the ancient Hindoos, and have never had a Kapila or a Panini among them, they have far excelled that people in the practical part of a nation's development. In history and politics, in social economics, in practical applications of science, and in useful inventions, they are incontrovertibly superior. The Hindoos have not yet learned to write history or to record facts; they have never been able to construct a political system for their country capable of becoming universal and permanent; and after long neglecting to imitate from the Chinese the art of printing, they are only now beginning to adopt it from Europeans. In the practical qualities that constitute the greatness of a nation the Chinese are superior.

There is everything, then, to ensure to inquiries into the literature and social condition of China interesting results. But it is necessary to limit the field of inquiry. There have been many books written on that country, with a chapter on everything. It is this circumstance that renders them unsatisfactory to those who seek information on some particular subject. For example, on the character of their religions there still remains much to be said. Those who have described China have spoken with some fulness of detail on the Confucian system, but they have given too little attention to the religions of Buddha and Taou. There is room, then, for a work like the present, which sketches the religious condition of the people at the present time from actual observation. Space is wanting in a volume like this to enter adequately into the subject. It will, perhaps, prove the forerunner of one larger in dimensions, that may do a little more justice to many of the questions that here occur to be considered, and also attempt the narrative of the birth, progress, and existing state of the religions of China.

We Europeans do not yet know China. It assumes to our imaginations a certain quaint and ludicrous aspect, which interferes with a correct opinion of its condition. The first who visited it were travellers of the Middle Ages, who, even if they had not found in it a country resembling in its civilisation Europe as it then was, would have given to their descriptions of it a mediæval colouring, because they were themselves mediæval men. The picturesque pages of Sir John Mandeville, and the more detailed accounts of Marco Polo, told such wonderful things of China, that their readers did not feel sure whether they were dealing in fact or fiction. Ever since that time the Western world has agreed to look at China through a coloured glass, as, indeed, the inhabitants of that country look at us. We see in them much that is singular and provocative of laughter, and they imagine that we exhibit characteristics just as adapted to excite the sense of risibility.

In acquiring a true view of a nation, there is nothing more helpful than an acquaintance with its religious opinions. They are too intimately connected with the spiritual and intellectual life of a nation not to be excellent exponents of its true character, and too real not to demand very grave consideration. The religions of India and China are invested with an interest high in proportion to the advancement in science and the arts of those who believe them. God has left these nations to the unassisted light of nature and reason for an unusually long period. They have had ample opportunities for doing what man by wisdom can do, to find out God as He is in Himself and in His relations to us. The history of all heathen religions is the history of the ineffectual efforts made by mankind to seek after God, to know the nature and certainty of our immortality, and to devise means of salvation. There will always be, as there always has been, the intermixture of priestcraft and kingcraft with these religions; but their prime element is found in the natural longings and hopes of a religious kind that men have. It is these that give to priests and statesmen the opportunity to use popular superstitions for their own advantage as engines of power. All this comes very clearly to view in the religions of China.

Two results will be observed to follow from a careful study of the religion of the Chinese. The real life of the nation will be better understood, and questions connected with natural theology will receive some fresh illustrations. It will be shown, by new examples, how men, who have not the light of Christianity, seek for something better than they possess, and how they try to satisfy themselves with a substitute, extremely unsatisfactory though it may be, for those truths which revelation teaches.

The most noteworthy name in all Chinese history is that of Confucius. He was one of those who, unaided, except by the light of calm reflection, read more clearly than most the lessons conveyed in the unwritten book of God's law. A true sage was Confucius, one who reasoned soberly and practically on human duty; a man to attract towards himself high veneration on account of his personal character and the subjects and manner of his teaching. He lived in the sixth century before Christ, a hundred years later than Buddha, and a hundred years earlier than Socrates. He found a religion already existing in China, with a very practical system of morals, which first and last has always given it its special character. No character in history is less mythological than Confucius. He is no demigod whose biography consists chiefly of fable, but a real person. The facts of his life, the personal aspect of the man, the places where he lived, the petty kings under whom he served, are all known. He was a critic of the ancient books composed by earlier sages. He wrote a history of the times immediately preceding his own. He edited the national book of history, the "Shoo-king." He published a collection of national poetry. He attempted to give a philosophical character to the ancient divining book called the "Yih-king,"—not surely because he had any predilection for divination, but because he revered the memory of the celebrated men who had transmitted it. So high was his respect for antiquity, that he could not think slightingly of the system of divination which had been practised by the best Chinese kings up to and beyond the boundary line between history and fable. He also edited a work upon the state religion which described the rites, popular and imperial, which are to be performed to the superior powers.

Confucius taught 3000 disciples, of whom the more eminent became influential authors. Like Plato and Xenophon, they recorded the sayings of their master, and his maxims and arguments, preserved in their works, were afterwards added to the national collection of the sacred books called the Nine Classics.

There was nothing ascetic, nothing spiritual, in the religion of Confucius. The questions to which it replied were, How shall I do my duty to my neighbour? How shall I best discharge the duty of a virtuous citizen? It attempted no reply to the higher questions, How am I connected with the spiritual world beyond what I see? What is the destiny of my immaterial nature? How can I rise above the dominion of the passions and of the senses? Another religion attempted to reply to these inquiries, but it made poor work of the answers.

Contemporary with Confucius, there was an old man, afterwards known as Laou-tsoo, who meditated in a philosophic mood upon the more profound necessities and capacities of the human soul. He did so in a way that Confucius, the prophet of the practical, could not well comprehend. He conversed with him once, but never repeated his visit, for he could not understand him. Laou-tsoo recommended quiet reflection. Water that is still is also clear, and you may see deeply into it. Noise and passion are fatal to spiritual progress. The stars are invisible through a clouded sky. Nourish the perceptive powers of the soul in purity and rest. A philosopher, called Chwang-chow, who seconded him in these researches, was not only very meditative and fond of soaring high in the region of pure ideas, but was also sarcastic and controversial. He threw ridicule on the want of philosophical depth exhibited by Confucius, and extolled the doctrine of Taou, the name which the system of Laou-tsoo had assumed. Their followers were called Taouists; but it was not said by the leaders of the new sect how their principles should be practically carried out, so that their disciples were left to choose what discipline and mode of operation they pleased to constitute the religious life and to effect its objects. They became alchemists, astrologers, and geomancers, or else they adopted the hermit life. It was not till many years after that they imitated, from the Buddhists, the monastic system and idol worship.

It was in the first century of the Christian era that Buddhism entered China from India. In obedience to a dream, the Emperor Ming-te sent ambassadors to the West to bring back a god from thence. They returned with an image of Buddha; and soon after some monks from the banks of the Ganges came to the Chinese court to propagate their religion. During several centuries this new faith struggled for existence and influence in the country. The emperors treated it with alternate patronage and persecution. The Buddhists from India came peaceably, teaching the Chinese to revere their pompous ritual and their placid, benevolent, and thoughtful divinities. They spread among them the doctrine of the separate existence of the soul, and its transmigration into the bodies of animals. They also pleased their imaginations with splendid pictorial scenes of far-away worlds, filled with light, inhabited by Buddhas, Bodhisattwas, and angelic beings, and richly adorned with precious stones, charming animals, and lovely flowers. In this way they enticed the Chinese into idolatry.

The difference between Buddhism and Brahmanism consists very much in this. The Buddhists place the popular Hindoo divinities in a very humble position. They allow them to exist, but they give them very little power; they are made to act as listening pupils or as keepers of the door to Buddha and his disciples. The common Hindoos suppose these same divinities, Brahma, Seeva, Shakra, &c., to have very great influence, and to be constantly exercising a control over human affairs. They erect temples specially to them, deprecating their anger, and earnestly desiring their protection. The Buddhists pay them no such honours. There is no terror to them in the name of a god. They believe that higher power belongs to Buddha, the self-elevated man. In this there is one essential difference between the two religions.

There is a remarkable, though a less, distinction between the Buddhism of China and of Tibet. In regard to philosophy there is little or no difference; but in Tibet there is a hierarchy which exercises political power. In China this could not be. The Grand Lama and many other

Lamas in Mongolia and Tibet assume the title of "Living Buddha." In him most of all Buddha is incarnate, as the people are taught to think. He never dies. When the body in which Buddha is for the time incarnate ceases to perform its functions, some infant is chosen by the priests who are intrusted with the duty of selecting, to become the residence of Buddha, till, in turn, it grows up to manhood and dies. No Buddhist priest in China pretends to be a "living Buddha," or to have a right to the exercise of political power. In Tibet, on the other hand, the Grand Lama, as chief of the "living Buddhas," not only holds the place of the historical Buddha, long since dead, acting as a sort of high-priest, he also exercises sovereignty over the country of Tibet, ruling the laity as well as the clergy, and being only subordinate to the lord paramount, the Emperor of China.

In the study of Buddhism, the distinction between the northern and southern form should be always kept in view. It is to Burnouf that we owe the first clear separation of these two chief parties into which the Buddhists are divided. The priests of Ceylon, Birmah, and Siam have their sacred books in the Pali language, which is later in age than the Sanscrit. The monks of Nepaul, Tibet, China, and the other northern countries where this religion is professed, either preserve the books of their religion in Sanscrit, or have translations made immediately from Sanscrit. Sanscrit is the mother of Pali, and was spoken quite late in some of the mountainous kingdoms of Northern India. Another great distinction is in the books themselves. The fundamental books of both the great Buddhist parties appear to be the same, but the northern Buddhists have added many important works professing to consist of the sayings of Buddha, yet in reality fictitious. They belong to the school called the Great Development School, which is so denominated to distinguish it from the Lesser Development School, common to the north and the south. In the additions made by the northern Buddhists are included the fiction of the Western Paradise and the fable of Amitabha and Kwan-yin, the Goddess of Mercy. These personages are exclusively northern, and are entirely unknown to the south of Nepaul. In the south the Hindoo traditions in respect to cosmogony and mythology are adhered to more rigidly; while in the north a completely new and far more extensive universe, with divinities to correspond, is represented to exist in the books, and is believed to exist by the people.

The Buddhism of Mongolia is derived from Tibet, as that of Corea, Japan, and Cochin China is from China. There are no more devout adorers of the Grand Lama than the Mongols, and on account of the religious predilections of these rude tribes, the Tartar emperors have always paid great respect to the priests who follow the Tibetan form of Buddhism. Several large monasteries exist at Peking and at Woo-tae-shan-in-shanse, where many thousand Tibetan and Mongolian *lamas* (the Tibetan name for monk) are supported at the expense of the Government. In the countries to the east of China, the translations made from Sanscrit into Chinese are employed. The names of divinities are also preserved, as are the schools into which the Chinese Buddhists have become divided on account of their differences in opinion on matters of philosophy.

All these forms of Buddhism have come from a common origin. It was Shakyamuni, who, according to some authorities, lived in the seventh century before Christ, that instituted the monastic life of Buddhism and the practice of public preaching. The Buddhists of China very seldom now discharge the duty of public preaching, but the name is kept up, and a room in the monasteries is set apart for it. This great religious leader lived to a ripe old age, and taught many disciples. His doctrines spread rapidly during his life and after his death. His remains were universally revered as eminently sacred, and worthy of religious adoration. A hair, a tooth, a piece of bone, a particle of hair in a transformed state, were preserved in temples, or had costly tombs erected over them or near them. This was the origin of the pagodas of China. A pagoda is an ornamental tomb erected over the remains of a Buddhist priest, or intended for the safe keeping of holy relics. This original design has, however, often been departed from, and buildings of this sort are erected in many cases as ornaments to monasteries, and because the neighbours believe that in the presence of a pagoda they have security from certain calamities that might befall their agriculture, their trade, or their dwellings.[1]

After some time Buddhism became the favourite religion of the kings of India. Buddha himself, the historical person distinguished with that title, belonged to the Kshatrya, or royal caste, which predisposed them in his favour. But early in the Christian era the Brahmans exerted themselves to destroy the new religion that had sprung up in India. They succeeded at last in driving it out of Hindostan. This persecution led to the wide propagation of Buddhism in the neighbouring countries. When the Chinese Heuen-tsang visited the sacred places of his religion, near Benares and Patna, in the seventh century, he found that Buddhism had very much declined. It was no long time afterwards that it almost entirely disappeared from India.

The chapters of this work are a series of sketches, illustrative of the religious condition of the Chinese as affected by the mutual relation of these three religions to each other. There are other religions in China, and something is also said of them; but these three are far the most influential in point of numbers and social position.

Researches into the religions of mankind have a high interest of their own; no subject out of the domain of pure truth can have more. But perhaps the most important circumstance in studies of this nature is the bearing

---

[1] Many details on the subject of pagodas are collected by Mr. Milne in his work "Life in China."

that they have upon the future spread of Christianity. These systems take the place in the belief of mankind that ought to be held by the doctrines of the Bible. In subverting the ancient idolatries of Europe, learned arguments against them and apologies for Christianity were written. To overthrow the religions of the East, the Christian advocate there must make great use of the press. The careful study of the articles of a heathen's faith, and of the superstitions to which his religious susceptibilities cling, becomes necessary. The work now in the reader's hands is a sort of introduction to these studies in the Chinese field.

England has now opened China to the Christian world. The attention of the statesman, the merchant, and the man of science, is drawn to it as a country that must henceforth be the scene of increased European enterprise. Commerce must thrive there in a growing ratio. Travellers in pursuit of new information in geography, geology, and natural history must be attracted there from all countries where these sciences are studied with zeal. Various foreign powers will struggle there for predominating influence. None of these different classes of men who visit China, or study it through books, can be expected to pass by its religious condition; but this subject is most important of all to those who desire to see the Christian faith becoming triumphant there over all opposing systems.

Christianity was said, by some of the early Romish missionaries, to have been introduced into China by the Apostle Thomas. This statement, they said, there was evidence for in the traditions of the Chinese. The Buddhists speak of a celebrated ascetic named Tamo as having come from India by sea early in the sixth century. His full name in Sanscrit was Bodhidharma. There is no want of particular information respecting him as to his religious opinions and his biography. There were at the time 3000 Hindoos in China helping to propagate the Buddhist faith. The early Romish missionaries, having very insufficient information on Chinese history and religions, caught at the name Tamo as a Chinese form of the word Thomas, and the description of his personal character, as a severe ascetic and worker of miracles, decided them in regarding him as identical with the Christian apostle.

Whether Christianity was preached in that country before the time of the Syrian Christians we do not know. The Jews arrived there much earlier than the Nestorians. If there were also teachers of Christianity, all historical traces of them are wanting till the Tang dynasty. What we know of the Nestorian missions extends from A.D. 636 to 781, the period included in the Chinese monument erected by the converts of those missions, and containing a short history of them, with an abstract of the Christian religion. This monument, found buried in the soil two centuries ago, shows that though afterwards they declined and disappeared, it was not from want of zeal in the first missionaries. For the first century and a half they extended themselves rapidly. Their bishops and archbishops were appointed from the schools in Mesopotamia, the headquarters of the missions. It was the Syrian missionaries that first taught Christianity to the Mongols, and introduced among them the art of writing. The present Mongolian alphabet, which is that used by the Manchoos in China, is a modification of the Syrian. Prester John was a Tartar prince, who became the neophyte of the same zealous missionaries. Like the other Oriental churches, the Nestorians gradually lost their ardent faith and evangelistic enthusiasm. Their missionaries ceased to visit China, and the converts there gradually diminished, till the last remains of them were lost in the troubles that in the fourteenth century attended the expulsion of the Mongols from China. Native authors speak of three foreign sects as having existed in the seventh century in China: the Roman (Ta-tsin),[1] the Manicheans (Mani), and the Mahom-

[1] Some Romanist writers translate Ta-tsin, Judæa. Mr. Wylie, in his interesting and valuable notes on the Nestorian tablet at Se-ngan-foo, prefers to render it Syria.

medans. By the "Roman" they mean the Nestorian Christians, who belonged, at the time they reached China, to the Eastern Roman Empire, and who assumed the name that they found already in use in China to designate the part of the world from which they came. It is curious to find traces of the Manicheans in China. The word Mani can scarcely mean any other religionists than they, and church history tells how widely they were spread in the time of Augustine. A circumstance still more curious is, that Manes derived part of his system from the Buddhists. So Neander tells us. Resident in Persia, he had Christianity on the west, Buddhism on the east, and the system of Zoroaster in his own locality. His religion was derived from these three sources. Referring to Chinese history of a time very little later, we find notices of his sect, of the Parsees or fire-worshippers, of Christianity in the Nestorian form, and of Buddhism, existing side by side. Buddhism only was become the popular faith through all China. The other three were but striving for existence, and in a few centuries they entirely died out.

The next attempt made to introduce Christianity was by the Papal missionaries of the Mongolian period. One result of the extraordinary career of Zinghis Khan was the opening of the way for travellers to and fro across the vast plains of Central Asia. What was impracticable while the nomad races of Tartary were without a head, and while Asia was split into small kingdoms, became easy of accomplishment when the short-lived empire of the Mongols was formed. It was then that the Polos resided for some time in China, and that our own Sir John Mandeville served as a soldier for several years under the Emperor of China. It was then, also, that Archbishop John of Peking, a missionary from the Pope, attempted, during a lengthened residence, to establish a permanent mission in the metropolis of the Grand Khan.

In the time of Queen Elizabeth, the Roman Catholic Church recommenced its efforts to propagate Latin Christianity in China. This time they were more successful, for they made greater exertions than before. It was the age for new enterprises. America and the way to India had been discovered a hundred years before, and missions had been founded in the Portuguese settlements in the East. The system of Copernicus had been published to the world, and Protestantism was victorious in Germany. The wonderful Cathay was once more open to the knowledge of Europeans, and there was a vast nation of infidels to be converted to the true faith. While Catholicism was on the wane in Europe, it might be extended by missionary operations in Asia. The Jesuits resolved to enter on this new field. Enthusiastic men have never been wanting to enlist under the banner of Jesuitism. They are charmed by the grandeur of its plans and the glory of the life to which it invites them. The Papacy was sagacious enough to see that youths of noble and self-denying zeal could have assigned to them no more suitable occupation than that of preaching Christianity in China and other heathen lands. Hence there came a succession of men from the Jesuit schools, who, for high scientific culture and devotion to their religion and their order, have not been surpassed by any body of missionaries in any age. The character of the converts belonging to the Romanist communion at the present day in China is probably superior to what it is in India and in some other heathen countries, for many among them may be met with who have a good acquaintance with the doctrines and facts of Christianity, while the Roman Catholic converts in India are, as a class, extremely degraded. Unfortunately, Catholicism must everywhere carry with it the worship of the Madonna, the masses for the dead, the crucifix, and the rosary. Some of the books the Jesuits have published in Chinese contain the purest Christian truth; but it is an unhappy circumstance that they must be accompanied by others which teach frivolous superstition. We should be better satisfied on meeting with converts of enlightened minds and apparently devout feeling, if we did not meet with many more who, instead of revealing intelligence and piety, have nothing to show as evidence of their Christianity but a crucifix and a picture.

The prospect of the introduction of true Bible Christianity into China is upon the whole highly favourable and encouraging. The number of conversions that have taken place in the free ports since the war of 1842 will well bear comparison with those of other countries where missionaries labour. Among the native preachers that have been trained to assist the foreign missionaries, there are some devoted men and eloquent expounders of Bible truth. At Amoy, five hundred converts abstain from worldly business every Sabbath-day, and meet for praise and prayer in God's house. Near to Ningpo there are some interesting little communities that have sprung up amidst the village population through the operations of native catechists. In the region called Sanpoh, noted for the roughness of its inhabitants, the labours of these men have been so far aided with the blessing of God that the nucleus of two or three bodies of village Christians has been originated, which are likely to thrive in respect of numbers and of zeal. In the neighbourhood of Shanghai, missionaries have frequently succeeded in effecting a residence in several cities and towns. On two occasions the British consul has, at the instance of Chinese government officers, recalled one of his countrymen to Shanghai. But several residences of some months in duration have been effected, and the rite of baptism has been administered to converts in three cities and several villages as the result of these rural efforts. At the present time the work of conversion progresses in an increasing ratio, and there is much reason to take a sanguine view of the probable spread of Bible Christianity in China.

There is a hindrance to the Protestant missions which did not meet the agents of the propaganda. The practice of opium-smoking, entailing much personal suffering and family wretchedness, is a great hindrance to the success of missionary efforts. The introduction of opium by foreign merchants has given to the nations engaged in the traffic an ill name among the Chinese. England has the greatest share in the dislike that the Chinese feel for those who bring opium to their shores. They remember that we fought for freedom of trade in this deleterious article of commerce; and now they will remember also that it was through our influence, employed in the hour of our success, that their Government was induced to class it with legitimate imports. These things grievously interfere with our good reputation among the people of that country, and lead them to feel a prejudice against our religion. Missionaries from Great Britain have not a fair field for their efforts in China while the national honour is still stained by the cultivation of the poppy and the preparation of opium under the immediate direction of the Indian Government. If free trade may not be interfered with, our Government, at least, should not make the providing of opium for the Chinese market a national act. Every British missionary would rejoice if he could say to those who so often ask him why his countrymen bring opium, "Our nation has nothing to do with the traffic or with the preparation of this drug." He could meet the questions and taunts of his Chinese auditors far better if he were able so to speak.

This is not the place to enter upon the opium question, except to show, as has just been done, its bearing on our missionary operations. On these its effects are too mischievous and too painful not to produce depressing thoughts in every missionary's mind. But a correction needs to be made of the mistaken opinion, that the Chinese have rendered opium contraband only for fear of losing their silver. This error has been committed by some who, with the means of information at their command, ought to have known the Chinese better. Mr. Crawfurd said once at Leeds, in a lecture on China, "The moral branch of the argument, as used by the Chinese, is a mere make-weight to assist the real one, which is, that opium was robbing China of the precious metals."

These words, used by one who had been many years resident in the East, were adapted to convey quite a wrong impression, and to do harm in proportion to the experience and authority of the speaker. The reason of the antipathy of the Chinese to opium is, that it injures the moral character of individuals, involves them in habits which dissipate the wealth of families, robs men of the right government of themselves, renders them indolent and sensual, and too often occasions them a wretched existence and an early grave. Certainly there has been quite enough in the rapid spread of opium-smoking to alarm the Chinese. If such a habit had grown up in our own country in as short a time, the alarm with which it would have been witnessed would have been caused far more by deep moral and religious sentiments than by the circumstance that it would seriously affect our money market. Much more must it be so with the Chinese, who thoroughly understand what morality is, while they know little of the modern science of political economy.

CHAPTER II.

IMPERIAL WORSHIP.

The imperial worship of China is ancient, elaborate, and solemn. At the establishment of each new line of emperors fresh regulations in regard to sacrifices are enjoined, but it is usual to follow old precedents to a very large extent.

The study of the old Chinese worship is specially interesting, because it takes us back to the early history of the Chinese people, and introduces us to many striking points of comparison with the patriarchal religion of the Old Testament, and with the worship of the kings of Nineveh, Babylon, and Egypt.

In the year 1644, at Peking, the first of the Manchu line of emperors, on the first day of the tenth lunar month, proceeded to the altar of Heaven and Earth to offer sacrifice, and announce that he had mounted the throne of China.

The prayer in which this announcement was made was in great part as follows:—

"I, the son of heaven, of the Great Pure dynasty, humbly as a subject dare to make an announcement to imperial Heaven and sovereign Earth. Though the world is vast, God[1] looks on all without partiality. My imperial grandfather received the gracious decree of Heaven, and founded a kingdom in the East, which became firmly established. My imperial father succeeding to the king-

---

[1] God is here *Te*, an abbreviation of Shang-te, the ancient name for God in China. It is used in place of the second personal pronoun, which could not be employed without a breach of reverence.

dom, extended it till it grew wider and more powerful. I, Heaven's servant, in my poor person, became the inheritor of the dominion they transmitted.

"When the Ming dynasty was coming to its end, traitors and men of violence appeared in crowds, involving the people in misery. China was without a ruler. It fell to me reverentially to accept the responsibility of continuing the meritorious work of my ancestors. I saved the people, exterminated those who oppressed them, and now, in accordance with the desire of all, I fix the urns of empire at Yen-king at present. I am told by all that the divine assistance must not be left unrecognised or repaid by ingratitude, and that I ought to ascend the throne, and restore order to the ten thousand kingdoms.

"I, receiving Heaven's favour, and in agreement with the wishes of the people, on this the first day of the tenth month, announce to Heaven that I have ascended the throne of the empire, that the name I have chosen for it is the Ta-tsing (Great Pure) dynasty, and that the title of my reign is, as before, Shun-che.

"I beg reverentially of Heaven and Earth to protect and assist the empire, so that calamity and disturbance may soon come to an end, and the empire enjoy universal peace. For this I humbly pray, and for the acceptance of this sacrifice."

Officers were despatched at the same time to the Temple of Ancestors, and to the altars of the spirits of Grain and Land, to offer sacrifices and make similar announcements.

The chief centre of the religious solemnities embraced in the imperial worship is the altar of Heaven. This is in the outer city of Peking, and is distant two miles from the palace.

There are two altars, the southern, which is called Yuen-kew, or "round hillock," and the northern, which has upon it a lofty temple, called Che-nien-tien, "temple for prayers for (a fruitful) year."

Beside special occasions, such as the establishment of a

dynasty, the conclusion of a successful military campaign, or the accession of an emperor, there are three regular services in each year. They are at the winter solstice, at the beginning of spring, and at the summer solstice. The first and last of these are performed on the southern altar, the second at the northern.

The spectacle is most imposing. The Emperor proceeds the evening before, drawn by an elephant, and accompanied by grandees, princes, and attendants, to the number of about two thousand. He passes several hours of the night within the park of the altar of Heaven, in a structure called Chai-kung, or Palace of Fasting, which corresponds to the "Lodge for passing the night while upon the road," mentioned[1] in the classical work "Chow-le."

Here the Emperor prepares himself by quiet thought for the sacrifice. He spends the time in silence; and, to remind him of the duty of serious meditation, a copper man fifteen inches high, attired as a Tauist priest, is carried in the procession, and placed before him on his right, as he sits in the fasting-hall. The image bears in its hand a tablet inscribed, "Fast for three days." It is intended to assist the Emperor to keep his thoughts fixed. The idea is, that if there be not pious thoughts in his mind, the spirits of the unseen will not come to the sacrifice. The three fingers of the left hand of the image are placed over the mouth, to teach silence to the monarch of three hundred millions of people while he prepares himself for the ceremony.[2]

The altar of Heaven consists of three marble terraces, circular, and ascended by twenty-seven steps. The uppermost of the three terraces is paved with eighty-one stones, arranged in circles. It is on a round stone in the centre of these circles that the Emperor kneels. Odd numbers

---

[1] Loo-tsim-che-shï, "road sleeping-house."

[2] It was Choo-tai-tsoo, founder of the Ming dynasty, who gave the order to have this image made for the purpose above stated, A.D. 1380.

only are used, and especially multiples of three and nine, in the structure of this altar.

As the visitor stands on this terrace, he sees on the north the chapel for preserving the tablets, beyond it a semicircular wall, and farther still the buildings connected with the north altar and temple. This temple is ninety-nine Chinese feet in height, and has a triple roof, with blue tiles. Both altars are ascended by four flights of steps, towards the four cardinal points. Behind the visitor, a stone's throw from the altar on the south-east, is the furnace for the burnt-sacrifice, in which a bullock is consumed to ashes. On the south-west are three lofty lantern poles, the light from which is very conspicuous in the darkness of the winter night at the solstice, when the kneeling crowd, headed by the Emperor, is engaged on the successive terraces of the altar and the marble pavement below in performing the prostrations appointed in this the most solemn act of Chinese worship.

The two altars, with the park, three miles in circuit, which surrounds them, date from A.D. 1421, when the third emperor of the Ming dynasty left Nanking, and made Peking the capital. At first Heaven and Earth were worshipped together, according to the appointment of the Emperor Tai-tsoo; but in A.D. 1531 it was decreed that there should be separate altars for Heaven and Earth.

The upper terrace of the great south altar is 220 feet in diameter, and nine feet high; the second 105 feet in diameter, and eight feet high; the third and lowest is fifty-nine feet in diameter, and eight feet one inch in height. The entire height, then, is twenty-five feet two inches, but the base is already raised five feet by a gradual ascent. The low encircling wall is roofed with blue tiles.

In place of the green porcelain furnace on the south-east for the burnt sacrifice, there was anciently an altar on the south called Tae-tan. The word *tan*, "altar," shows that in the time of the "Le-ke," one of the classics, which uses this term in describing it, it was an altar, and not a furnace.

The altar on which the Emperor kneels, and where the written prayer is burned, corresponds to the Jewish altar of incense. The furnace, or rather the altar, which it now represents, corresponds to the Jewish altar of burnt-offering. The furnace is nine feet high and seven feet wide, and is placed outside the low inner wall which surrounds the altar; and when the smoke and flames are ascending, and the odour of the burning flesh is spreading on every side, that part of the sacrificial ceremonies takes place which is called "looking at the flame" (*wang liau*).

Outside of the furnace is the outer wall, distant 150 feet from the inner. Beside it is the pit for burying the hair and blood of the victims, a ceremony instituted apparently with the idea that it would be possible in this way to convey the sacrifice to the spirits of the earth, just as the smoke and flame of the burnt-offering convey the sacrifice to the spirits of heaven.

It is impossible here to avoid seeing a striking resemblance to the Roman sacrifices which contained the burial ceremony, with a similar idea attached to it, in their worship of the terrestrial divinities.

This and the holocaust seem to link the Chinese sacrifices very closely with the ancient religions of the Western world.

The animals are slaughtered on the east side of the altar, everything appertaining to the kitchen requiring to be upon the east side.

They consist of cows, sheep, hares, deer, and pigs. Horses were formerly used, but not now.[1] The house where these animals are kept is on the north-west of the altar, near the hall in which the musicians and dancers who take part in the sacrificial ceremonies meet to practise for these occasions.

---

[1] Animals offered in sacrifice must be those in use for human food. There is no trace in China of any distinction between clean and unclean animals, as furnishing a principle in selecting them for sacrifice. That which is good for food is good for sacrifice is the principle guiding in their selection.

The idea of a sacrifice is that of a banquet; and when a sacrifice is performed to the supreme spirit of Heaven, the honour paid is believed by the Chinese to be increased by inviting other guests. The emperors of China invite their ancestors to sit at the banquet with Shang-te, the supreme ruler. A father is to be honoured as heaven, and a mother as earth. In no way could more perfect reverence be shown than in placing a father's tablet on the altar with that of Shang-te. Yet, at the same time, another idea is present: the Emperor desires, in fulfilment of the duty of filial piety, to pay the greatest possible honour to his parent. The natural love of parents, and the selfish wish to exalt their own lineage, have doubtless often had more force in the minds of emperors, when settling these matters, than any disinterested wish they might feel to honour Heaven. But then, again, they do as they are advised. The experienced and aged statesmen with whom they take counsel act according to precedent, and invariably recommend the placing of the Emperor's ancestral tablets on the altar of sacrifice with that of Shang-te. To their opinion the emperors have always assented. Of the five Tartar dynasties that have at different times ruled China, there has never been one that has not accepted the Chinese religion, and this not, it may be, from state reasons only, but because the old religion of the Tartar races was essentially the same as that of China.

On the upper terrace of the altar the tablet of Shang-te, inscribed "Hwang-tien Shang-te," is placed, facing south, immediately in front of the kneeling Emperor. The tablets of the Emperor's ancestors are arranged in two rows, facing east and west. Offerings are placed before each tablet.

Large and small millet, panicled millet and rice, are boiled as if for domestic use. Beef and pork in slices, with and without condiments, are presented in the form of soup. Salt fish, pickled fish, pickled slices of hares and of deer, pickled onions, bamboo shoots, pickled parsley and celery, pickled pork and vermicelli, come next. The condiments used in making the dishes are sesamum oil, soy, salt, pepper, anise seed, and onions.

The fruits offered are such as chestnuts, sisuphus plums, water chestnuts, and walnuts.

Wheat flour and buckwheat flour are made into balls, with sugar in the middle, and afterwards stamped so as to become flat cakes.

Three cups of *tsew*[1] are placed in front. Next comes a bowl of soup. Then follow eight rows of basons, making twenty-eight in all. They consist of fruit, basons of rice and other cereals boiled, pastry, and various dishes.

Jade stone and silk offerings intended to be burnt are placed behind these twenty-eight dishes. Then there is a whole heifer, with a brazier on each side for burning the offerings.

Behind the heifer are placed the five worshipping implements of Buddhism, namely, an urn, two candelabra, and two flower jars.

Behind these are more candelabra, and the table in the south-west corner at which the Emperor reads the prayer.

On the second terrace, on the east side, the tablet of the sun is placed, and also that of the Great Bear, the five planets, the twenty-eight constellations, and one for all the stars. On the west side is placed the tablet of the moon spirit, with those of the clouds, rain, wind, and thunder.

I do not know why some of the dishes are looked on as unsuitable for these spirits; but it is curious to notice that four of the twenty-eight dishes used in the offerings to Shang-te and to the spirits of the deceased emperors are here wanting. No jade stone offerings are presented: a full-grown bullock takes the place of the young heifer.

---

[1] *Tsew* is, in China, either distilled or not distilled. It is the Mongol and Turkish *arahi* and *arrack*, and the Japanese *sak*. The number three is expressive of honour. The same mode of showing respect is employed in the sacrifices to the Earth spirit and to the Emperor's ancestors.

The five Buddhist implements and the gold lamps and censers are all omitted.

In the offerings to the spirits of the stars, a bullock, sheep, and pig, all full grown, are included. In other respects the offerings are nearly the same as to the sun and moon.

Twelve pieces of blue silk are burnt in honour of Shang-te, and three of white in honour of the emperors.

Seventeen pieces of silk, yellow, blue, red, black, and white, are burned in honour of the spirits of the heavenly bodies, and wind and rain.

Several kinds of incense are used. All are composed of fragrant woods ground to sawdust, and then made up into bundles of sticks or pastilles of various shapes.

The Emperor is the high-priest, who acts personally or by deputy in all the public sacrifices performed for the sake of obtaining rain or securing freedom from calamities. His position then is like that of the patriarchs in the religion of Genesis. He combines the offices of chief magistrate and high-priest.

The particulars of his duty as priest of the people are such as offering prayer for a good year, presenting the offerings, and worshipping. Besides these, he previously inspects the animals in their sheds when living, and afterwards when slain and made ready for the sacrifice.

On proceeding to the robing-tent, he washes his hands and puts on sacrificial robes. He then, guided by the directors of the ceremonies, mounts the altar and stands near the kneeling cushion, while all the princes and nobles take their places on the steps and terraces of the altar or on the stone pavement below. When told to kneel, he kneels. When told to light incense and place it in the urns, he does so. When led to the tablets of his ancestors and told to kneel before each and kindle incense sticks, he does all this. He is afterwards led back to the chief tablet, and there he performs the ceremony of the three prostrations and nine knockings of the head. In this he is immediately imitated by the attendant worshippers in their various positions.

The music, which has been in course of performance by the appointed 234 musicians, stops. The Emperor is led to the table on which are placed the offerings of jade and silk which are to be burned. Here he kneels, having the heifer behind, offers the jade and silk, and rises. The officers whose duty it is to sing here interpose with a song descriptive of the presentation of the bowls of food. Other officers bring up these bowls, together with hot broth, which last they sprinkle three times on the body of the heifer. Meantime the Emperor is standing on the east side of his tent.

More music is now performed, the piece being called "The song of universal peace."

Upon this follows the performance of the ceremony of presenting the bowls of food before the various tablets by the Emperor.

Then the first cup of wine is presented, the Emperor officiating. Appropriate music is performed.

The officer in charge of the prayer places it on the table intended for this use, and it is there read by the Emperor. It is, at the sacrifice in February, couched in such terms as the following:—

"I, your subject, by hereditary succession son of heaven, having received from above the gracious decree to nourish and console the inhabitants of all regions, think with sympathy of all men, earnestly desirous of their prosperity.

"At present looking to the approach of the day *Sin* and the spring ploughing, which is about to take place, I earnestly look up, hoping for merciful protection. I bring my subjects and servants with offerings of food in abundance, a reverential sacrifice to Shang-te. Humbly I pray for thy downward glance, and may rain be granted for the production of all sorts of grain and the success of all agricultural labours."

The remainder of the prayer is an encomium upon the deceased emperors worshipped on the same occasion.

After reading this prayer, the Emperor takes it to the table for silk offerings and the jade sceptre. Here, kneeling, he places it in a casket with the silk, and then makes some more prostrations.

The second presentation of the cup of wine now takes place, and after it the third, the Emperor officiating.

The music here takes the name "The song of excellent peace," and "The song of harmonious peace."

The band of musicians on the pavement below, numerous as it is, is no larger than that of the dancers, who move in a slow step through several figures. When the songs are ended, a single voice is heard on the upper terrace of the altar chanting the words, "Give the cup of blessing and the meat of blessing." In response, the officer in charge of the cushion advances and kneels, spreading the cushion. Other officers present the cup of blessing and the meat of blessing to the Emperor, who partakes of the wine and returns them. The Emperor then again prostrates himself, and knocks his forehead three times against the ground, and then nine times more to represent his thankful reception of the wine and meat.

The assemblage of princes and nobles all imitate their lord once more at this point. An officer calls, "Remove the viands." The musicians play a piece suitable to this action, and another called the "Song of glorious peace."

The spirit of Heaven is now escorted home again to the tablet chapel on the north of the altar.

The crier then chants the words, "Carry away the prayer, the incense, the silk, and the viands, and let them be reverently taken to the Tae-tan."

Tae-tan is the old classical name of the altar of burnt-offering, a name still retained, while for long centuries the altar has given place to a furnace.

The crier calls, "Look at the burning." The proper

music is played, and the Emperor proceeds to the spot set apart as most suitable for observing the burning.

The officers upon this take the tablet on which the prayer is written, the worshipping tablet, the incense, the silk, and the viands to the green furnace, within which they are placed and burned.

At the same time the silk, incense, and viands offered to the tablets of the emperors are taken to the large braziers prepared for them, and there burned.

The ceremonies here terminate, and the Emperor returns to the palace.

The spirit of the worship may be partly judged of from the hours at which it is performed.

At the south altar it must be at midnight, because that is the hour called *Tsze*. Tsze is the first of the twelve hours, and was applied to the eleventh month, or December. The sun is at Tsze when he passes the winter solstice. The day was divided into twelve parts, because there are twelve lunations in a year. It was natural to begin counting the months from the time when the sun was at the lowest point. The time of the solstitial sacrifice of winter should be regulated on the principle that the hour Tsze is on this account most suitable.

When the spring sacrifice takes place near the beginning of the year, the time chosen at present is the first glimmering of the dawn. But formerly midnight was the hour.

The sun is worshipped at the Sun altar at four o'clock in the morning, and the moon on the Moon altar at ten in the evening.

Not having a true science of nature, the Chinese mind puts circles and symbols, and the distinction of even and odd numbers, in its place. Their philosophy is a numerical or symbolic philosophy. That learned Chinese is a rare person who can divest himself of the idea that his cycles of ten, of twelve, and of sixty, represent something substantial in nature, and may be received as necessary truth. Hence most of the Chinese are by birth and training believers in astrology. Without it they cannot be born, marry, or die. Their fortune-tellers are found to be fundamentally all astrologers and believers in numerical cycles, although they are classified as physiognomists, phrenologists, or adepts in palmistry or geomancy.

Wherever the cycles of astrology and the distinction of the male and female principle can be introduced in common life, whether in medicine, the choice of sites for houses and graves, going on a journey, or ordering a new suit of clothes, there they will be found.

It would be impossible, in fixing the hour of the sacrifices in which the Emperor takes part, that there should be a neglect of the secret laws of nature, which are believed to be brought to view in the cycles of astrology.

Something may be perceived of the ideas of the Chinese in regard to their sacrifices from the discussions which have taken place as to whether the spirits of Heaven and Earth should be worshipped together or separately. When the present temple, with its three roofs, was first made in the time of Yung-lo, it was not intended that there should be a separate altar to Earth. Two altars were made, the northern and the southern; the united worship was performed at the northern, and the colours of the three roofs of the temple erected on it were yellow, red, and blue, comprising the appropriate colours of heaven and earth. A century later a discussion was instituted on the propriety of the united worship. In consequence of this discussion, and in accordance with the opinions of the majority of those who were consulted, it was decreed that the worship of Earth should in future be separately conducted. The altar of Earth was constructed on the north side of the inner city, in an open space beyond the walls.

The character of the Chinese imperial worship at the Earth altar is substantially the same as at the altar of Heaven, except that instead of the worship of star gods and the sun and moon we have that of the spirits of mountains, rivers, and seas.

The account given by Herodotus of the religion of the ancient Persians shows that it consisted of much the same usages as those now found in the Chinese imperial worship. The great objects of nature were adored. The heavenly bodies, the mountains, and rivers, were supposed to have divinities presiding over them, and to these deities sacrifices were presented.

This characteristic comes clearly into view in the worship at the altar of Earth.

There are two terraces to the altar. One is sixty feet square, and six feet two inches high. The other is 106 feet square, and six feet high. Only even numbers are made use of in the construction of the altar. Yellow tiles are employed in roofing the walls. The steps on each of the four sides are eight in number. A ditch surrounds the altar. It is 494 feet four inches long, eight feet six inches deep, and six feet wide.

Between the altar and the ditch is a wall six feet high, and two feet thick, and within it are four open gateways. Outside of the north gateway, a little to the westward, is the pit for burying the prayer and silk, which are offered to the spirit of Earth. Beside it is the spot where the silk offered to the spirits of the emperors worshipped at the same time is burned.

On the upper terrace, when the sacrifice takes place, are arranged the tablet of the spirit of Earth facing north, and those of the emperors facing east and west.

On the lower terrace fourteen Chinese and Manchoo mountains are represented by fourteen tablets, and the seas and rivers of China each by four tablets. Half of the mountains, seas, and rivers occupy the east terrace, and half the west. The seas are simply north, south, east, and west. The mountains and rivers are worshipped by their names, and they are selected on account of their size and sacredness.

In the sacrifice to Earth, the burial of the prayer and the silk, it is to be noted, takes place at a spot on the north-west. The tablet, according to the present arrangement, faces to the north, and the spirit, therefore, has the ceremony in sight. The west is, as being on the left hand, the position of honour. The Emperor, after the presentation of the three cups of wine, is directed to proceed to a certain station on the altar where he can conveniently observe the process of burying, which here corresponds to the burning of the prayer and silk in the sacrifice to the spirit of Heaven.

The prayer is as follows :—" I, your subject, son of heaven by hereditary succession, dare to announce to How-too, the imperial spirit of Earth, that the time of the summer solstice has arrived, that all living things enjoy the blessings of sustenance, and depend for it upon your efficient aid. You are placed with imperial Heaven in the sacrifices which are now presented, consisting of jade, silk, the chief animals used for food, with various viands abundantly supplied."

The Emperors Tae-tsoo, Tae-tsung, She-tsoo, &c., are reverentially appointed to be sharers in the sacrifice.

The spirit of Earth is the only spirit beside the spirit of Heaven to whom in prayer the Emperor styles himself a "subject."

The colour of the jade presented is yellow. The prayer is written on a yellow tablet.

The twenty-eight dishes, the three cups of wine, and the solitary bowl of soup are the same as at the temple of Heaven. The gold lamps are wanting, as also the gold censers, one pair of the candelabra, and the flower-vases.

The designation Shang-te is applied to the spirit of Heaven only.

The burying of the silk is limited to the spirit of Earth. In the case of the offerings to the emperors whose tablets are on the altar with that of the spirit of Earth, they are burnt in a brazier as at the altar of Heaven.

The musical instruments are the same for the spirit of Earth as for the spirit of Heaven, viz., two kinds of stringed instruments, two kinds of flutes, &c.—sixty-four in all;

but the bell is gilt for the sake of having it yellow. The two hundred and four musicians and dancers, instead of blue, wear black robes embroidered with figures in gold. Blue, on the other hand, is the colour used in the worship of Heaven.[1]

The music is accompanied by words arranged in irregular verse. There are six lines of poetry, four of which rhyme. The poetic particle *hi* occurs in the middle of each line, dividing it into two clauses. Each line has six, seven, eight, or nine words in it. There are nine or ten pieces of poetry at each sacrifice, and they are sung to as many melodies with instrumental accompaniments.

When the emperor sends an officer to perform his duties at the sacrifice, the details are much less complex. The cup and meat of blessing, the tent, the music, and other accessories are omitted. The same omissions occur if the Emperor's son is deputed to perform the ceremonies. These omissions clearly show that a priestly character is attributed to the Emperor by virtue of his office.

The presentation of food and wine to the spirits who are worshipped indicates that the Chinese idea of a sacrifice to the supreme spirit of Heaven and of Earth is that of a banquet. There is no trace of any other idea. The burning of sacrifices does not appear to have among this people any notion of substitution. There is in the classics in the "Shoo-king," perhaps the most important of them all, a statement respecting the ancient Emperor Cheng-tang, B.C. 1800, to the effect that he acknowledged himself, in the name of the people, to be a sinner deserving punishment, and requesting that the punishment to be inflicted on the people might be inflicted instead upon him. So far as this, it may be said that substitution is familiar to the Chinese in connection with sacrifices. But the sense of life for life, the animal dying in place of man, is not known to them.

---

[1] Yellow and brown are both expressed by *hwang*. The earth colour here meant is the light brown of the soil in North China, but black is the colour of the north. The altar of Earth is the "north altar," *Pei-tan*.

The imperial worship of ancestors constitutes one of the most important portions of the official worship.

The imperial Temple of Ancestors is on the south-east of the *Woo-men*, or chief gate of the palace. It is called *Taimeaou*, the "great temple," and is divided into three principal *tien* or halls, and several smaller.

The front *tien* is used for the common sacrifice to all ancestors at the end of the year. The middle *tien* contains the most important tablets, each in its shrine. Emperors and empresses are placed in pairs. They begin with the grandfather of Shun-che. All face to the south. Ten generations are now represented. The sacrifices on the first day of the first month in each of the four seasons are offered in this hall.

Confucius said that the dead are to be sacrificed to as if living. There must, therefore, be clothing as well as food. Chests of clothing, with all articles complete, such as mats and stools, are found here carefully stored, and are presented with the sacrifices.

In front of this hall is a court, on each side of which are secondary halls containing tablets of certain meritorious persons who are appointed to be guests at the sacrificial banquets. Relatives occupy the eastern hall, and loyal officers the western.

In the court on the east is a brazier for burning the prayer offered to ancestors, and the silk offered to them and to the relatives. On the west is another brazier for burning the silk offered to meritorious officers. At the gate in front there are exhibited twenty-four ancient spears.

The back hall contains the tablets of the great-grandfather and grandmother of Shun-che, and of three generations preceding. The book from which this account is extracted was published A.D. 1721, and subsequent changes in the arrangement will, of course, be found in later editions.

The times for sacrifice are not only the first of every

third month and at the end of the year, but whenever great events occur.

The Emperor, when informed that the time has come for inspecting the prayer, proceeds to the *Paou-ho-tien* or *Chung-ho-tien*, both of them state halls in the palace. The prayer, written on a yellow tablet, is presented and approved.

The sacrifices are offered in the middle and back halls of the ancestral temple at the same time, in order that all the imperial ancestors, remote as well as near, may enjoy them.

The tablets of emperors and empresses are arranged in pairs. Each has his wife with him, and husband and wife are placed side by side. One set of offerings is presented before each married pair. Each emperor occupies the east side. On his left are placed clothing and silk. On the right of the tablet of the empress there is clothing, but no silk.

Why this distinction? Can it be that there is something peculiar in the silk? Is there some ancient idea connected with burnt-offerings which is not alluded to in the usual doctrine, " Sacrifice to the spirits as if they were living?" If this were all, why should not the silk be given to the Empress? She would need it for clothing as much as the Emperor.

Yet she shares in the silk placed near the animals, as will be seen in the following plan of the offerings :—

	TABLET OF EMPRESS.	TABLET OF EMPEROR.	Two pieces of silk.
Table and stools with clothing.	Three cups of wine.	Three cups of wine.	Table and stool with clothing.
	Two bowls of soup.	Two bowls of soup.	

		Twenty-eight dishes.	
Reader's table.	Pig.	Cow.	Sheep.
		Silk.	
	Candle.	Incense.	Candle.

The dishes are the same as those used in the sacrifices to the spirits of Heaven and Earth. They are placed before the Emperor and Empress in common.

This seems to show that the exclusion of women from the social meal is not so ancient as the time when the sacrifices were instituted. The Emperor and Empress can have their meals together when dead, though they may not when living.

The prayer is read from a table on the south-west, chosen because it is the point of greatest humility, the east being the position of honour.

An officer reads the prayer upon his knees, in the name of the Emperor. The prayer states the Emperor's descent as son, grandson, &c., as the case may be. Then follows his proper name, which is not permitted to be written or pronounced by any of his subjects. The prayer proceeds to say: "I dare announce to my ancestor that I have with care, on this first month of spring (or any other of the four seasons), provided sacrificial animals, silk, wine, and various dishes, as an expression of my unforgetting thoughtfulness, and humbly beg the acceptance of the offerings."

The prayer contains the titles of all the deceased emperors and empresses prayed to, amounting to twelve or twenty words in each instance.

Six poems are sung, each to a different melody. Some of the names of these airs are the same as those used at the sacrifices at the altar of Heaven. Each poem has eight lines of four or five words each, except the first, which has twelve lines. Six of these lines have rhymes. Here follows a specimen: "Ah! my imperial ancestors have been able to become guests with supreme heaven. Their meritorious acts in war and peace are published in all regions. I, their filial descendant, have received the decree of heaven, and my thought is to carry out the aims of those who preceded me, thus ensuring the gift of long prosperity for thousands and tens of thousands of years." This is sung when the Emperor presents the silk.

The musicians sing in the Emperor's name, and the pronouns and other peculiar terms are so employed that if he sang them he could use them as they are. This is very manifest in the following poem:—

"The virtue of these my ancestors has opened this celestial succession. I dare to say that I, their child, enjoy the complete result. The virtue I wish to make a return for is boundless as bright heaven. While with sedulous earnestness I make this third presentation of wine, my heart rejoices."

The Emperor must not call himself "your subject." He must say "your filial descendant, the Emperor."

The act of prostration embraces kneeling three times, and knocking the head nine times. The same is done by attendant officers, who imitate the Emperor's act. This ceremony is performed first at the arrival of the spirit from the shrine in which ordinarily it remains.

The meat of blessing and cup of blessing occurs in this sacrifice as in that at the altar of Heaven. It is, as there, not used except when the Emperor himself performs the ceremony.

At the presentation of wine an officer places a cup before each of the tablets representing the ancestors, male and female, of the Emperor.

That an officer should read the Emperor's prayer for him in his presence is peculiar, for in the service at the altar of Heaven the Emperor reads the prayer himself.

After the prayer the Emperor is directed to knock his head three times against the ground, which he does. Upon receiving the cup and meat of blessing, he again performs the full ceremony of prostrations and knockings, and the same occurs again after this twice more, at the removal of the viands from the tables, and before his return to his palace.

This ceremony being so burdensome as to entail on the Emperor the necessity of kneeling sixteen times, and knocking the forehead thirty-six times against the ground, is an indication of the importance attached to filial piety, and to the character of the Emperor as an example of virtue to all his subjects.

The burning of the prayer and silk offered to the emperors shows that they and the empresses are classed among the spirits that belong to heaven, and not to those that belong to earth. This is important in connection with the text in the book of poetry where the soul of Wen-wang is said to move up and down in the presence of Shang-te. The use of the word *shen,* " spirit," in the name *shen-choo,* for " tablet," and in the phrase *ying-shen,* " meeting the spirit," to escort it from its shrine to the place of sacrifice, implies the same thing.

At the new year a sacrifice is offered to the spirits of those ancestors, male and female, whose tablets are in the back hall of the Tai-meaou. On the Empress's birthday the same thing takes place.

The number of musicians is two-thirds of those that perform at the temple of Heaven.

Another ancestral temple of the emperors is within the palace. It is called Feng-sien-tien, and is in the eastern portion of the palace. Beside this there is the temple at the tomb of each emperor.

A very important branch of the imperial worship is the sacrifices to the gods of land and grain. The altars to these spirits are on the right hand of the palace gate. Their position corresponds to that of the Temple of Ancestors.

The altar of the spirit of land, *Shay,* consists of two terraces, both ascended by flights of three steps. The upper terrace is covered with earth of five colours. Yellow occupies the middle, blue the east, red the south, white the west, and black the north.

On the south-west of the altar is a spot for burying the victims. The tablet to the god of land, *Shay,* is on the terrace on the east. That to the god of grain, *Tseih,* is on the west. Both face north. There are two tablets occupying the position of guests; *Hea-too,* called Kow-lung, looks west, and *How-tseih* east. The last of these was superintendent of husbandry to the Emperor Yam; the first was officer of Hwang-te. They represent, it may be safely said, the founders or chief promoters of Chinese agriculture.

The worship takes place in the middle months of spring and autumn, and on occasion of important events when announcements are to be made to them.

The sacrifices are the same as in the worship of ancestors and of the temple of Earth, as regards the twenty-eight dishes, but a bullock, pig, and sheep are all offered, and the jade and silk to be burnt are placed beyond the three animals.

This account of imperial worship must here cease. I will add one remark. Every impartial investigator will probably admit that the ceremonies and ideas of the Chinese sacrifices link them with Western antiquity. The inference to be drawn from this is, that the Chinese primeval religion was of common origin with the religions of the West. But if the religion was one, then the political ideas, the mental habits, the sociology, the early arts and knowledge of nature, should have been of common origin also with those of the West.

The argument for identity of race thus becomes very strong, and is supported by the close resemblance of a mass of common linguistic roots,[1] found to be alike in sound and sense.

---

[1] See on this subject Dr. Schlegel's "Arya Siniaca," and my "China's Place in Philology."

CHAPTER III.

TEMPLES.

The most conspicuous buildings in a Chinese city are the yamuns and the temples. The officers of Government reside and transact business in the former, and they are often spacious and handsome. The temples are very numerous, belonging as they do to three religions. They are of all sizes and descriptions. One of those best worth examining is that of Confucius. It is placed in a large area ornamented with trees and water; in close connection with it are the Government examination-hall, the temple containing the tablets to the national sages, and that in which the distinguished persons of the city are commemorated on monumental boards.

The hall of sages contains the tablets of seventy-two persons ranged on each side of Confucius, and revered as his most distinguished followers. On the tablets are their names and titles. The sages before the time of Confucius are not represented here, the temple being dedicated specially to this philosopher. He is called "the most holy ancient sage Koong-foo-tsze." By the Jesuits this word was Latinised into Confucius. On the entrance gates there are inscriptions such as "The teacher and example for ten thousand generations," and "Equal with heaven and earth."

Sacrifices to Confucius are offered at the vernal and autumnal equinoxes. Oxen and sheep are slain, and the carcases, denuded of the skin, are placed upon stands in front of his tablet. The mandarins are present on the occasion at three o'clock in the morning. The flesh of the ox and the other animals is afterwards divided among the resident literati who may desire it, and eaten by them. The character of the temple is funereal. After entering the gates, the visitor passes through a long avenue of cypresses to the chief hall, and the tablets and the mode of placing them are the same as in the funereal temples raised to deceased ancestors. No image is placed to Confucius, except very rarely, and when it is used, it is merely as a statue for ornament, not as an idol for worship. The tablet, however, is worshipped. It is called "the place of the soul." When Confucius is worshipped, prayers are not made use of; the worshipper is mute, while he prostrates himself to express his reverential respect for the virtues of the sage. Those who have rank and property in China join with the learned class in professing to despise all religions but that of Confucius. They associate his name with their ancient national polity, their literature, their system of universal morality, and, indeed, with all the elements of their civilisation. So great and good was he, that they regard him as infallible. Yet he himself was distinguished for humility, and would never have dreamed of claiming infallibility; nor would he have wished to be in that high position of dignity to which his followers have raised him.

Their reverence for him takes the place of a religion. Children are taught to make their bow to Confucius when they enter school; and when, years after, they appear in the examination-hall to take their degrees, they repeat this act of reverence. They do not, indeed, suppose him to have the attributes of a god, but they pay him religious respect, as the embodiment of all that is sacred and good.

Near the Confucian temple is a smaller edifice to the memory of the virtuous women of the district. A tablet is placed to each, and incense is burnt before it on certain occasions. The temple to virtuous women is of much less pretension in size and ornament than that of Confucius and the seventy-two sages. It is sometimes erected in other localities. We saw one on the island of Tung-ting, near Soochow, in memory of the women of that island. It was on high ground, in a beautiful situation, in sight of some of the other islands that stud the northern part of the Tae-hoo lake. The rock on which it stands is limestone, furnishing excellent materials for mason-work. Some time since an application was made to Government to prohibit quarrying for stone at this spot, as disrespectful to the temple. The request was granted. We noticed that a part of the limestone was crowded with fossil shells.

There is an agricultural temple (*tan*) in the neighbourhood of every Chinese city. In it is a tablet to Shin-nung, the fabulous emperor who is said by the Chinese to have taught their forefathers agriculture. There is another to the spirits of the hills and rivers and those that preside over grain. The officers visit this temple in early spring to sacrifice before these tablets, and to plough a small plot of adjoining ground. They do this as an example of industry to the agricultural population, as an intimation that the labours of the field are to commence, and as an appeal to the divinities that watch over the interests of the farmer for a prosperous year.

The prevailing character of these and other temples belonging to the Confucian religion is funereal. They are the abodes of the dead. The name of the tablet, Shin-wei or Ling-wei, "the place of the soul," denotes that the spirit is supposed to be present there.

The character of Buddhist temples is different from this. They are not for the dead, but for the living. They contain halls where images are placed to represent the expositors of Buddhist doctrine addressing an auditory. Buddha, who is styled "the teacher of the present world," occupies the centre, and inferior personages are placed on his right and left. The Buddhist temple is a residence for monks who have retired from the world—a monastery—as well as an assemblage of buildings in which images are grouped to be worshipped according to their rank—a temple.

A funereal temple, such as that of Confucius, or of the ancestors of a family, is called "*meaou*," while Buddhist monasteries or temples are termed "*sze*." How numerous buildings of both kinds, as well as those bearing other names, are in China, every one who has travelled there knows.

I have in my recollection, as I write, a town with a large population built at the foot of a hill in the eastern silk region of China. The hill, formed of a bright red stone, is crowned with a pagoda, commanding an extensive view. On entering the adjoining temple, the visitor passes through some neatly-furnished rooms, in which he sees a series of Buddhist idols of clay, with their customary expression of benevolence and thoughtfulness. Beyond them is a fountain dedicated to some divinity, and a cave where images of the Goddess of Mercy, Kwan-yin (the Kanon of the Japanese), and of her two attendants, are seen set up in niches in the rock. At one end of the town, in the plain below, is a ruinous temple, in much worse condition than its fellow upon the hill. On each side of Buddha stands a row of clay statues, representing the Devas of Hindu mythology, with their Sanscrit names. Here are Brahma, Indra, Shakra, and other divinities, so well known in the land which boasts its 300,000,000 of gods. They are a part of the assembly that honours Buddha by reverent attention and offerings of flowers.

Near Hoochow, a city not far from this place, I visited some large monasteries, embosomed among hills, very retired from the common haunts of men, and fit for those who love rural sights and sounds. Here are quiet cells where he who wishes to live in undisturbed solitude may do so. On one of these hills, that of the White Magpie, there is a fine view of Tae-hoo, the great lake of Soochow, and the monastery is surrounded with groves of bamboo and other trees. On another, the landscape embraces Hoochow and the well-watered plain in which it lies. The view extends to the mountainous region where the peaks of Teen-muh-shan and its adjacent hills tower up to 4000 or 5000 feet above the level of the sea. To such retreats the mandarin wearied with public business, or the shopkeeper who has been unsuccessful in trade, will sometimes betake himself in search of the pleasures of solitude for the remainder of his existence.

There are wilder regions than this to the south-west of Ningpo, which have become the favourite abode of such refugees from the disappointments of the world. Thousands of Buddhist monks are here gathered in large convents in a bleak and dreary situation, where for several miles round there are no towns or villages. Here, among mountains of considerable elevation, a few shepherds' cottages are the only human habitations, except the abodes of the monks. Many of these ascetics, wishing to carry their self-denial to the furthest extent, are unwilling to reside in the monasteries, where there would be in the society of their fellow-monks some compensation for the loss of worldly enjoyment. They build a hut of reeds and straw in the hollows of the mountain, or in some spot sheltered by groves of trees, and here they live alone, with no companion but the little image of the god Buddha, and no employment but the burning of incense to him or chanting prayers. Their food is brought them from the neighbouring monastery, and they have no family cares, and no need to seek a living by labour. The monotony of their existence is only varied by an occasional visit to their brethren who live in the monastery which supports them, and whose rules they have to obey.

I went many years ago to this celebrated place, where Chinese Buddhism is to be seen in its glory, and where the style of the temples and the mode of living among the monks may be observed to the best advantage. It was the 18th of April, a fine time of year for visiting the mountainous regions of China, that we found ourselves, a party of three, crossing a beautiful pass on the way to Teen-tae. All the morning, after sleeping in a quiet monastery—for in such parts of China monasteries are the only inns—we had been following the windings of a noisy stream, running through a narrow valley. Now and then, as we turned a corner, we came in sight of a pretty cascade rushing down an abrupt face of rock. More than once we crossed the stream on a bamboo raft instead of a ferryboat, where the water was too deep to be forded by pedestrians, and yet too shallow for oars or sculls. At last we began to ascend the pass. All around were hill-tops, six or eight in number, their sides covered with azaleas in full bloom. The stream far below had an evident partiality for the same winding curve which is followed by the Wye near Chepstow. The view of the neighbouring hills we thought extremely beautiful, but the most striking effect was witnessed by us on reaching the top of the pass, where the landscape in a moment doubled itself, and we saw the upper course of the stream in the valley in the direction of the celebrated Buddhist retreat, to reach which was the object of our journey. We thought we had never seen such a profusion of flowers as were spread, growing wild, on each side of our path. This pass is called Chaou-yang-ling. Leaving it, we proceeded for another day, and after sleeping at a wayside inn, arrived in the evening at a monastery in the district of Teen-tae, called Tsing-leang-sze. The principal monk was very polite, gave us good accommodation, and passed much time in discussing with us the principles of Buddhism.

Beyond this, as we proceeded, we found that large monasteries were placed at about five miles apart all through this mountainous tract of country, which is otherwise inhabited only by a few cottagers. In these establishments the Oriental monasticism is seen surrounded with all the attractions of natural scenery, and in the temples the modes of conducting service may be witnessed in the most complete and elaborate form. Near one of the monasteries is a fine waterfall, sixty feet in height, surmounted by a natural rock bridge. It is fourteen feet long and eight inches wide, and has been well worn by the steps of passers-by, who go across it to worship at the shrine placed at the other end of the bridge. It is in the midst of a richly-wooded dell, in which there are several temples. The priests who reside in them say that they hear at early morning, in the adjoining groves, what they call the Lohans chanting Buddhist prayers, but they never see them. In the shrine at the end of the bridge are five hundred little figures cut in stone to represent the Lohans, or, as they are termed in Sanscrit, the Arhans. These figures are so small that they do not look more than half an inch in thickness. We passed the night at Hwa-ting-sze, a monastery 3000 feet above the level of the sea. It consisted of an extensive range of buildings thatched with straw, a rare thing to see in China. The principal hall has in it nearly the same images in all these monasteries. Buddha sits in the centre, an idol of clay, gilt over its whole surface, and seated on a gigantic lotus-flower. On his right is usually Ananda, and on his left Kashiapa, two Indian disciples of Buddha. Sometimes the place of these two disciples, the one the writer of the sacred books of the religion, and the other the keeper of its esoteric traditions, is occupied by two other representations of Buddha, namely, Buddha past and Buddha future.

At Koh-tsing-sze, a very old monastery, lately rebuilt at great expense, we found that there were two hundred resident priests. We saw there ten priests shut up together in a hall dedicated to the Buddha of the western heaven. They were obliged by vow to remain there for three years, keeping up their melancholy chant all day and all night. While some are sleeping the rest continue their monotonous chant. We went in among them and gave them some books, which they received with strong demonstrations of pleasure.

In each of the monasteries is a large hall dedicated to the five hundred Lohans, supernatural beings, who are supposed to make Teen-tae their chief place of abode. These halls, built to accommodate five hundred life-size statues, are necessarily large. On each side of the gateway of a Buddhist temple is a tower, the one for a bell and the other for a gong, which are struck on festival days, on the arrival of visitors, and in services for the dead.

In the vicinity of the Koh-tsing monastery is a nine-storied pagoda, of great antiquity. The pagoda is a very frequent appurtenance of Buddhist temples. Its object was originally to form a tomb for deceased Buddhist priests, or to be a repository for relics of Buddha and other venerated personages. They are now employed in China as erections in honour of Buddha, and for purposes of geomancy. They are supposed to ensure prosperity to the neighbourhoods in which they stand. An outside gallery is usually carried round each story, and to its roof is attached a circle of small bells, which are rung by the wind. When the wind rises and the tinkling of the bells is heard, the priests say that it is the tribute of praise to Buddha from inanimate nature.

In a complete Buddhist monastery, beside halls for images of various divinities, there are apartments for the abbot and monks, a large dining-hall, a library, reception rooms for visitors, and out-buildings for the culinary department.

On entering the principal gate, the visitor first arrives at the chapel or hall of the gods (in Chinese, *teen*) who are subordinate to Buddha, and are represented as guarding the doorway to the abode of the great hero, or teacher of gods and men, as he is styled.

Passing this, there will be seen, not seldom, an imperial stone monument, bearing an inscription, and protected by a roof on pillars; and immediately behind it is the great hall of Buddha.

The pagoda at Koh-tsing is more than a thousand years old, and the traditions of the monastery are equally ancient. During so many generations as have passed from the time of its foundation to the present day, there have arisen not a few legends of hermits and Lohans connecting themselves with the pagoda and monastery, and either residing in the woods and caves of the surrounding hills, or making transient visits to them. This is true indeed of all the Teen-tae region, and the tombs and various relics of many celebrated Chinese Buddhists are preserved there, with care, and are visited with great interest by travellers.

As we bade adieu to Koh-tsing and turned our steps towards the plain, we felt that we were leaving behind us a remarkable region. Among these hills, all of them high, and one of them reaching an elevation of 4500 feet, several thousands of monks and hermits are congregated. We thought of Mount Sinai and the numerous societies of Christian monks that formerly retreated there from the Syrian and Egyptian cities, and who left as their memorial the inscriptions that have recently become so famous. We tried to gather from the comparison of Eastern and Western monkery some light on the philosophy of asceticism. On descending into the plain, we were reminded that we were in the native land of the mulberry-tree and the silkworm. The leaves were being gathered by women and children for the Paou-paou, "the precious ones," as the worms are affectionately termed by the country people. Coming amongst a dense population, and noticing the marks everywhere visible of a thriving industry, we felt inclined to wonder why so many of the Chinese should prefer the secluded life of a mountain hermitage or monastery to the pleasures and activities of society. Besides the other reasons that may lead men to prefer a monastery among the mountains for their home, there must be sometimes a feeling of sincere faith in the religious opinions that they have adopted, and a longing of the heart after something that cannot be obtained except in religious meditation.

It is time to introduce the reader to another class of temples—those of the Taouist religion. Some of them are called Kung, *palace;* and the endeavour is made in these to represent the gods of the religion in their celestial abodes, seated on their thrones in their palaces, either administering justice or giving instruction.

In the larger Taouist temples, often called Kwan, a greater number of divinities is found in the various halls and side apartments of the building. The sages noted in the history of the Taouist sect, the gods of the various heavens spoken of in its books, the star deities, and the cyclic gods, who preside over the years of the national sexagenary cycle, have images to represent them according to their ranks.

Besides these edifices there are temples to the State gods, the god of war, and the protectors of cities and towns. They are called Meaou, their character being like that of the above-mentioned temples of the Confucian sect. They are intended for honour to the dead, and the deceased heroes and statesmen to whom they are dedicated are all chosen by the Government to their places in the national pantheon. Those who hold official positions in any city visit these temples on certain public occasions, though it is not always with a friendly intention that they thus give their countenance to the sect of Taou.

Let the reader imagine himself, on the morning of the new or full moon, wending his way to the temple dedicated to the patron god of a Chinese city, the *Ching-hwang-meaou.* If early enough, he will have the opportunity of witnessing an interesting ceremony. The mandarins of the city are there to listen to the reading of one of the imperial lectures addressed to the working classes on their special duties. There are sixteen of these lectures. In them the Emperor speaks to the people as a father to his children:—" You ploughmen, spinners, and cultivators of the mulberry-tree, should be very diligent in prosecuting your respective callings. For what is the country to do for food and clothing unless you are so?" It was the Emperor Kanghe—" the great Kanghe," as he is justly called by the Jesuits in their letters—who instituted this custom, which was first put in practice in the reign of his son, early in the eighteenth century. In one of the lectures, to the public reading of which by the town-clerk the officers of Government and a small audience listen with respect, an attack is made on the idolatrous religions of the country. The people are warned that they should not frequent the Buddhist and Taouist temples, nor take part in the idolatrous village festivals held on certain days. The imperial censor calls the Buddhist priests the drones of the community, creatures like moths and other mischievous insects, that thrive on the gatherings of others, while they do no honest work themselves. When he has finished his remarks on these two heterodox religions, the Emperor proceeds to criticise certain other sects. Among them, he says, is the *Teen-choo-keaou* (Roman Catholic Christianity). "That," he says, "is the religion of Western men. Now these men from the West are clever in the mathematical sciences, and on this account they are employed in the astronomical tribunal to calculate eclipses and the courses of the heavenly bodies. But as to their religion, it is not accordant with the orthodox doctrine. You people should not by any means believe in it."

CHAPTER IV.

CONFLICT OF RELIGIOUS PARTIES IN CHINA.

The existence of three national religions in China has occasioned a perpetual conflict of religious opinions among the people of that country. Great diversities of sentiment are found there upon religious subjects. Between the literary class, the followers of Confucius, and the multitude, the adherents of Buddha and Taou, there has always been a want of cohesion. The former feel no little pride in asserting that they never worship images. The latter defend them as a useful symbolism. Fortunately for the permanence of the Confucian system, it has always had the balance of intellectual and political influence on its side. The best writers have supported it in books and condemned the other systems, while the Government has often persecuted the Buddhists and Taouists, and even when its patronage has been extended to them, its approval was given because it thought that their doctrines agreed with those of the great national sage.

An example was given in the preceding chapter of the protests constantly repeated on behalf of the orthodox Confucian government of China against the Buddhist and Taouist religions, and also against Christianity. For some centuries, however, the dominant party has ceased to persecute the other two national religions. It has fallen into the habit of toleration, and contented itself with condemnatory protests on public occasions. Catholic Christianity was new, and it has been several times severely persecuted by the rulers of the present dynasty. But the state of public relations between Christian nations and China has now changed. After 1843, when foreigners went to Shanghai to reside, the town-clerk quietly omitted the passage referring to Christianity, when reciting in course the fortnightly lectures, and he was not called to account by his superiors for this polite concession to the feelings of the newly-arrived residents, so reluctantly admitted to the "central flowery land."

When the graduates of a province, or one of its subdivisions, meet for examination and to receive degrees and other honours from the imperial examiners, copies of the sixteen lectures, known as the Sacred Edict, are frequently distributed among them. This is one of many modes by which efforts are made, not only for the encouragement of virtuous industry and moral conduct among the people, but to keep up the old hostile attitude of the orthodox religion, that of the Government and the scholars, against other systems.

Some examples will now be given of the feelings that the scholars have as individuals respecting the worship of the popular divinities, the clay gods, and high-roofed temples, blackened with incense-smoke, that they see round their homes. I know a man of fine intellect who looks with contempt on idolatry. While the mass of his fellow-townsmen are willing worshippers of idols such as those described, a few like him will be found in every Chinese city fully sensible to the degradation of idolatry. I remember, on a bright starlight Sabbath evening, holding a lengthened conversation with him on the character and claims of Christianity. Possessed of clear reasoning powers, and naturally fond of scientific inquiries, he felt no doubt or difficulty respecting the existence and character of God. He freely admitted that the principal doctrines of Christianity are so evident and just, that all ought to believe them. From the character of his mind he was prepared to accede at once to everything shown to be reasonable. But those parts of Christianity which appeal to a heaven-born faith in the heart, rather than to the reasoning faculties, these were a stumbling-block to him. He said, for example, that the doctrine of universal depravity is nothing different from the Chinese dogma on the same subject. Many philosophers of his nation, he contended, had held that in addition to the good element in human nature (conscience, or the moral sense) there was a gross principle, evil in its influence, residing in the domain of the passions and operating through them. This germ of evil is not from heaven, but springs up of its own accord, in consequence of the soul's attachment to matter, and grows side by side with the knowledge of good and evil which is bestowed by Heaven. So also he did not oppose the doctrine of the Trinity; but when miracles and the divinity of Christ were spoken of, he was reluctant to accept them. They appeared to him as things hard to be understood. But whatever his objections to the religion of Jesus Christ, he preferred it much to the systems of idolatry prevailing in his own country. He did so at least theoretically, but his want of faith in idolatry did not prevent him from giving his donation, when asked, towards the expense of maintaining worship in a Buddhist monastery.

Another instance of conflict in matters of opinion is found in the method of criticising the sacred books recently introduced within the Confucian school. Previous to the present dynasty, an old-fashioned mediæval philosophy had ruled the minds of the literary class with a sway almost as powerful as that of Aristotle over the schoolmen. Choo-foo-tsze was the Coryphæus of this philosophy. One of its tendencies was atheistic; it denied the personality of God, and held that the Shang-te of the classics—the supreme ruler, as revered in the ancient Chinese monotheism—is nothing but a principle. This principle, called Le (*reason*), underlies all existences. All things are the manifestations of it. Sometimes it is spoken of as a law of a moral or intellectual kind pervading the world. At other times it is nothing but a very fine material essence.

This was the conception to which the idea of God was reduced by the middle-age Chinese philosophers, about the time of the European schoolmen. In their hands Providence is nothing but the spontaneous action of a law, and creation nothing but the self-originated beginning of such action. This clearly is atheism. Recent Chinese authors have felt that such a system was unsatisfactory, and they have returned to an older one, which regarded the personality of God as a fundamental point; and though it had no very distinct view on the subject of creation, made such statements in regard to the providence of God, as to show that the early Chinese had conceptions of the Divine Being far in advance of most pagan nations. Modern Chinese writers, when speaking on the question, Whether the God of the classics is a personal being, or a principle, ask :—" Can a principle become angry? Can a principle be said to approve the actions of men, and be pleased with the offerings of men? Yet these acts are ascribed to God in the classical books. God, therefore, cannot be a principle, but must be a personal being."

This new criticism on the interpretations of the school of Choo-foo-tsze was exceedingly well timed, for the influence of that school had been such that not a few native scholars might be properly denominated atheists or pantheists. A moderately well-read Chinese, who has not imbibed the spirit of this new school, will say to the missionary of our purer faith :—" We are worshippers of God too. He is present in all nature. The world is God. When we inquire into science, celestial or terrestrial, we honour God." Identifying nature with God, such men find no difficulty in reconciling Christian views of the Deity with the cold and cheerless abstractions of such a philosophy as that of Choo-foo-tsze.

Sufficient attention has not yet been given to the remarkable change that has occurred in Chinese authorship during the last two centuries as bearing on religion and philosophy. Authors on China have limited themselves too much to the older system, which has had its day, and has now given place to more rational opinions, at least among the better instructed class of Chinese readers. At the same time, it must be allowed that the views they repudiate still hold their ground with the mass of so-called Confucianists; for in that country the opinions of a new school can only become universally known after a long period. The *vis inertiæ* of Chinese institutions renders change difficult. In course of time probably there will be a new system inaugurated in the Government examinations, and the sentiments which the influential writers of the present day call in question will perhaps be publicly renounced. The multitude will wait till this is done before taking the trouble to inform themselves on the particular opinions of their best thinkers and authors, much more before adopting them.

CHAPTER V.

HOW THREE RELIGIONS BASED ON DIFFERENT PRINCIPLES EXIST IN CHINA.

THE susceptibility of the Chinese to become converts to Christianity cannot be held doubtful, if their past and present religious history be well considered. The study of their literature, and personal observation of their customs and modes of thought, lead directly to this conclusion.

The light in which the Chinese too often appear to the foreign observer is that of the ludicrous and fantastical almost exclusively. Next to this, they are usually represented as avaricious, conceited, and untruthful. Writers like M. Huc prefer the comic to the real, and the pleasure they take in drawing an amusing picture prevents their doing justice to the good points of the national character they endeavour to describe. The good-natured sketches of Mr. Fortune, and the philosophic views of Mr. Meadows, represent the country and its people much more correctly than the overflowing fun and vivacity of this author would allow him to do. The writer who means to be predominantly comic will not give a fair view of any people among whom he travels. He will overlook the deeper and more influential elements of character, and fix his eye too much on the effervescing qualities.

China presents a fine field for observing the mutual influence and conflict of those ideas which have most to do with the formation of character—the religious and the moral. We have there three great national systems existing in harmony. Three modes of worship, and three philosophies underlying them, have been there for ages interacting on each other. Sometimes they have been in conflict, but usually they have preferred a state of peace. The Chinese would rather have toleration than persecution. They did not drive out the intruding religion that came to them from India, as the Japanese did Christianity in its Roman Catholic form. Nor did Confucianism expel the Taouist religion, as the Brahmans did Buddhism from the land of its birth. The Chinese quietly adopted all these religions, after a limited period of persecution, and now they exist side by side not only in the same locality, but, what is more extraordinary, in the belief of the same individuals. It is quite a common thing in China for the same person to conform to all the three modes of worship. The flexibility is very convenient to the governing powers in the State. Any divinity they may wish to have worshipped by the common people will be admitted at once into their pantheon without difficulty. While they comply with the will of their governors, they also feel superstitious reverence for the new god. They believe that the Emperor has the power of appointing the souls of the dead to posts of authority in the invisible world, just as he does in the visible. When they see his image in a new temple in appropriate costume, seated in his shrine like any other god, they will soon learn to adore him as willingly as any of the old divinities with whose names they have been long familiar.

There is a temple in a retired spot in the city of Shanghai, built to the memory of a Chinese hero who died in battle in the first English war. He fell at the capture of Woosung by the British forces. He held the highest military post that a Chinese can hold, that of Te-tae, the rank of Tseang-keun being limited to the Manchoos. This hero, Chin-te-tae, appears in the temple, carved in wood, the size of life, and the likeness is said to be very good. The honours of deity are paid to him, and though there are few visitors to the temple now, doubtless the superstitious faith of the inhabitants in this new divinity assigned to them by

Government authority, will increase with the lapse of years, and his worshippers will become more numerous. This at least is the common order of things in China. The neighbours evidently think there is a certain sacredness attaching to this new temple. It is the spot which they selected to place the body of the Shanghai city magistrate who was killed at the capture of that place by a rebel force five years ago. After the re-entrance of the Imperialists, the coffin of the slain mandarin was publicly exhibited there for some days. A biography of him was written by a scholar of the neighbourhood, in which he was classed among the patriotic and the loyal who had died in the discharge of the trust committed to them by the Emperor. The best reward for such persons is considered to be the bestowal of divine titles and sacrifices by command of the Emperor.

The readiness with which new religious ceremonies are received among the people has allowed the three religions to interact very extensively on each other. It will be worth while to point out instances of this interaction, and also to show how they co-exist harmoniously. This will be interesting to all students of the religions of the world, as well as to those who have at heart the Christianisation of the whole human race. China is the only instance of a country where three powerful religions have existed together for ages without one of them being successful in destroying the rest.

The remaining religions of China are exclusive, and those who belong to them consider it their duty not to conform to the rites of other systems. Of these, the Mohammedans are most numerous. In the northern provinces it is said that they often compose a third of the population. Though the Chinese Mohammedans are probably the most lax of all believers in Islam, they keep up among themselves a spirit of resistance to idolatry, refusing to adore any but *Chin-choo,* "the true Lord." They did not require us to take off our shoes when we entered their mosques, as the foreign visitor must do in India or Ceylon, but they have more than once claimed fraternity with us as being opposed, like them, to the worship of images.

The Roman Catholic converts in China amount to nearly a million; a large number in itself, but small when compared with the remainder of the population.

Leaving these two bodies of religionists out of view for the present, an attempt will now be made to show the mutual influences of the three great systems that may be properly called national.

The religions of Confucius, Buddha, and Taou are truly national, because the mass of the people believe in them all. They are far from feeling it inconsistent to do so. Philosophers may not know what to do with a fact like this; but it is true nevertheless. Those who themselves have a devoted love of truth, and feel strong convictions of certain things, do not understand how any one should belong to three religions at once. Hence some writers have parcelled out the Chinese among these systems, assigning so many millions to one and so many to another. In estimating the number of Buddhists in the world, one hundred and eighty millions of Chinamen are placed by one author at the head of his enumeration of nations. He has obtained this number by halving the whole population; a process conveniently short, but far from giving a true view of the case. If it serves for other races to refer every individual belonging to them to some one religion, it will not answer for China. Some other mode of classification must be employed. The majority of the inhabitants in that country comply with the worship of more than one religion, believe in more than one mythology of gods, and contribute to the support of more than one priesthood.

What is the cause of this indifference? Why do they care so little about finding out what is the truth and holding to it? Several answers may be given to this inquiry. They are superstitious, but wanting in conscientiousness. They accept legends as true without examining whether there is any good evidence for them or not. They care more to have divinities that seem to meet their wants, and can do for them what they wish to be done, than to have truth and certainty to rest upon. This is one answer.

Another circumstance that helps to explain how it is that the Chinese believe in three religions at once is, that these systems are supplementary to each other.

Confucianism speaks to the *moral* nature. It discourses on virtue and vice, and the duty of compliance with law and the dictates of conscience. Its worship rests on this basis. The religious veneration paid to ancestors—for that is the worship of this system—is founded on the duty of filial piety. The moral sense of the Chinese is offended if they are called on to resign this custom.

Taouism is *materialistic*. Its notion of the soul is of something physical, a purer form of matter. The soul it supposes to gain immortality by a physical discipline, a sort of chemical process, which transmutes it into a more ethereal essence, and prepares it for being transferred to the regions of immortality. The gods of Taouism are also very much what might be expected in a system which has such notions as these of the soul. It looks upon the stars as divine. It deifies hermits and physicians, magicians and seekers after the philosopher's stone and the plant of immortality.

Buddhism is different from both. It is *metaphysical*. It appeals to the imagination, and deals in subtle argument. It says that the world of the senses is altogether unreal, and upholds this proposition by the most elaborate proofs. Its gods are personified ideas. It denies matter entirely, and concerns itself only with ideas. Most of the personages adored by the Buddhists are known to be nothing but fictitious personations of some of these ideas. The Buddhist worship is not reverence paid to beings believed to be actually existing. It is a homage rendered to ideas, and it is only supposed to be reflex in its effects. Their worship is useful as a discipline, but not effectual as prayer. The Buddhist, if he can obtain abstraction of mind from the world in any other mode, need not pray or worship at all.

These three systems, occupying the three corners of a triangle—the moral, the metaphysical, and the material—are supplemental to each other, and are able to co-exist without being mutually destructive. They rest each on a basis of its own, and address themselves each to different parts of man's nature. It was because Confucianism "knew God, but did not honour Him as God," that the way was left open for a polytheism like that of the Buddhists. In the old books of China, God is spoken of as the Supreme Ruler. He is represented as exercising over mankind an infinitely just and beneficent providence. But the duty of prayer is not enjoined. No worship of God by the people is permitted. It was only by the Emperor acting vicariously for the people that the Deity was adored in that country. The system of Confucius wanting this, was more a morality than a religion.

Buddhism came to fill this vacancy. Individual faith in God, with a rational mode of worship to accompany it, could not be a result of the religious teaching which preceded it in China, nor were they inculcated by it. In Buddhism, the Chinese found objects to adore of mysterious grandeur, and richly endowed with the attributes of wisdom and benevolence. The appeal thus made to their religious faith was strengthened by a pompous form of worship. Processions and the ringing of bells, fumes of sweet-smelling incense, prayers, chanting, and musical instruments, were their aids to devotion. No wonder that these additions should prove welcome to the religious susceptibilities of a nation which had hitherto been restricted within the bounds of a system almost exclusively moral, and which discouraged the worship of God by the mass of the people.

How Taouism meets certain other wants which the other two systems fail to gratify, we will now show by an illustration:—It was a cold morning in January when a missionary walked, on one occasion, to a temple near the west gate of Shanghai. There is a medical divinity much honoured who resides in this temple, to heal, as his worshippers think, the ailments of those who pray to him. The Taouist priest in charge addressed the foreign visitor with a somewhat unexpected exhortation:—" You come to our country giving us good advice. Now let me address a little to you. Your religion does not meet the requirements of the people. When they worship, they wish to know whether they can grow rich, and recover from disease; but, in the case of believing in Jesus, there are no benefits of this kind to be looked for." He pointed to the little image, representing some physician of a former dynasty, sitting in its shrine in a dim light, just visible through the opening of the curtains. "See," said he, " here is the god, ready to tell the believing devotee what medicine he needs, and to guarantee its healing effect. Look at the inscriptions fixed on the roof above, and on each side of the shrine. They describe his marvel-working power." He was asked who placed those tablets there. " They are," he replied, " the offerings of persons cured by this divinity. In the Central Kingdom, the setting of the tablets in the temples by individuals is customary, and they are intended to commemorate benefits received from the divinities to whom they are dedicated." A visitor from a village in the country, at a distance of some miles, now appeared, and went through the usual ceremonies. He was asked, "Why do you not consult a physician? This idol is dead wood. It cannot see or hear. Why apply to it?" The devotee answered with great simplicity, " I do not know what my disease is, how then can I apply to a physician? It is on this account that I ask the god. He will heal me. I have come a long way on purpose. His fame is very widely spread." He was again asked, "Will you not go to the foreign free hospital?" He answered, " It is not the right time of day, and besides,

I like to come here; and why should I not?" He was asked again, "Do you know that this burning of incense and seeking for oracular information at an idol's shrine is displeasing to God? It is as unwise, therefore, as it is unreasonable, to apply to this god to tell you what medicine you should use." At this point the Taouist priest came to the defence of his system. "You believe in Jesus. We believe in our gods. Religions differ according to place, and every country has its own divinities. We have Kwan-kung, for example, the god of war, and other divinities, holding the same place among us that Jesus does among you." He was asked, "How can these supposed gods benefit you? They are but the imaginary representatives of men belonging to your nation who long ago died." The Taouist asked in reply, "Is it not the same with Jesus? He also is long since dead. What benefit do you expect from Him?" He was then told, "We do not make an image of Him, place it in a shrine, and cast lots before it, expecting to learn by so doing how a disease is to be cured. The parallel is not accurate. The benefit we expect from Him is, that He will help us in becoming virtuous, and in attaining a happy future life. The object of our religious books is to free us from sin, and Jesus, who still lives in heaven, is able to secure us this." The reference to books led him to remark, "We have our books, too, to exhort men to virtue." He took up a copy of a well-known work, often distributed gratuitously in China by those who devote money to the printing and circulation of religious tracts among their countrymen. "This," he said, "is the Kan-ying-peen (Book of Retribution); all that it contains is intended to make men better. It promises long life to the good, and all kinds of calamities to the wicked. Our object is the same as yours, to make men good." He was reminded that, according to the doctrine of this book, happiness and misery were the rewards of virtue and vice, and that this did not agree with the system of divination on which his temple depended for its support; and was asked why he encouraged those who frequented it to expect good from the throwing of sticks on the floor, and the shaking of lots together in a wooden cup, if good and ill fortune were awarded to men by Heaven only according to character. To this the priest of Taou replied, as he sat surrounded by his boxes of medicines, arranged in pigeon-holes, with his recipe book on the table before him, from which he selected the appropriate nostrum under the guidance of the oracle, "If the person who comes to worship is wicked at heart, he will not be heard, the oracle will fail." "But," it was remarked, "if he be only virtuous, he need not come here at all. The great thing is to be good."

It is curious to notice how the upholders of the most degrading superstitions will invariably maintain that they are auxiliary to virtue, and that they rest upon the soundest principles of morality. Taouism, as it is popularly believed, is one of the most abject of all the religions that the world has known. There is much in it which is so wretchedly mean, that the examination of it is quite disspiriting, and the reflection often occurs—Can the soul of man sink so low as this? This poor Taouist doctor gained his living by a trade no more respectable than that of a gipsy fortune-teller. The history of his sect is that of a succession of necromancers who could call up spirits at their will, of dreamers who expected to discover the art of transmuting all metals into gold, and of a few philosophers who, though their aspirations were a little higher, have failed to lend any air of dignity to a system hopelessly mean. Yet this man contended, as the conversation was continued, that believers in his religion strove after virtue. It was by virtue, he said, that they looked for immortality. The genii who reside in forests and mountains, who have left the haunts of men for ever, and escaped the necessity of dying, have arrived at this good fortune by the force of their goodness. He confessed, however, that in modern times there are none so good as to become immortal in this way.

The missionary reminded him that if he really wished men to be virtuous, some better method to make them so might be found than the keeping open of a temple like that. The idols with their gay ornaments, the hanging lanterns, the burning of candles and sandal-wood, and the apparatus for divination, would not promote the virtue of the community. They are all the work of human hands. There is nothing divine in them. "Such is our custom," observed the villager. "Customs differ according to place." The priest felt a little nettled, and remarked, "If you were to fall into a river, Jesus would save you from drowning, I suppose. He would come and draw you out of the water. You honour Jesus, and it is very well for you to do so. But He does not preside over China. He is not the God of our country, and it would be of no use for us to pray to Him." Of course neither of these two men were prepared to admit what they were then told, that Jesus is the true God, and that in Him is eternal life.

This incident shows how the Taouist system works among the Chinese. Its appeal is made to the lower wants of their nature. It invents divinities to promote the physical well-being of the people. The gods of riches, of longevity, of war, and of particular diseases, all belong to this religion. Such a system could not fail to be popular among all those whose spiritual nature has not been wakened into activity. The number of such persons in China is overwhelmingly vast. Their appetites are gross, and Taouism has supplied to them a suitable pabulum.

We have already assigned two reasons for the existence, side by side, of three national religions in China. The first was, that while the people of that country are prone to superstition, they neglect to inquire into evidence. They have no literature of evidences corresponding to our evidences of Christianity, nor have they formed their notions on logic into a science. The second was, that these religions address themselves particularly to different parts of human nature. We shall add a third. These three systems are all supported by the weight of authority. Confucius professed to tread in the steps of the ancient sages of his nation. It is a favourite proverb among the Chinese, *Kin puh joo koo*, "the moderns are not comparable with the ancients." Since the time of Confucius, men of mark in China have lent their influence to uphold the same system, and it has always been the religion of the State. But while the influential authors and the emperors of the successive dynasties have never deserted the Confucian standard, many of them have shown attachment to Buddhism. Last century the Emperor Keen-lung gave the palace of his grandfather at Hangchow to the Buddhists to be a monastery, and wrote with his own hand an inscription on a monumental tablet to be placed on its roof. The literature of that religion, in more than 1000 volumes, is published by Government with public funds. Numberless prefaces to Buddhist works have been written by emperors and authors of great repute. The influence of Buddhism is discernible in the productions of many of the most influential writers. The Buddhist priesthood has been and is recognised by many public acts of the Government. Buddhism is supported as the national religion among the Tibetans and Mongols, and large establishments of Lamas belonging to these nations are maintained at Peking at the imperial expense.

Taouism, perhaps more than Buddhism, may be considered a State religion. All the State gods, such as the god of war, Wen-chang the god of literature, and the very numerous patron gods of cities and country towns, belong to the Taouist religion, and are required by imperial edict to be worshipped according to the forms of that religion. The officers of Government, resident in particular cities, regularly visit the temples of these State gods on certain occasions. Confucianism is theoretically the only religion of the State, but practically Taouism is not less so. Besides this, the influence of the philosophy of the Taouist system on great writers, and the characteristically national tone of its legends, and of the more frivolous and nonsensical portion of its doctrines, help to show that it is properly described as national, and why it has come to be so.

At the present time a city cannot be without its temples, nor can these temples be suitably taken care of without inviting Buddhist or Taouist priests to assist. The protector of the city must have a temple where worship is performed specially on the 1st and 15th of each month. There are no persons so well adapted to undertake this duty as the priests of Taou.

CHAPTER VI.

INFLUENCE OF BUDDHISM ON CHINESE LITERATURE, PHILOSOPHY, AND NATIONAL LIFE.

THE reader is now invited to give his attention to some sketches of the influence of Buddhism on the national life of the Chinese. It has been unquestionably great. The Hindoo mode of thought is more speculative and philosophical than the Chinese. The practical Chinese mind had not amused itself with visiting those subtle depths of speculation which were familiar to the Hindoo. They could not invent an abstract philosophy like that of Buddhism, but they could follow it, and understand it when translated into their language. In the early part of the Christian era, translations of a vast number of philosophical and other works were made from the Sanscrit. They taught the Buddhist doctrines in an elegant form, which could not fail to attract readers in a cultivated nation like the Chinese. Some traces of their influence will now be pointed out as found in the works of celebrated authors.

The priests of this religion are fond of fountains and caves. In order to impart to them an air of sanctity, they invent legends of the appearance of divine personages in their neighbourhood, or attach to them some reminiscence of the visits of remarkable men. The poet Soo-tung-po was regarded by them as one of their best friends, though he never abandoned Confucianism. To keep him in remembrance, and to show their gratitude for the verses he wrote in praise of their mode of life and their doctrines, they have dedicated to him more than one wayside spring where he is said to have halted on a journey. I have seen some of them when travelling in the province of Chekeang. They were pointed out by the resident priests as Se-yen-tseuen, the spring where the poet washed his inkstone.

Another poet, nearly of the same period, was Taou-han. He has described a visit to one of the most famous monasteries in China, the Teen-chuh-sze, at Hangchow. This ancient establishment is, in its modern form, of most magnificent dimensions. Its name is derived from that of India, which was called Teen-chuh by the Chinese when they first became acquainted with it (or at least when their books first mention it), about the time of Christ. There were about 700 priests belonging to this establishment when I visited it twenty years ago. It is in a mountain hollow about three miles from the city. A long paved road leads to it, bordered by shrubberies, and ornamented with numerous monuments to the dead, either tombs, or those erections called *pai low*, constructed of upright and horizontal slabs of granite, and sculptured with the names and virtues of remarkable persons. The poet sketches the appearance of the monastery as he arrived there in the evening. After walking for some time up the path, which was shaded by a thick overgrowth of cypresses and pines, he came in sight of the temple. He describes the lofty gateway, through which the visitor, passing by the four gigantic guardian deities who stand as sentinels at Buddha's door, enters the great court. He notices the great hall where Shakyamuni Buddha appears, enthroned on a vast lotus. On each side and behind was a wilderness of cloisters, side-rooms, sleeping-rooms, and apartments for the monks according to their gradations. He passed the night there, and noticed the contrast between the silent groves outside, and the halls of the monastery echoing at intervals during the night with the chanting of prayers and the striking of bells. From his window he saw the moon shining on the lake, and the sound of running brooks fell on his ear. The peculiarity of his temporary lodging-place led him to think of the land of the Brahmans. He then tells how he fell into a pleasant reverie, in which the chain of cares that had wound itself round him was broken, and his mind felt free to wander in the realms of abstraction.

Every large monastery has its printed history, and such poems as the preceding are carefully preserved in it as the homage paid by literature to religion. The priests of this old monastery still entertain visitors hospitably. The abbot was very friendly in his manner when my companion and I were there, so much so that he recommended an adjoining piece of ground for building a Christian temple. He thought that the Buddhist and Christian religions might be maintained very harmoniously in this close proximity to each other. He added some remarks on the hostility shown by Christian missionaries to idolatry, and recommended that they should exhibit what he chose to represent as a more liberal spirit, and cease from their attacks upon the customs of other religions.

The influence of Buddhism on Chinese philosophy is seen in the writings of Choo-foo-tsze, and other authors of his time. He was a man who left a very deep and long-enduring impression upon the literature of his country. The most modern school of authorship has, indeed, changed its tone respecting him. It charges him with an imperfect system of criticism, and with yielding to Buddhist influence in his peculiar philosophy and his mode of interpreting the ancient books. But till recently he was considered as almost a second Confucius. He was undoubtedly one of China's greatest men, and was the most prominent among all the authors of the middle-age period in that country. Relics of such a man are preserved with affectionate veneration. I have seen a harp that belonged to him. It was in the possession of a native gentleman, an amateur in harp music. He carried it with him when travelling, as the most precious of his curiosities, and played upon it to amuse his friends. I heard him perform a tune intended to represent a quarrelsome discussion between a woodman and a fisherman. It was a five-stringed instrument. The strings were modern, but the wood looked very old. Whether it had seen seven hundred summers and winters, and had actually been played on by the great philosopher, I will not undertake to say. But Confucius, as well as his commentator, was, it is said, very fond of music. When Choo-foo-tsze was a child, and just able to talk a little, a noted scholar, a friend of his father, pointed to heaven and said, "See, that is heaven." The child answered, "And what is there above heaven?" The scholar only replied by a look of astonishment at the intelligence these words exhibited. At five years old he went to school, and comprehended the whole meaning of the "Book on Filial Piety" at the first reading. He wrote on the margin, "If any one has not this, he is not a man." When he went with other children to play upon the sandy channel of a mountain stream, he would leave them, and busy himself with marking upon the sand the eight diagrams that form the basis of Chinese philosophy. When he was a young man he studied with avidity the books of Buddha and Taou. He did this only to increase the range of his reading. He never became a convert to their opinions. They left, however, a marked impression upon his mind. He speaks in terms of glowing admiration of one of their books—the "Leng-yen-king," in which there is an elaborate argument to prove that none of the objects presented to us by the senses are real.

This author and his contemporaries, when they read the subtle treatises of the Buddhists on philosophical questions, felt ashamed of the simplicity of their own system, and tried to impart to it an air of scientific refinement. The diagrams of Fuh-he, which he had drawn on the sand in his childhood, were nothing but lines, arranged parallel to each other in certain varying forms. It was said by sages that these diagrams contained within them the system of the universe. Bare symbols may be made to mean anything; and it was easy to affirm that these lines, the most ancient relic of the art of writing that the Chinese possess, represent the formation of the world. Confucius added that the Great Extreme, or Tae-keih, was at the beginning of all things, but he did not describe precisely what the Great Extreme was. The school to which our author belonged were not satisfied. New additions were made, too abstract to be detailed here, to the doctrine of the Tae-keih.

An attempt was made to define the Great Extreme. Confucius probably meant by it nothing but a boundary in time—the commencing epoch of the gradual formation of all things. Our author and his friends, fresh from the perusal of works which denied the existence of matter, and also that of a Supreme Creator, ventured on the assertions, that the Tae-keih is identical with the ultimate reason (Taou-le), and with God (Shang-te); that creation is a spontaneous process, not effected by an agent; and that there is no personality in God. This was the form they chose for their national philosophy. Very different it is from the old Chinese system, in which no doctrine is more manifestly an article of faith than the personality of God, although it does not expressly say that He was the Creator, self-existent and eternal.

It was the teaching of this modern system which Commissioner Yeh brought forward in his conversations with Mr. Wingrove Cooke, as detailed in his work, "China in 1857-58." In the very graphic and interesting account there given of the commissioner, he (Yeh) speaks sometimes in the character of a Chinaman of the genuine Confucian school; as when he says, "Tien means properly only the material heaven, but it also means Shang-te (supreme ruler); for as it is not lawful to use his name lightly, we name him by his residence, which is in Tien." At other times he falls into the phraseology of the modern school, where he says, "Shang-te and Taou-le (reason, the ultimate reason) are one and the same thing." He speaks afterwards of the personage worshipped by the Taouists as Shang-te, a priest of that religion who lived in the Han dynasty: "Shang-te," he says, "is a Taouist *Taou-le*." This is a specimen of the facile way in which the Chinese will in conversation pass over from one stand-point to another, without giving the slightest intimation of their doing so to the interrogator. To understand such men as Commissioner Yeh, it is necessary to distinguish between the different systems they are familiar with. The ancient and modern Confucian philosophy must be separated, and the peculiarities of Buddhism and Taouism properly considered. One of Mr. Cooke's conclusions is, that "the Confucian philosophy recognises only nature, self-produced, active, but will-less and unintelligent." But this is the view of the modern commentators on Confucius, not of Confucius himself. They began to speak in this way after Buddhism had taught them how to construct a system of negative instead of positive doctrines. It was the Hindoo mind that led the way in the hardy assertion that nature may subsist without God. The philosophers of China yielded to the wish to become speculators on the laws of the world, and retaining the phraseology that they found in Confucius, proceeded to eliminate such ideas as that of a personal God and of moral retribution, as administered by a person, and when they had reduced the universe as much as possible to abstractions, concluded the process by identifying the terms of their philosophy. This is just what is done by the German when he says that reason, God, knowledge, being, and thinking are identical expressions. It is not easy to say from Mr. Cooke's narration which view Yeh preferred—the old doctrine of a personal God, who dwells in heaven, and whose name it is not lawful to use lightly; or that of the sophistical modern school, which finds nothing at the basis of nature but a principle. The scholars of his nation are now forming themselves into two parties, holding these opposite views, and it would be interesting to have known under which banner he would have preferred to enlist. We incline to think that he would have chosen the former, according to which God is known simply as the Supreme Ruler, infinitely just, good, and powerful. This is the real faith of the Chinese. For the sake of argument, they will speculate and sophisticate, or they will repeat the sophistries of others; but the deeper principle of national religious faith will assert itself in their more earnest moments, and they will return to a more reasonable system.

Mr. Cooke arrived at another conclusion from the opinions of Yeh, namely, that the Protestant missionaries are wrong in using the term Shang-te for God, because it is the name of a created being. If it is the name of a created being, it is so only in the opinion of a modern philosophical school; but even in this case the word "created" does not convey the idea contained in the corresponding Chinese expressions. What they mean is rather development than creation. They may speak of Shang-te being developed from the ultimate principle; but if this modern school had such a dogma respecting the origin of Shang-te—a subject not alluded to in the old literature of the country—this circumstance would not necessarily render that term less suitable to be used as a translation for our word God. How can we expect them to have in all points correct views of the Divine Being?

The influence of Buddhism in producing modifications in the philosophy of the Chinese is, although perfectly visible, not acknowledged by those who have become subjected to that influence. But there are not wanting very numerous assertions of the most unqualified kind, that the two religions are identical in their principles. For example: Commissioner Yeh told Mr. Cooke that "the Taoli of Confucius is at one with the Taoli of Buddha." There is a class of books published, frequently for gratuitous distribution as religious tracts, maintaining this view. The Buddhist reasons that there is nothing real but Buddha, that the mind is Buddha, and that to attain to the state of

Buddha it is only necessary to watch the mind and follow out our own nature. This is what a priest of that religion would probably give as an answer, if asked to put in two or three sentences the essential features of his system. It is very common for the Confucianist who is favourably disposed to Buddhism to say that in these statements the term Buddha, "intelligence," is put for what he calls "reason" (*le*) or "nature" (*sing*), and that they amount to nothing more or less than the doctrine that human nature is originally good, and that the path of reformation and perfection lies in following out our nature. It is in this way that they assert the identity of the Taou-le of Confucius and of Buddha.

I knew a native scholar of great ability who had been a Buddhist priest in his youth. Not satisfied with his prospects as a member of the monkish fraternity, he resolved to let his hair grow, and return to Confucianism. There is no comparison between the respectability of the two religions, and the scope that they afford for those who have energy and enterprise. My former acquaintance was ambitious, and abandoned the cloistered seclusion of a monastery to try his fortune in a wider field. His Buddhist reading, however, made him think favourably of that religion. He said to me on one occasion, "All countries have their sages. We have Confucius. Buddha was the sage of India. The Mongols have the Dalai Lama, and the Mohammedans Mahomet. You in the West have Jesus. It is necessarily so in the arrangements of Heaven. You speak of Adam in your Scriptures. He is no other than our Pan-koo."

This show of liberality is very common with the Chinese when conversing with foreigners upon Christianity. It springs partly from politeness, which induces them to admit, for the time, the equality of the religion of their foreign interlocutor with their own. It comes in part, also, from the circumstance that they do not claim a divine character for Confucius. They regard him as nothing more than the wisest of men. They never speak of him as God, nor do they claim inspiration for his words. They can afford, then, to admit that other religions are as suitable for other nations as theirs is for them, if they enjoin a good morality. An ethical test is the only one they know. When the evidence of a new religion is presented to them, they at once refer it to a moral standard, and give their approval with the utmost readiness, if it passes the test. They do not ask whether it is divine, but whether it is good. This tolerant mode of viewing other religions is one of the effects of the introduction of Buddhism into China.

The Chinese having this mode of viewing religions as equally good, the difficulty often felt by the Christian missionary in persuading them to believe in the religion of Christ will be easily perceived. He may prove its divinity, but this does not go far with a latitudinarian people, who give their assent equally to all systems that have a good moral code.

The influence of Buddhism on Confucianism is seen most palpably in the mixing of its rites with the worship of ancestors. Of all religious ceremonies, the people of China think this the most important. It is related of some of the high officers that they will visit their ancestral chapel in the morning to pass some time in self-examination, having the feeling that they are likely to discharge this duty more faithfully in the presence of the holy tablets which preserve the remembrance of their forefathers, and act as a sort of guardian *penates* in protecting and consecrating their homes. To look upon these tablets is to a Chinese like an appeal to his honour. He dares not commit any act that will bring dishonour on his ancestral name. He feels rewarded when he has done anything that he is conscious is not unworthy his ancestors. It is reverence for them that constitutes the most powerful religious sentiment in his mind.

The Buddhist masses for the dead afforded the opportunity of showing in a palpable manner the regard felt for ancestors. The ancestral worship is simple. Simplicity marks the style of the funereal temple and the family cemetery. The common eye, not satisfied with simplicity, was pleased with the rich dresses, genuflexions, and processions of the Buddhist monks, and especially with the preparations that they undertake to make for the soul of the departed in the invisible world.

These additional rites are performed in the family home, not in the ancestral temple. The Hindoo metempsychosis allows great scope to the fancy in imagining the condition of the departed soul in the next world. I saw on one occasion, at Kwun-shan, a large paper house burnt. It was intended to be the residence of the deceased in Hades. Kwun-shan is a city passed by the traveller on his way from Shanghai westward to Soochow. The walls include a much wider space than is needed by the population; but the deficiency of inhabitants is made up by a busy suburb outside the gates on the river-side. A hill crowned with a pagoda within the city is its principal ornament, and forms a landmark for many miles round. From this hill the city presents a very umbrageous aspect. The Chinese are fond of trees in their cities, and this gives them a very pleasant habitable appearance.

My fellow-travellers and I followed a funeral procession that we met in the streets, and were admitted to the house where the principal ceremonies were to be performed, without difficulty. We went in with a crowd of other strangers through the open doors, as is commonly done in China on such occasions. The paper house for the departed soul was near its completion. It was about ten feet high and twelve feet deep. It contained a sleeping-room, library, reception-room, entrance-hall, and treasury. It was furnished with paper chairs and tables. We saw boxes of paper money carried in. A paper image of the dead appeared in the interior seated in state. There was a sedan chair, with bearers, and also a boat and boatman, for the use of the deceased in the unseen world. A table spread with food was placed in front of the house. A party of Buddhist priests now came forward and walked in procession, striking bells and chanting. As they passed round the house they threw rice and wheat upon it. The family came forward and worshipped their deceased mother, for whose use the house was built. They wore white cotton cloth and sackcloth, white cloth shoes, and white cotton braid at the ends of their pigtails, instead of the usual silk braid, used as a terminal decoration to that ornament. The Chinese think that in mourning costume the material should be uncoloured, and they therefore employ white. In this they resemble the ancient Jews, who wore sackcloth, as being a coarse, uncoloured material, on occasions when they desired to make an outward expression of grief. After the act of worship, some shots were fired, and then a light was applied to the fragile paper fabric, and in a moment it was in flames. It stood in an open court within the family residence.

According to the doctrine of metempsychosis we are all passing through a succession of lives, some past and some to come; and the life on which we are about to enter may be sufficiently like the present to allow of provision being made for our comfort there in a way such as that just described. Rich Confucian families in China are in the constant habit of performing similar ceremonies for the dead. *Ab uno disce omnes.* And although the individual, when appealed to, will say that they are of no use, that he does not believe in their efficacy, and only permits them in conformity to local custom, it is quite possible that in most cases, under this pretended infidelity, there may be no little faith in the metempsychosis, and in the validity of Buddhist rites founded on that doctrine. Men, from their natural constitution, will have some belief in a future state. This comes from the teaching of the internal monitor, "the divinity within us that points out a hereafter, and intimates eternity to man." While Christians were slow to convey the truth to China's teeming multitudes, the Buddhists seized upon their opportunity, and fed with Hindoo fictions the craving after some knowledge of the future life which they found among this and the other nations they visited.

Faith in the Hindoo view of the future state is very common among the Chinese Confucianists. It does not amalgamate well with their own system. The two doctrines are far from dovetailing nicely together. They know this, and are not offended when the Buddhist view is denied. They revere it less than the teaching of Confucius, but still they have some faith in it. They conform to Buddhist ceremonies, and believe to some degree that they are valid and efficacious. If obliged to make their choice, they would prefer the doctrine of Confucius, but since it is not expected in China that a man should restrict himself to one religion, they conform to both without caring for the contradiction and inconsistency that such a course involves. This need not surprise us, when we recollect how a faith in witchcraft and fairy mythology among many of our own people existed several centuries after Christianity had become the national faith.

CHAPTER VII.

INFLUENCE OF BUDDHISM ON CHINESE LITERATURE AND SOCIAL LIFE—*Continued.*

THE illustrations contained in the last chapter of the influence of Buddhism on the literature and national life of the Chinese will now be continued by the citation of a curious passage from a scientific tract published some years ago at Hangchow. The author is treating upon modern European astronomy. He had read of the discovery of Uranus and Neptune, of the motion of the sun attended by his planets among the fixed stars, and of the statement that the fixed stars themselves are suns shining upon planetary systems of their own. He is trying to comprehend this for himself, and to make it plain to his reader. He first takes for comparison a scene very familiar to a Chinaman's eye. He imagines the hall of a rich man's mansion ornamented by a large number of hanging lanterns. They are seen by the visitor as he walks under them to be hung from the ceiling in lines and circles according to a regular plan, but when looked at from a distance, the rows of lanterns appear to cross each other in a very confused manner. He does not give in his adhesion to the modern European astronomy without an attempt to show how much of it was known to his countrymen before. He quotes ancient Chinese authors who had said that the earth is round, and that it moved from west to east; that in winter it travels to the north-west, and in summer to the south-east, passing over the middle points of its journey at the equinoxes. These things are said in very old books, and we must allow the ancient Chinese all the credit they deserve for them, although, like the theories of Nicetas and Pythagoras, they were not commonly believed in at the time.

Not content with this, he proceeds to say that the Buddhist cosmogony has anticipated the modern European astronomy: "Their books speak of a great, a middle, and a small universe of a thousand worlds. I used to wonder at the falsity and absurdity of such descriptions of the universe until I read the new astronomical views of the men from the West, who say that through boundless space are scattered numberless nebulæ made up of thickly-clustered stars. They also say that the stars sprinkled over the heavenly vault are so many suns, each of them having several earths revolving round it. They tell us also that the Milky Way is a nebula, and contains within it the sun as one of its component stars. The sun is the nearest to the earth of all the stars, and therefore he appears to us much larger than they do. What the men of the West have discovered by astronomical instruments agrees remarkably with the opinions of the Buddhists. I cannot but admire the sagacity of these men. By the light of their wisdom they were able to discover without the use of instruments the vastness of the universe. Is not their sagacity far superior to that of the followers of Confucius, who never imagined the existence of numberless other worlds spread through the region of infinite space?" He then states that the long periods of revolution of the more distant planets resemble what was said by the Buddhists of the heavens in their cosmogony. In the paradise of Tushita, for example, four hundred of our years make one day. In that of Shiva, a thousand six hundred years of our time constitute one day.

We see here the first effect of European science on the mind of a scholar, himself a Confucianist, but well read in Buddhist literature. Nothing can be more palpably fictitious than the system of the world to which he refers. The inventors of the cosmogony of the Northern Buddhists were metaphysicians who denied the existence of matter, and when they spoke of immense assemblages of worlds in various parts of space, only intended them to be the imaginary abodes of imaginary Buddhas, partaking in no way of reality. These Buddhas, with the realms over which they reigned, were symbols of ideas, and nothing more. The Chinese reader of their works, looking at things from his practical, unimaginative point of view, will, as in this case, mistake their object, and see in these ideal creations of the subtle Hindoo intellect proofs of a sagacity that he thinks can bear comparison with that of those European investigators who possessed the power to discover the unknown truths of nature—with the genius of such men, for example, as Copernicus and Newton. It is known from experience that when the geological periods in the history of the earth are mentioned to intelligent Chinese, they will remark, " That is just like what we have read in Buddhist books before." These books speak of an endless succession of Kalpas, or periods of alternate formation and decay. According to this view, the world is subject to incessant changes under the dominion of fate. This fate is exercised in agreement with the laws of moral retribution, so far as it refers to living beings. In relation to the physical world, it causes it to pass through four periods, those of formation, conservation, decay, and destruction. As often as this fourfold process is completed it begins again. This system of the world occurs to the mind of the follower of Confucius when he hears of the theories of modern geology. The living author already quoted from says the appearance of new stars, and the disappearance of old ones, as described in Western astronomy, accords with the Buddhist account of the history of worlds.

When such men read the Mosaic narrative of creation, they will be likely to bring forward an objection to it from modern geology. They have, then, to be met with the same arguments which are addressed by defenders of Divine revelation at home to those that impugn its authority. The Christian missionary in China must be prepared to meet there cultivated men, who will oppose him with the arguments of an infidel logic, just as he will also find dense masses of population whose religious faith consists of gross superstitions. All the opposition that intellectual activity and degrading superstitions can unitedly bring against Christianity will be likely to exist in a country like China. This will not surprise those who remember the character of the resistance made to Christianity in India by the educated class. Educated Hindoos prefer to attack the religion of Jesus with weapons drawn from the armoury of infidelity, rather than with those furnished by superstition. So it will be in China in the coming contest. To be forewarned is to be forearmed.

Similar instruction may be derived from another work lately published by a Confucianist at Soochow. Protestant missionaries are now hoping to establish themselves at this, among other great cities that are to be opened to the Christian traveller. They may meet there with the writer of the work we refer to, and with other men who think like him. How these men think, and what opinions they hold on science and religion, may be learned from a book like this.

He attacks Matthew Ricci, the first Jesuit missionary in China, for teaching the Ptolemaic system of the world. He states that the doctrine of nine crystalline spheres encircling the earth like the coats of an onion, the uppermost of them all constantly carrying the other eight, which contain the stars and planets, along with it, is absurd. He also criticises Copernicus. He allows that the earth has a motion round its own axis, but not round the sun.

To what this author says upon Christianity, allusion will be made in a subsequent part of this work. At present I shall only refer to his views on Buddhism. He has a section upon supernatural beings. These include those personages commonly worshipped as divinities, and also the souls of ancestors. He says the worship of the gods and genii of Taouism, the belief in fabulous islands whose inhabitants enjoy perpetual youth, and the use of charms and divination, are comparatively modern in China. He proceeds to animadvert on the doctrine of hell and the metempsychosis, or the "revolving wheel" of life and death. It came from India, and it was when Buddhism was taught, he complains, that China heard for the first time of a return to life after death, of a judge of men's actions in Hades, of birth into another world, and of the acts of the present life being recollected in a future one. All these things come, he says, from the ever-active human mind, which spontaneously believes in these doctrines, and likes to put faith in various supernatural beings. Whether we assert or deny them, we cannot feel sure that we are right. We only know this, he thinks, that all religious doctrines and customs come out of the mind itself. His conclusion is, that men have a natural tendency to believe in these things, that differences in opinion on religious matters depend on the country where they exist, and that there is no ground of certainty respecting them. He finds a proof of his opinion in the separation of the soul at death, when, according to the common Chinese doctrine, the ethereal and grosser parts of the soul return to their respective sources, the Yang and Yin. These are the male and female principles, the two elements that pervade all nature. The soul having been divided in this way, he argues that it cannot be supposed capable of living again. How then, he asks, can the spirits that are worshipped, and which are popularly believed to be the souls of deceased men, be really still existing? The life of man, and of living things generally, depends on the union of these two principles, and ceases with their separation. He asserts his disbelief in the reality of the beings worshipped by his countrymen as gods on this ground. It may appear a very insufficient argument to us, but this is the form that his thoughts take upon the subject. He rests his denial of the being of the gods upon the dogma that the soul cannot have an individual conscious existence after death. His countrymen suppose that the soul, like the body, is compound. There is the rational soul, that which thinks; the animal soul, which presides over the body; and a third which is the seat of the passions. Immortality is secured if these parts are kept from separating. The discipline of the Taouist sect is intended to effect this. But our author disbelieves in the possibility of preventing the parts of the soul from becoming scattered. Yet he admits that the souls of ancestors should be worshipped, because otherwise the great duty of affectionate respect to parents would fall into neglect. The popular divinities should also be worshipped, because it is a good thing for men to be controlled by a sentiment of veneration for superior beings.

Surely the Christian revelation, coming to men with Divine authority, and fortified by objective proofs, is remarkably suited to the state of mind of this writer. Buddhism does not profess a Divine origin. It is nothing but the work of the human intellect and imagination, operating on a large scale, such as might be expected in the product of Hindoo pantheism. It elevates philosophy above God. It is subjective and human. It does not address the Confucianist with a voice of authority as from God. He looks at it, as he thinks Confucius himself would have done, if it had entered China in his time. The words of the great sage recur to his memory. He repeats them rapidly over. "Abundant is the beneficent activity of the supernatural powers." This seems to favour belief in them, and reverence for them. He cites another familiar extract: "Honour the supernatural powers, but keep them at a distance." The sage of China thinks we should not have too much faith in or reverence for the gods. There is nothing certain and tangible in what we know of them. Let us discharge the duties we owe to men. It will be better to make up our deficiencies towards them than to give our attention to beings of whom we know so little. It is with these sentiments that our author closes his chapter upon the Kwei-shin (the gods). He is something more of an unbeliever than his master, but he defers to his master's teaching. He opposes one human religion with the dicta of another human religion. Neither of these systems claims any other authority than that of eminent men for their doctrines, and the common conscience of mankind for their morality. Christianity, taking higher ground, resting upon Divine inspiration and external historical evidences of its Divine source, will, it may be hoped, when rightly understood by men like our author, be felt to supply what the religions of his country have failed to give him. He declines to believe in the gods of Buddhism and Taouism, because they have been imagined by the human mind, and rest on no proofs of their own. Christianity has that sort of evidence and of certainty that will meet his requirements, if he can be brought to understand it. But at first, when Christianity is offered to the educated Chinese, they will look at it from the Confucian stand-point, and condemn it as belonging to the same class of religions as Buddhism. This we shall have the opportunity of illustrating by extracts when we discuss the present attitude of literature in that country in respect to Christianity.

The city where this author resides, Soochow, had before its capture by the Taipings, a population of a million two hundred thousand. The wall is twelve English miles in length, and there are very populous suburbs. Is he a fair representative of the opinions of his fellow-citizens? The views of the scholar, sending forth a pamphlet on science and religion from the seclusion of his family mansion, may be expected to differ from those of the multitudes who, bent on business or pleasure, throng the streets in his vicinity. To illustrate their sentiments on the doctrines of Buddhism I will here refer to what I have seen among them. A friend and I were once taken to the official residence of a mandarin of the third class. He led us through his suite of apartments, which were handsomely furnished in the best Chinese style. He had a large Spanish oil-painting of a lady, which, instead of being hung on a wall, was covered up and kept in a cupboard. He valued it very highly. In the innermost of his apartments upstairs we found what seems to have been the most sacred thing to him that his house contained. It was the shrine and image of Kwan-yin, goddess of mercy. On the table beside it was a copy of the book of prayers used in the worship of this divinity. It was not one printed in the common Chinese mode, from wooden blocks, but an impression from stone tablets, on which these prayers had been engraved five centuries ago by a celebrated artist, and which are preserved as an important antique relic in some Buddhist temple. Before the image sticks of incense were burning, which had been fresh lighted that morning. A follower of Confucius should not, if consistent, worship Kwan-yin, nor keep her image in his house. But we found that our mandarin friend had the innermost corner of his residence devoted to this superstition. He would profess, like his fellow-mandarins, to disbelieve in the efficacy of worship of this kind, but this little incident taught us that the professions of a follower of Confucius are no index to his private belief. Temples are to be seen in nearly every street of a Chinese city; but this is not enough to satisfy the disposition of the inhabitants to practise idolatry. They will also have a private chapel in their own houses if it be practicable, which they may visit each morning for the performance of an act of worship.

Take another example of the extent to which Buddhism is believed in a city like Soochow, from the class of artisans. When residing as a missionary at Shanghai, I had been on one occasion denying the doctrine of a former life. Popular Buddhism in China, carrying out to the full the belief in the Hindoo metempsychosis, maintains a previous life to account for our present one, quite as strongly as it insists on our present life being followed by a future one of retribution. A tailor from Soochow, who formed one of the audience, remarked that there must be some cause for the misfortunes of our condition in this life, and that that cause was in the sins of a former state. It was stated to him in reply, that our present calamities are the result of the sins of our ancestors, and that they can be accounted for in this way, without the supposition that we ourselves had lived and sinned in the person of some individual of a former generation. He was then asked why Kwan-foo-tsze, the deified hero of an ancient dynasty, had never appeared again in times of danger to save his country, and why Confucius had not been born into the world afresh to restore the nation to virtue and good order? If his doctrine of a former life were true, and the same person might appear in the world at different periods, great men like these would not fail to be recognised on their second arrival. He replied, that if Confucius had not appeared among mankind a second time, Kwan-foo-tsze had done so, and that not very long ago, in the reign of the Emperor Kanghe.

The opinions of this artisan may be taken to illustrate two things—the notion that the common Chinese have of another life, and that which they entertain of the incarnation of divine persons. They see a law of retribution pervading the world, and human life is to their conceptions so enlarged as to embrace an indefinite number of past and future periods. These successive lives may be passed in this world, or in heaven, or in hell, or in some intermediate localities. Thus, the soul of a woman may, as a reward for virtue, on entering the world a second time, inhabit the body of a man. Chinese women frequently pray for this. A wicked man may become, as a punishment, a sheep, or an ant, or a bird. The retribution is decreed by a sure but invisible and impersonal fate, the same law of fate that regulates the succession of worlds, which are constantly being created and destroyed afresh in the order of the ever-revolving Kalpas. According to this view, the region through which the soul may wander during the interminable series of lives through which it must pass includes all the palaces of the gods, and of other beings possessing a different nature from that of man, as also the abodes of punishment for the wicked. How strongly the common Chinese believe in these Buddhist opinions may be shown by a reference to the fact that they trace bodily calamities to sins in a former state of existence. On one occasion a patient in an hospital at Shanghai, when asked by a missionary if he knew himself to be guilty of sin, looked significantly at his diseased foot, and asked, "How can I be without sin? I must have committed some crime in a former life."

The other notion that the preceding conversation illustrates is that of the incarnation of divinities. Personages like Kwan-foo-tsze, the god of war, may appear again and again in successive centuries. In the event of his reappearance, the person whose body he inhabits will be noticed to have the qualities of the long-deceased hero by the more sagacious of his contemporaries. The incarnation takes place in such a way that the individuality of the person in whom the divinity resides is not destroyed.

The Taouists, who have been servile imitators of the Buddhists in very many points, adopted from them this mode of increasing the importance of certain personages to whom they wished to pay especial honour. They say of Laou-keun, the founder of their religion, that he was born into the world several times before and after the date of his historical appearance.

The popular phraseology of the Chinese language furnishes, on examination, abundant evidence of the very extensive influence of Buddhist ideas. The Chinese speak of certain localities, which they call *teen tang*, the "heavenly paradise," and *te yuh*, "earth's prison," and which correspond nearly to our terms heaven and hell. These terms, not found in the books of the Confucian religion, are universally familiar to all classes of the people. Christian missionaries, in teaching the Bible doctrine of retribution, make use of these names for heaven and hell, as being the best equivalents they can find. The consciousness of immortality, natural to men, has among the common Chinese people been moulded into this form. When stripped of a Buddhist dress, such conceptions constitute, like the other parts of natural religion, a preparation for the reception of Christianity.

The common notion in China of merit attaching to charitable actions, and the forgiveness of sins for the sake of them, comes from Buddhism. The phrase *yin kung,* "invisible merit," is very much in use. It means merit that wins the approval of invisible beings, and ensures a reward from them. All acts of kindness and benevolence are thus designated. The performance of a mass by Buddhist priests for the rescue of a soul from one of the prisons in hell is called *kung tih,* " merit." The distribution of money and food to the poor, and the repairing of roads and bridges, are spoken of as meritorious actions, which will be sure to bring rewards from the unseen powers that watch human conduct. Such actions are called simply *haou she,* "good acts," a phrase which has become a synonym for almsgiving. The Chinese beggar, when he calls to passers-by for money, is understood to be asking charity, although he says only, *Tso haou she*—" Do a good action." He frequently adds the phrase, *Sew tsze sew sun*—"Act virtuously, that you may obtain sons and grandsons." These expressions have come into use because Buddhism has promulgated the idea that virtue consists in exercising kindness towards those who suffer. The Confucian notion of virtue is rather that of doing one's duty. The Buddhist conception of it may be gathered from such phraseology as this, which is universal in China in the speech of the common people.

Many of the most frequently used phrases for retribution are Buddhist, in fact all those that allude to rewards and punishments in a future state. The sight of a great act of wickedness will suggest to a bystander to say that the perpetrator deserves to be confined in a prison in hell, eighteen stories deep. A good action is supposed to excite the regard of the invisible good beings that inhabit the air. In a popular romance, "The Tale of a Guitar," a young wife is very assiduous in performing the offices of filial piety to her husband's parents. He has deserted her and them, and is living in the metropolis in the enjoyment of the highest wealth and rank, the reward of his talents. During his absence, a famine deprives his family at home of the means of subsistence. His parents die of hunger, and are buried by his wife, who had been living for some time on the husks of the rice with which their lives were supported. She prays at the grave, and proceeds to raise over it a mound of earth with her own hands. Celestial soldiers in the sky, seeing that this pious task was wearisome and exhausting to her, came to her aid. For every spadeful of earth that she threw on the grave, a thousand more were thrown by invisible hands. Several terms are employed to express an influence of this sort exerted by the virtuous among mankind upon celestial beings. They say *kan ying joo hiang*, "the influence" on the part of virtuous persons, and "its response" on the part of celestial beings, are "like the sound" of a bell when struck by a clapper, in the rapidity of the effect that is produced. The phrase *paou ying* expresses protection given as a reward for virtue, or in answer to prayer.

Maimed beggars appeal to the bystanders to pity them on the ground that they are "at present in hell," their phrase being *heen tsae te yuh*. In doing so, they acknowledge themselves to be sinners of a very deep dye. Of this their calamity is considered to be a proof.

These and similar notions obtained from Buddhism prevail universally among the people of China, as shown by the constant use of expressions such as those, a few of which have now been given. They prove how extensively Buddhism has influenced a population that is still nominally Confucian.

CHAPTER VIII.

CONFUCIAN AND BUDDHIST NOTIONS OF GOD.

This chapter and the next will be devoted to the consideration of the opinions the Chinese hold respecting God. Intelligent men among them, who have become familiar with Christianity, say that the ancient Chinese were undoubtedly more religious than the modern. The frequent mention of God, under the denomination Shang-te, in the earliest books of the nation, may be regarded as a proof of this. I remember a Chinese, of fine intellectual appearance, having made this statement. It was not to be wondered at, he said, that the ancients, being much nearer the time of Adam, should be more imbued with the spirit of piety towards God, than men belonging to modern days, when tradition has become obscured by time. The further back we went in time, he observed, the more near to coincidence would the traditions of his nation be with ours. Our Chinese friend was reminded that the first princes of his country were said, in the ancient books, to have worshipped not God only, but also the spirits of mountains, and rivers, and of other parts of nature. Their religion, then, could not be regarded as the same with ours, because they offered sacrifices to other beings beside God. But these spirits, he replied, are the same that are called angels in your Bible.

With all due respect to the opinion of the native scholar to whom reference is here made, it is perhaps more correct to regard these beings, supposed to inhabit different parts of nature, as deriving their origin from the human imagination. The movements seen in nature, the indications of

universal life which perpetually meet our eyes, suggest to
the observer the presence of supernatural beings. The
Chinese very early had the conception of powerful beings,
subordinate to God, regulating the course of events in the
physical and intellectual universe. They called them
shin.

There are inconsistencies in the views held by the
Chinese respecting the duty of worshipping God. Many
followers of Confucius seem to recognise this duty when
they offer incense to Heaven on the new and full moons.
On those days they proceed to the square open court round
which the family home is built, and there, under no cover-
ing but the sky, they kneel and pray, or burn incense, to
Heaven. Yet it is common to hear the Chinese say, that
Heaven should be worshipped only by the Emperor in the
name of the nation, and that the God of heaven is too
majestic and glorious for a common man to dare approach
Him as a worshipper. The people and the officers of
Government should worship the subordinate divinities that
preside over the cities or districts to which they belong.
This is the theory, but it is not strictly carried into practice. Some profess to worship Heaven once a year, others
twice a month. They often speak of adoring Heaven and
Earth, as if they meant two divinities by those terms. The
presence of gross material views in their minds leads them
away from the one invisible Ruler to the world which He
governs. Then, having their thoughts fixed on the world
instead of its Maker, they imagine a duality of ruling
powers, the two spirits of Heaven and of Earth. This is
favoured by the prevailing philosophy, which sees a duality
all through nature. Often do the Chinese argue, as they
think triumphantly, in a way like the following:—The sun is
yang, the moon is *yin* (or light and darkness respectively).
Man is *yang*, woman is *yin*. The south is *yang*, the north
is *yin*. The rational soul, *hwun*, is *yang;* the physical
soul, *pih*, is *yin*. Heaven is *yang*, earth is *yin*. They
conceive that in a chain of antithetical expressions like

these there is contained a perfectly obvious and irrefragable proof of their favourite dualistic philosophy. Here is their weakness. It is the clinging to ancient system that keeps their minds closed against truth when it comes to them in a novel form. They will not go out of their old-fashioned tracks of thought. It was through this mode of thinking that they readily adopted the conception of two ruling powers in nature, which they call Heaven and Earth. Instead of saying that they worship God, they will more frequently say that they worship Heaven and Earth. The husbandman, at harvest, when he has gathered in his sheaves, acknowledges that it is his duty to *seay teen pac te*, to "thank Heaven and worship Earth."

The spiritual element has been very little developed in the minds of this people; they have not had Divine revelation to train and guide the spiritual faculties. This is the cause of the confusion of ideas which the common people in that country often exhibit, when they do not separate between heaven and God. They are not accustomed to the conception of a purely immaterial being. Their notions of God are materialised. They confound Him with the place where He resides, and with the world that He has created. But the error of the common people is not more mischievous than that opposite one of the modern philosophical school that has identified God with an abstract principle, and maintained that there is no distinction between God and *le*, "reason," the law of the world.

They have more easily fallen into these views, because the three national religions have been occupied with objects very different from that of representing God as the Father of the human family, who must be expected to make His will known; so that, when missionaries speak of God's commands, their auditors will sometimes ask, "What are God's commands? We did not know that He had any. In what way can He teach us anything?" They have not been led to look at religious truths and duties as communicated and enjoined directly by God. This renders it hard to persuade them that idolatry is a sin, as being forbidden by Divine authority. They consider idols to be symbols, and nothing more. They see that it may be foolish to worship them, but they do not so easily perceive that it is wicked. Though they are in the habit of recognising the right of a father in his family, and a king in his kingdom, to issue special commands, they are not accustomed to think of God as being likely to do so. The ancient Chinese believed in God as a personal, active being, the ruler of heaven and earth, just, powerful, and merciful; but it was not to be expected that this belief and tradition of theirs by itself would, through the long ages that have intervened, preserve a clear knowledge of God among their descendants. It has been seen that they have fallen into very great errors. If the attributes of God, according to the common notions of the Chinese, were examined, they would prove a most manifest need of the light of revelation. For example, let us take the omnipresence of God. They object to the doctrine that Jesus is the Son of God, because, if He were Divine, He would have left heaven without a government when He came into our world. That they should attempt to disprove the Divinity of Christ in this way, shows that they have no proper conception of the omnipresence of God.

With regard to creation, they know of no law but spontaneity and self-development in the construction of the existing universe. They consider that all things have come to be as they are of themselves. They do not conclude, from the marks of design and contrivance which are exhibited in nature, that there must have been an intelligent Contriver. Some other heathen nations have been familiar with this argument of natural theology, but the Chinese not so. All their descriptions of the origin of the world are pervaded with the idea of spontaneous production. When the Christian doctrine of creation is presented to them, and illustrations of the infinite wisdom of God in it referred to, they admit them to be reasonable, but they do not feel it to be a necessity that they should resign their own idea of the spontaneous origin of the universe. They do not speak of the *works* of nature or the *works* of God, when gazing on the ever-moving panorama which that universe offers to the eye. They prefer to denominate it the "living heaven" and the "living earth." "Why," they have often been asked, "should you speak of those things which are dead matter fashioned from nothing by the hand of God, as living beings? Heaven and earth are surely not *persons?*" "And why not?" they have replied. "The sky pours down rain and sunshine. The earth produces corn and grass. We see them in perpetual movement, and we may therefore say that they are living."

These opinions, widely diffused among the mass of the people, if not acceded to by the more intelligent, materially interfere with correct views of God. The idea of creation most familiar to the Chinese mind is that there was a monad at the beginning. This first atom separated into two. The two atoms became four, the four were changed into eight, and the eight gave origin to all things. If the Chinese are asked how this process was commenced and continued, they answer, that "it came of itself."

Preoccupied with this particular cosmogony, they do not feel any necessity for a creating agent, nor are they led to meditate on the wisdom of God as displayed in His works. While, then, we find that the Confucian religion is monotheistic, recognising one Supreme Ruler, the tradition of whom the Chinese had from the earliest period of their history, they have been left with very insufficient notions of some of the Divine attributes. This religion has failed to represent the agency of God in creation and in providence, so clearly as to preserve the mass of the nation from grossly erroneous views of the Divine nature and from the neglect of prayer. A young man of the artisan class had come from a neighbouring village, a few years since, to the city of Shanghai, and, entering a missionary chapel, had heard an address on Christianity. The auditors were invited to express their opinions on the subject of religion. This man was the most ready to comply. He adopted a flippant style of remark indicating no little admiration of his own cleverness. He had heard, he said, for seven or eight years, occasionally, foreigners advocating their religion, and he had studied it with many other systems of belief without arriving at any satisfactory conclusion. He was acquainted, he said, with no fewer than thirty or forty religious systems, and he had discovered something wrong in all of them. Christianity seemed to be good, but he feared that there would be found defects in that also. He allowed that our opposition to idolatry and incense-burning is reasonable, and asserted that he had long given them up, but he considered that he ought to adhere to the worship of ancestors according to the national custom. The prohibition of this observance by Christianity must prevent his becoming a believer. He was recommended, seeing that he could not find satisfaction in any of the religions he had examined, to abandon these restless inquiries, and look to God to be instructed in answer to prayer. "How," he asked, "can instruction from God be obtained?" "The foreign teacher means," remarked a bystander, volunteering an answer, "that God will speak to you in a dream at night." "No," said the missionary, "He will teach you from His Holy Word, this book. In the course you have hitherto taken, you cannot expect to obtain settled convictions. Try a new method. Instead of weighing with a minute accuracy the respective merits of this and that system, seek your own personal salvation from God, and the forgiveness of sins." "Sins!" he exclaimed, "I have no sins." He was again asked, "Do you pray to and thank God for His goodness?" "No," he said. When reminded that the neglect of those duties was sin, he replied again, "I do not know which God (Shang-te) to believe in. There are many." He was met with the reply, "There is but one God. How can heaven have two suns, or a kingdom two sovereigns?

Surely you should worship Him. He made heaven and earth." "But how," he replied, "can I know that He created heaven and earth?" He was answered, "You are not at liberty to deny that the world had a Creator. This house in which we are sitting must have had a builder. To speak as you have done is to deprive our Maker of His glory. You would do better to submit to God and seek His forgiveness." He did not attempt to refute the argument from design, nor did he acknowledge its validity. He proceeded to defend himself with weapons of another kind. "You differ from the Roman Catholics. How can I tell whether you or they are right?" The conversation, as it continued in this new channel, need not be further detailed. What has been given serves to illustrate, with respect to the knowledge of God, the effect of the Confucian system, which this individual professed to follow, upon the very large class of persons whom he may be taken to represent.

When we leave the region of Confucian thought, and enter into that of Buddhism, we find the notion of God appearing in a form differing from that which meets us elsewhere. This religion is professedly atheistic. It denies that there is an eternal God, the Creator of the world. The gods that it admits the existence of are subject to mortality like men, and limited in their power. But this atheism is that of subtle logicians, and it cannot become the faith of common men. The feeling natural to man that there is a Divine Power present in the universe must express itself. If the activity of divine beings do not exhibit itself in creation, it may do so in providence. The powers attributed to the Buddhas and Bodhisattwas are supposed to be exercised in answer to the prayers of men, and they take the place of God in the minds of common believers in that religion.

The use of the word *poosa* in Chinese is in some respects like that of God. The lower class of people say that all success in life, for example, depends on the protection of

Poosa. This word is a shortened form of the Sanscrit term Bodhisattwa. Originally it is merely a designation of a class of Buddha's disciples. Their progress in knowledge gives them power over nature, and they exert that power, it is supposed, for the good of mankind. They are men elevated to their position by wisdom. Their office is to teach rather than to govern, but the power to control physical nature develops itself in them spontaneously, as they make progress in comprehending and exemplifying the doctrine of Buddha. The Poosa feels more sympathy with the lower wants of men than the Buddha does. Buddha is freed from desire. He knows nothing of common feelings. His aim is very lofty and abstruse. The disciple who is far advanced in the path of enlightenment can appreciate his teaching. But the Poosa is more within the reach of human sympathies. He is prayed to for relief from sickness, for riches, and other benefits appertaining to the animal nature of man. Both Fuh and Poosa are trusted in as God by the Chinese Buddhist. Both are relied on for protection and salvation. Buddha or Fuh is highest in rank, but Poosa is nearest in sympathy. They are both viewed as having divine power and benevolence. They are alike in pitying mankind, or seeking to save men from misery, and in aiming to do so by teaching. They also resemble each other in the circumstance that they are both nothing but exalted human nature. They differ, however, in rank. The highest of all conditions is that of Buddha. There is no step beyond this except the Nirvana, where personality is lost in an eternal, unchangeable state of unconscious existence. It is here that the distinction disappears between person and state, and between thought and being. If Buddha does not enter at once into the Nirvana, he retains his personality and his conscious activity merely for the sake of mankind. But he lives always upon the verge of the abyss of the Nirvana, ready to sink into it the moment that his appointed work of instructing and saving living beings is completed.

The next step in the scale of being, below that of Fuh, is Poosa. The person who has attained to this rank must become Fuh before he can enter the Nirvana. So that he is not supreme, nor absolutely perfect, nor does he exercise creative power, nor is he exempt from change, nor without the need of improvement, all which things are inseparable from the true notion of God. Poosa is a learner at the feet of Buddha, while himself a teacher of others, and Fuh has still to make the transition into the Nirvana. These things show that Fuh and Poosa are far from exactly corresponding to the notion of God; and this will be further evident from the meaning of the words—Buddha signifies *perception*, and Bodhisattwa *knowledge* and *pity*.

Such are the beings on whose power and desire to save common Buddhist minds rest as they should do upon God. The faith that they ought to give to Him they give to them.

The principal Buddhas that they thus revere are Shakyamuni, the historical founder of their religion, and Amitabha, who presides in the western heaven, the paradise of the Northern Buddhists. It is the image of Shakyamuni that is seen occupying the centre in almost all temples of this religion in China. Kneeling and bowing are the attitudes of worship. Oral prayers are used or not as the worshipper pleases. Though the image of this Buddha is everywhere seen, yet he is not so much trusted to and prayed to for the common blessings that men need as is Amitabha. Amitabha is the guide of the disciple to paradise. He is therefore called "the guiding Buddha"— Tsie-yin-fuh. His immediate providence in the salvation of the disciple seems to be more recognised than that of Shakyamuni. His name is very much used as a charm. It is constantly heard from the lips of the *hoshang* or monks in daily conversation, and it forms the burden of their prayers while performing morning and evening worship in monasteries. The common phrase Omitofuh is the Chinese form of the name Amitabha Buddha, or Amida

Buddha, as he is called in the Mongolian language. There are many other Buddhas whose names are occasionally mentioned, but they are much less known than these two.

Of the personages honoured with the name of Poosa, Kwan-yin, the goddess of mercy, is best known. This divinity is represented sometimes as male, at others as female. At present, for convenience' sake, we use the feminine pronoun. She is often represented with a child in her arms, and is then designated the giver of children. Elsewhere she is styled the " Kwan-yin who saves from the eight forms of suffering," or " of the southern sea," or " of the thousand arms," &c. She passes through various metamorphoses, which give rise to this variety in names.

In Buddhist books, descriptions are given of what is designated the true Poosa. His feelings are very benevolent, and his pity for the victims of misery that he sees prompts him to seek their rescue from their unhappiness. I remember an aged Buddhist priest who had spent his life from his boyhood in discharging the duties of his monastery. His head bore the usual mark of admission to the order of which he was a member, viz., twelve indentations made in the skin with hot iron immediately above the forehead. He said every one who instructs his fellow-men in virtue is a true Poosa, and any act of real charity and self-sacrifice is that of a Poosa.

So far as this, Poosa is a human being, animated with the wish to teach and save men, but other illustrations of the use of the word will show that it is oftener used, in popular phraseology, as denoting powerful protectors belonging to a supernatural order of beings. Chinese worshippers will sometimes say, for example, that they must spend a little money occasionally to obtain the favour of Poosa, in order to prevent calamities from assailing them. I saw an instance of this at a town on the seacoast near Hangchow. The tide here is extremely destructive in the autumn. It often overflows the embankment made to restrain it, and produces devastation in the adjoining cottages and fields. A temple was erected to the Poosa Kwan-yin, and offerings are regularly made to her, and prayers presented for protection against the tide.

About two years before the capture of Canton by the English forces, Yeh-ming-chin, the governor of the province to which that city belongs, was engaged in exterminating large bands of roving plunderers, that disturbed the region under his jurisdiction. He wrote to the Emperor on one occasion a despatch in which he said that at a critical conjuncture in a recent contest, a large figure in white had been seen beckoning to the army from the sky. It was Kwan-yin. The soldiers were inspired with courage, and won an easy victory over the enemy.

The principal seat of the worship of Kwan-yin is at the island of Pooto. Here he (or she) takes the place of Buddha, and occupies the chief position in the temples. We were on our way there once from the island of Chusan, when two priests begged to be allowed to proceed there in the same boat. They had travelled far, and had visited the cities and mountains where the Buddhist worship in China is most flourishing. One of them spoke of *che-hwei*, " wisdom." He said, in answer to our questions, that it was to be obtained by prayer, and that prayer should be offered for it to Kwan-yin. He was reminded that this personage was altogether unreal, and was asked why he should not rather pray to God for wisdom. He could not worship God, he said. Kwan-yin was the divinity to whom he prayed. The claim of God to be worshipped he denied, but afterwards admitted it. He asserted that Buddha was the creator of heaven and earth; yet when explanations were offered, he allowed, perhaps out of compliment to the foreign visitor, that creation was the work of God.

When the Buddhists have occasion to speak of Shang-te or God as he is known to the disciples of Confucius, they identify him with Indra Shakra, one of the chief Hindoo gods, and assign him no higher authority or wider kingdom. This remark will illustrate some parts of the following description. On the island of Pooto, sacred to Kwan-yin, as already observed, there are many small caves dedicated to the use of hermits, or venerated as having been formerly inhabited by holy persons who pursued that mode of life. In several of them, high up on a hill-side, may be noticed a small figure of Buddha, intended to remind the visitor of the self-denying and secluded life which Buddha led. The priests who resided in the adjoining monastery entered into conversation with their visitor from afar on the relative position of God and this self-elevated hermit. God, they said, was within the limits of the San-keae (the three worlds, heaven, earth, and hell), but Buddha, they maintained, extended his authority beyond these boundaries. They alluded to the imaginary universe of the Northern Buddhists, in which the visible one, the universe as known to us, occupies a small place in the centre. They confine the kingdom of the gods, among whom is Shang-te, to this small space. They were told that the universe of which they spoke, being simply the invention of former writers of their religious books, could not, however vast its proportions, constitute any real accession to the dominion ruled over by Buddha, nor help to place him above God. God, dwelling in heaven, was the true God of the world, and every world throughout space was subject to Him. One of the priests in the hall where this conversation took place, containing several idol shrines, remarked that there were thirty-three heavens, in one of which the God that foreigners worshipped resided. It was stated to him in reply, that, according to the views of the religion which he followed, the heavens he spoke of all rested on the crown of the Sumeru mountain, but in fact no such mountain existed; it was fabulous, like the imaginary island of Pung-lae, in the Eastern Ocean, and the abode of Se-wang-mu, the mother of the Western King. This personage is a mythological queen, whom old Chinese fable represented as dwelling on a summit of the Kwenlun chain in Tibet. The priest replied that the Sumeru mountain certainly did exist, and it was on its summit that the gods resided in their respective abodes. He was informed in answer that the ships of Western men had traversed the ocean in every direction, but had not discovered this mountain.

From what has preceded, it appears that Buddhism is atheistic, not in denying the existence of the ruler of the world, or of the gods of popular mythology, but in abridging the power and jurisdiction of such divinities. In ascribing to God a limited jurisdiction, subjection to birth and death, and subordination to the Buddhas and Bodhisattwas, they deprive Him in fact of His deity, while they allow the name of God to be retained.

The true source of this bold and infatuated attempt to reverse the fixed relations between God and man, the Creator and the creature, is found in the spirit of Hindoo philosophy. The human intellect, lifted up with pride, sought by the help of philosophy to exalt itself above everything that is called God. It rebelled against the authority of a personal God, and preferred to exercise faith only in a state, the Nirvana, where consciousness and individuality are lost; and life and death, thought and passion, good and evil, with every other antithesis possible to man, disappear in the absolute unity. It is true that the Nirvana is not peculiar to Buddhism, belonging as it does to other Hindoo sects. But it is here in the fiction of the two states, Buddha and Bodhisattwa, and the other grades beneath them, that the human mind has made the most systematic attempt to reduce Deity to insignificance, and to raise itself above the sphere in which Deity resides and reigns. We are amazed to find here the finite thinking soul audaciously imagining for itself, not only an accessible region beyond the actual universe, and outside of the dominions of God, but undertaking to lay down a pathway with the successive steps marked, by which those distant abysses of space may be traversed, and the world of the senses be left for ever behind.

The form of Buddhist temples exemplifies in a striking manner the relative position of Buddha and the gods. Four kings of the gods are represented in the vestibule. Their office is to guard the door by which entrance is obtained to the presence of Buddha. They perform no more dignified duty than to act as guards and as musicians to the greater personages who occupy the interior of the building. The central position is that of Buddha, who is seated on the lotus-flower in the attitude of a teacher. His countenance expresses the union of contemplation and benevolence, implying wisdom enabling him to teach, and compassion inclining him to save. The great Hindoo divinities, Brahma, Seeva, and Shakra, stand among the auditors, and they occupy a lower position than the personages called Poosa, Lohan, &c., who are scholars well advanced in the doctrine of Buddha.

The intention in this arrangement is to exhibit human philosophy as transcending Divine power, and personages of the highest rank in the visible universe listening submissively to the instructions of the earth-born sage. But the ideas of philosophers fail to be comprehended by the popular mind, and the common worshipper regards the gods whom he sees in a subordinate position as servants, and nothing more; while he trusts and prays to Buddha, the personation of philosophy, as a powerful divinity. He must obey the impulse of his nature to adore that which is divine, and he readily finds objects for his worship in personages so transcendent in wisdom as those bearing the title of Fuh and Poosa.

In the next chapter will be illustrated the notion of God as held by the Taouists.

CHAPTER IX.

TAOUIST NOTIONS OF GOD.

THE notions which the Taouist sect have respecting God and the gods deserve some examination. A sketch of them will form a suitable supplement to what has already been said of the views held on the same subject by believers in Buddha and Confucius.

The Taouist mythology resembles, in several points, that of many heathen nations. Some of its divinities personate those beings that are supposed to reside in the various departments of nature; others are men made into imaginary deities by a process of apotheosis. Among the gods originally belonging to particular portions of the natural world are sea and river gods, star-gods, and those that preside over meteorological phenomena and over the productions of the earth. On the sea-coast are found temples erected to the Spirit of the Sea, the King of the Sea, and the God of the Tide. On the banks of rivers the shrines of dragon-kings are common. The dragon is supposed to reside partly in air and partly in water. Any remarkable appearance in the sky or on the surface of the water is frequently pointed to as a dragon, or a phenomenon occasioned by the presence of a dragon. One of their divinities is called "the Ruler of Thunder," and another "the Mother of Lightning." Many of the stars are worshipped as gods. Some Greek philosophers supposed the stars to be living beings, and divine. The Taouists believe in a doctrine something like this. It is a characteristic instance of that materialism which marks almost all Taouist doctrines. The stars are regarded as the sublimated essences of things.

The world, for example, is made up of five kinds of matter, which contain each of them an essence or elementary substance. As the soul is an essence of matter, the purest form of matter in the body, so there are essences belonging to other things, which, when very pure, obtain a life and individuality of their own. They constitute the souls of coarse matter. Of these there is a series of five, which correspond to the five modes of subsistence found in material nature, viz., metal, wood, water, fire, and earth. These souls of the five elements rose, when highly purified, through the air to the region of stars, and became the five planets. Mercury is the essence of water, Venus of metal, Mars of fire, Jupiter of wood, and Saturn of earth. The fixed stars are also the essences or souls of matter, and other essences, believed to wander through space, impelled by an internal active life, are also called stars, although not visible in the heavens. In this way the word star has come to have, in the Chinese language, a meaning additional to the common one. A living material soul, the sublimated essence of matter, is so denominated. The process of thought in the materialistic philosophy of the Taouists was carried a step further. These stars and essences became gods. They were regarded as having divine attributes. The eye of the contemplatist of this school saw in the starry firmament the higher portions of the vast sea of ether of which our atmosphere forms the lower and grosser part. It is there that the star-divinities revolve. They look down from their region of purity and stillness on the world of men, and they influence the fortunes of men invisibly, but most powerfully. It was by carrying out this way of thinking that alchemy and astrology became an important part of the Taouist religious system. They are necessarily the two favourite sciences of a materialistic religion like this. The one deals in essences, the other in stars; and they have each had an extensive influence on the formation of the Taouist system of divinities, as well as on the Taouist doctrine of immortality, and of the method of self-discipline by which immortality is to be gained.

We may remark, by the way, that an interesting parallel may be drawn between the Chinese and the European alchemy and astrology. Great light on the signification and origin of these once famous studies of our mediæval period may be obtained from the same studies of the same kind that were pursued several centuries earlier in China. There is a remarkable analogy in the double meaning of our word *spirit* and that of the Chinese word *sing* (star) just pointed out. The terms for *soul* and for *essence*—in Chinese *shin* and *tsing*—are often convertible, as they are in our language. In China, however, the connection of alchemy and astrology as branches of one system, and 'that a religious one, are more clearly discernible than in the European history of these branches of knowledge, once called sciences.

In the legendary biography of the Taouist gods, it is common to say of them that a star descended and became incarnate in the person of certain noted men, who thus obtained their divine character. Wen-chang, the god who presides over literature, is a divinity of this kind. A small constellation near the Great Bear receives this name. The god who is prayed to by scholars to assist them in obtaining the reward of their exertions is Wen-chang, the divinity of whom we are now speaking. His representative in the sky is this constellation. A temple is erected to him in Chinese cities apart from that dedicated to Confucius. It may be seen built on an elevated earthen terrace, and, if my memory serve me rightly, of six sides, in imitation of the form of the constellation, which has the shape of a hexagon. Wen-chang is said to have come down to our world during many generations at irregular intervals. Virtuous and highly-gifted men were chosen from history as likely to have been incarnations of this divinity, and then legends were invented stating it as a fact. The regard paid to the god of literature by the class of scholars proves that the Taouist religion has had no little influence upon them, although they are professedly Confucianists, and should not, as such, give their adhesion to the tales of the Taouists.

Among the liturgical works used by the priests of Taou, one of the commonest consists of prayers to Tow-moo, a female divinity supposed to reside in the Great Bear. A part of the same constellation is worshipped under the name Kwei-sing. A small temple is erected to this deity on the east side of the entrance to Confucian temples, and he is regarded as being, like Wen-chang, favourable to literature. The word Kwei, in its written form, is a compound character. Its component parts are two other characters, *kwei*, "demon," on the left, and *tow*, the four stars forming a trapezium in the Great Bear (so named from a measuring vessel having that shape), on the right. A native writer, still living at Soochow, attempts to show that the whole story of the gods has sprung entirely out of the human imagination. One of the proofs that he adduces is the pictorial representation usually given of the divinity Kwei-sing. A demon-like personage is seen kicking with his foot the measuring vessel called *tow*. This mode of portraying the divinity in question was suggested solely by the meaning that happened to belong to the component parts of the character Kwei, and which were arbitrarily assigned many centuries before without any bearing on mythology. He very justly brings forward this circumstance as evidence that popular notions respecting this divinity had their source in the human imagination.

One of the twenty-eight constellations of the Chinese zodiac consists of six stars curved like a bow. It is called Chang, *to draw a bow*. Near it is a cluster of seven stars, known as "the heavenly dog." Chang, one of the genii of Taouist romance, is believed to be identical with the star cluster of the same name, and he is represented by painters and idol-makers with a bow in his hands, shooting the heavenly dog. The names of the constellations are much older than the mythological legends, of which the story of this personage is one. So that if any of the animal or human forms pictured on our celestial globes as aids to the memory in recognising the stars were to be appointed by priestly authority to be adored as gods, such an act would be a parallel one to what the Chinese Taouists have done. This gross and infatuated materialism has flourished in a country that has possessed for ages a cultivated literature and a highly-developed civilisation, a good moral code, and a long succession of philosophers and learned men. The mythology of which we are speaking has been greatly expanded during modern times in China, showing that nothing can be hoped for the improvement of that country in the knowledge of God unless Christianity be introduced among its inhabitants. At the period when its intellectual light has been at the highest point, the most extravagant additions have been made to its legendary mythology. At times when the arts and literature were most prosperous, superstition increased its proportions along with them, and spread amongst the population a multitude of absurd fancies, wild in their origin, and mischievous in their effects.

I met, on one occasion, a schoolmaster from the neighbourhood of Chapoo. He asked if I had any books to give away on astronomy and geography. Such works are eagerly desired by all members of the literary class. They feel a high respect for the knowledge Western men have on these subjects, the result of the information given them by the early Roman Catholic missionaries on these sciences. The inquiry was put to him—Who is the Lord of heaven and earth? He replied that he knew none but the pole-star, called in the Chinese language Teen-hwang-ta-te—*the great imperial ruler of heaven*. It was stated to him that it was a matter very much to be regretted that he should hold such views as this of the Supreme Being. When he was reminded of passages in the Confucian classics which speak of God as the ruler of heaven, independent of the visible creation, he admitted that he might be wrong. In the case of this man it is sufficiently evident that the notion of an independent, personal, spiritual Being, presiding over the universe, and distinct from it, had given place to a low, materialised conception of God.

The degraded notion that the Taouists have of God has allowed of their representing creation as effected by a material agency, instead of describing it as the work of God. I once asked a Taouist priest to show me some of his charms. They are pieces of paper bearing certain unintelligible marks. He declined to do so, on the ground that we do not believe in their efficacy. Their use was, he said, to frighten away demons, who did not dare to approach so wise and holy a divinity as the god of the temple, in one of the apartments of which we stood. The charms were sold in his name, and his protection was guaranteed to those who purchased them. It was observed to him that it was a groundless fancy to expect protection from such a god as this, and that our faith should be placed upon God the creator of all things. This priest denied that creation was God's act, and maintained that it was the act of a material agent which he called *Ke*—a word meaning a *very pure form of matter, vapour*. *Ke*, he said, was before God, and was the creator of all things. Its purer part rose and formed heaven, while its grosser portion became earth. He was reminded that *Ke* was a visible, material substance, capable of separation into parts, and it must therefore itself be a created thing. He admitted its material character, but denied the conclusion attempted to be derived from that circumstance. It was explained to him further, that we in the West were accustomed to think that the immaterial could produce the material and visible, but the material could not be the parent of the immaterial and invisible. We can conceive of the world of matter being created by God, a spiritual being; but we cannot conceive of matter becoming mind or soul by any process of creation or development. He proceeded to deny that God was invisible; and the conversation diverged to other subjects.

Before Buddhism came into China, and produced a very decided influence on Taouist ideas, the mythology of this latter religion was somewhat scanty. Besides the doctrine of Shang-te, and of the presiding spirits that dwell in various parts of nature, belonging to the Confucian religion, the ancient Chinese believed in a race of genii. They were men supposed to have attained to the honours of deity by their virtues. Some were fabulous persons, and others historical. At the time of Tsin-she-hwang, the builder of the Great Wall, about two centuries before Christ, many romantic stories were current of immortal men inhabiting islands in the Pacific Ocean. It was supposed that, in these imaginary islands, they found the herb of immortality growing, and that it gave them exemption from the lot of common men. That Emperor determined to go in search of these islands, but some untoward event always prevented him. One expedition that sailed never returned, and it was reported that those engaged in it had reached the islands, but were unwilling to come back, lest they should lose the treasure of immortality, so that their countrymen failed to secure the benefit of their discovery. The genii of mountains and of such islands are terrestrial genii. There is a higher class, called the celestial genii. They are supposed to ascend to heaven and reside there. The abodes occupied by the celestial genii are among the stars, or, higher yet, in the region of pure rest. In carrying out the conceptions of powerful beings inhabiting heaven as thus suggested, the Taouists obtained great help from the Buddhists. They imagined various regions in the sky, somewhat resembling the successive heavens of the Hindoos, and made them the residences of the new divinities that they chose to add to their pantheon. In the plan of a complete Taouist temple, provision is made for representing all the chief features of the modern mythology of that religion. The apartments devoted to the superior and inferior divinities correspond to the respective heavens in which they reside, and a certain number of the gods are selected for representation as specimens of the whole. Among these are some that resemble the Buddhas and Bodhisattwas of the sister religion, while others derive their origin from the ancient Chinese tales of hermits and genii. There are two elements, then, in the formation of their mythology — the primitive Chinese and the Buddhistic. The former—that of indigenous origin—has perpetuated the recollection of many fabulous and semi-fabulous individuals belonging to the early centuries of the nation's history. Among them are not a few hermits and alchemists, men of rigid morals, and having a fondness for solitude, seekers of the plant that confers immortality, and students of the hidden lore of mystics and magicians. Such beings are called *Seen-jin*. They form the mass of the inhabitants of heaven. The principal divinities are, however, Buddhistic. To Buddha correspond *Teen-tsun* and *Te*, and to Bodhisattwa *Tsoo*. Yuh-hwang-shang-te is the highest of all personages except the San-tsing. In his character as lord of the world and saviour of men he in part resembles Buddha. If this Shang-te is Buddha active, the San-tsing, or "three pure ones," are Buddha contemplative. They meditate on truth and doctrine, and communicate their feelings and ideas to men in language such as they can understand; one of the "three pure ones" is Laou-keun, the founder of the Taouist religion, in a deified form. The "three pure ones" are the Taouist trinity; as the "San-she Joo-lae," the "Tathagatha of the three ages," are the Buddhist trinity. In each case the trinity is a threefold manifestation of one historical person. That historical person is, in both instances, a man deified by his intellectual and moral advancement, bringing him at last to the summit of all excellence and power. Shakyamuni was represented by the Northern Buddhists in many different forms. One of the most common is the Buddha past, present, and to come. Three immense images nearly alike in form are thus designated. They are usually found in the larger Chinese temples, where it is desired to have idols of an imposing appearance. Little, however, is said of this trinity in the Buddhist books. Perhaps the reason why it has become common is not on account of any doctrinal importance belonging to this trinal manifestation of Buddha, but rather because an air of grandeur is thus imparted to the appearance of Buddha in the hall where he is worshipped.

Be this as it may, the Taouists have imitated the Buddhists in forming a trinity having its basis in the historical founder of their religion. Laou-keun, the philosopher thus distinguished, is styled, when represented as divine, the third person in this trinity. They say, indeed, that he was, in his human form, an incarnation of the third person in the San-tsing, wishing to make it appear that this trinity of divine persons, which is altogether of modern invention, is previous in time to Laou-keun, and in fact eternal.

The connection that the Taouist trinity has with the world is, like that of Buddha, one of instruction and benevolent interference for the good of mankind. The physical superintendence of the world is left to inferior divinities. In the view of both these religions, contemplation is above action. As a sage is esteemed a higher character than a warrior, so a divinity in the intellectual sphere is greater than a divinity in the physical. To save by teaching is greater than to save by power. This idea is seen very prominently in the grades of divinities in the Taouist mythology, as it is also in those of the Buddhist. The Fuh and the Poosa of the Hindoo religion are intellectual gods, and their sphere is regarded as higher and nobler than that of Brahma and Shakra, who rule rather in the physical universe. So in Taouism, the San-tsing are instructors, while Shang-te and the star-gods, the medical divinities, the gods of the elements and the deified hermits, are the rulers of the physical universe.

The Taouists take the Shang-te of the Confucian classics

to be identical with Yuh-hwang-shang-te, who is the chief god in their pantheon, excepting only the San-tsing. They assign to him the control of the physical universe, but they also make him an instructor of mankind. To connect him with the human race they have identified him with an ancestor of the hereditary hierarch of their religion, bearing the family name Chang. This hereditary head of the Taouist religion resides in the province of Keang-se, on the Dragon and Tiger mountain. In humanising the Shang-te of the classics, a birthday, as well as a name, has been assigned to him. His birthday is kept on the ninth of the first month. Very many spirits are employed by him in the control of the world. Towards the end of each year, these subordinate spirits, among them the kitchen-god, who have been engaged through the year in watching the conduct of mankind, go up to the palace of Yuh-hwang-shang-te in heaven, and present their report. After a certain number of days they descend again, and resume their office as inspectors of the moral behaviour of men.

Among the star-gods subordinate to the supreme deity of the physical universe just referred to, is a trinity known as the gods of happiness, rank, and old age. Three stars, or star-gods, thus designated, are among the commonest subjects for carving and painting in China.

Another favourite divinity is Tsae-shin, who presides over riches. He is identified with an ancient Chinese statesman, and is almost universally worshipped by those who engage in commercial pursuits. The extent of his worship is one of the most remarkable instances of the prevalence of superstition among the class of tradesmen and merchants. They trace their profits and losses in trade to the interference of this divinity. It is their faith in this god that has led to the erection of so many temples to his honour in Chinese towns and cities.

There is a very well-known triad of subordinate divinities, called San-kwan, the "three rulers." They preside over heaven, earth, and water, and it is said of them, in that part of the daily liturgical prayers which refers to them, that they are the three holy men who form a unity, and that they send down good and ill fortune on men and save the lost. In their collective unity they are called the three rulers who constitute one great god, *San-kwan-ta-te*.

The gods having invocations addressed to them in the Taouist prayer-books include several of a rank intermediate between Yuh-hwang-shang-te and San-kwan. They are the spirit of the earth, the north pole-star, the lord of the stars, some other star-gods, the ruler of thunder, the Buddhist divinity Kwan-yin, and the spirits of the sun and moon.

The following is a specimen of the attributes of these personages. The "father of thunder" is represented as passing through many metamorphoses and filling all regions with his assumed forms. While he discourses on doctrine his foot rests on nine beautiful birds. Thirty-six generals wait on him for orders. A certain celebrated book of instruction is said to have emanated from him. His commands are swift as winds and fire. He overcomes demons by the power of his wisdom, and he is the father and teacher of all living beings.

This description of the god of thunder is strongly tinged with a Buddhist colouring, and the same is observable in the characteristics of the other Taouist divinities. The style in which the books of prayers are written is thoroughly Buddhist. The same view is taken of the universe, of the wants of men, and of the interference of divine persons to remove them, as in that religion. Throughout there is a slavish adherence to the foreign model. China felt religious wants, which it could not supply from its own thinking. The Chinese had the notion of Deity, but could not unaided bring that notion into a form adapted for popular worship. When the Buddhist system arrived among them, they found in it a model that they could conveniently copy. The Chinese and the Hindoo mythology form an ill-assorted mixture. The additions made by the Taouists from this foreign source to their system fit it but clumsily, and the proof thus becomes so much the clearer that men will have gods to adore and some form of worship, and that however strong this craving, it cannot be met by the unassisted intellect. There must be the revelation of the true God in His Son Jesus Christ, before the desire men feel to know and adore the Divine can be satisfied.

A word should be added respecting the State gods of China. They are very numerous; each city has its patron deity. There are also tutelar gods to smaller towns. All such divinities are appointed by the State. Brave and loyal officers of Government, and men distinguished for public and private virtues, are honoured with a charge of this kind.

Among the most eminent of the State gods is Kwan-te, the god of war. By a recent decree of the last Emperor but one, he has been raised to the same rank with Confucius, who was before this the occupant of the first place in the State pantheon of canonised sages and great men.

Taouist priests are appointed to take charge of the temples of the State gods, but their worship does not constitute a principal part of the liturgical forms of the Taouist religion. These gods are admitted into the Taouist mythology as divinities more or less elevated in rank, and the worship of each is performed with attention only in the locality over which he presides. Temples to the god of war are, however, found everywhere.

It would have been interesting to inquire how far the views of the Taouists on a Divine Trinity are merely the result of the thinking faculties, or how far they should be regarded as traditional from the early ages of our race; or, further, what reason there is to consider them a truth in natural religion, at which, in some way, the human mind must, in its searchings, ultimately arrive. But this inquiry may be left in the hands of writers of theological books, and especially of those students, rapidly increasing in number, who are engaged in investigating the religions of the world.

CHAPTER X.

MORALITY.

ALL the world knows that the Chinese have a system of morality which, in theory, is remarkably pure. They may not be a peculiarly moral people when compared with the rest of mankind, but they have a better system of human duty than almost any other heathen nation, ancient or modern. Their sages have transmitted a multitude of excellent maxims, and have reasoned on moral questions, not seldom, very satisfactorily. Duty and morality are what every man can understand. To inculcate them is an easy task, because the appeal is made immediately to the conscience which God has bestowed upon all men. We cannot wonder that in Confucianism there should be found a good system of morality. Conscience and reflection guide at once to the discovery of it. The Jesuit missionaries, when they arrived in China, in the reign of our Queen Elizabeth, were charmed with the excellent doctrines of Confucius. They found there the Golden Rule of our Saviour in a slightly different form. The precept of Confucius was, "Do not to others what you would not that they should do to you." They also found in the common conversation of the people antithetical sentences and fragments of familiar poetry, exhorting to virtue and warning against vice. They are in daily use among all classes, from the rich and educated to the labouring poor. For example:—"Among the hundred virtues, filial piety is the chief. Out of ten thousand crimes, adultery is the worst." "Fidelity, filial piety, chastity, and uprightness, diffuse fragrance through a hundred generations." They spread through Europe the fame of the Chinese sages as excellent instructors in morality. Ricci thought that very many of them held views so good, that he felt no doubt they would be saved by the mercy of God in the next life. He says this in the rare and very interesting work, "De Christiana Expeditione ad Sinas," from which M. Huc has drawn much of the materials for his history of Christianity in China.

What is the Confucian morality on which such high encomiums have been pronounced? A follower of that sage would probably reply to this question by referring to the San-kang-woo-chang, "the three relations and the five constant virtues." The three relations, to which belong corresponding duties, are those of prince and subject, father and son, and husband and wife; the five virtues, whose obligation is constant and universal, are benevolence, uprightness, politeness, knowledge, and faithfulness. Politeness includes, in the Chinese meaning of the word, compliance with all social and public customs transmitted by wise men and good kings. The native term for knowledge means rather the prudence gained by knowledge. The word for faithfulness means both to be trustworthy, and also to trust to, and refers chiefly to friendship.

According to the Confucian school, the universal obligation to love mankind must be carefully limited and regulated by the social relations. It made a strong resistance on this ground to a socialist theory propounded by Mih-tsze, a Chinese philosopher who lived in the interval between Confucius and Mencius. The form that Confucianism, the orthodox Chinese morality, has come to assume has been constantly modified by controversy. This renders the historical study of it more interesting than it otherwise would be. Translations hitherto made of the Confucian books are somewhat dull, partly because the piquancy of the native phraseology is lost by transference to a foreign tongue, and in part also from the want of supplemental information on the important philosophical discussions that have taken place between rival sects, both contemporary with and subsequent to the time when the Chinese classics were written.[1] Mih-tsze laid stress on the circumstance that love to mankind ought to be universal and undistinguishing. He also founded the obligation to love on utilitarianism. He said, that if we all loved every other man in a perfectly undistinguishing manner, there would be no wars and no robbery. It is a remarkable fact that a Chinese writer three or four centuries before the Christian era should have these views. They are contained in works of the author which are partly spurious in their present form, but which are frequently cited and commented on in the writings of authors belonging to that age. The followers of Confucius made an energetic opposition to the doctrines of this philosopher, and insisted, as writers of the school of Butler might do against Bentham, and Paley, and the socialists, that the consciousness of right and wrong implanted by Heaven in the human breast must be made judge in matters of duty, and that the distinctions in the social commonwealth, arising from the political and domestic relations of men to each other, must be carefully preserved.

A striking resemblance between the discussions on moral philosophy in China and in Europe is found in the ambiguity attaching to the word *nature*—in Chinese *sing*. Bishop Butler says, when speaking of the ancient moralists of Europe, that they defined virtue as consisting in the following of our nature, and vice as deviating from it. He defended this doctrine, and guarded it from misconstruction by pointing out the different meanings of the word *nature*. The Confucianists have had to do the same in order to protect their orthodox doctrine of duty and conscience from abuse. One ancient school held that we

---

[1] We may expect a new translation soon from an able scholar, long resident in China, of a much superior kind to any we have had. Much has been done to meet this want by the insertion in Dr. James Legge's translation of Mencius of considerable portions of the writings on ethics of Seun-tsze, Mih-tsze, and Han-yii.

must follow our appetites, since they were natural to us. Another sect maintained that we must not follow our nature, our nature being bad. The orthodox party said our nature is good. The cause of our wrong-doing is in the passions that are born with us, and in superinduced habits.

When the European reader takes in hand the little "Three Character Classic," that forms the first reading-book in Chinese day-schools, he finds in the opening sentence the doctrine broadly stated, that man has originally a good moral nature — *jin-che-choo-sing-pun-shen* — and he thinks he sees in it a direct contradiction of the Christian doctrine of man's original depravity. If no friend to Christian theology, he rejoices in the fact; if he be a friend to that theology, he will be in danger of pronouncing a hasty condemnation on the author of the sentence just quoted. It belongs to Mencius, not Confucius, and was introduced by him into the orthodox system to serve as a barrier against the tenet of Scun-tsze, that the nature of man is bad. Many centuries after, during the time of our Middle Ages, discussions on the moral nature of man led to the adoption of new phraseology by the orthodox party. They said that there is a principle that leads men to do wrong, together with a principle leading them to do right, which two principles grow up together. The good nature is bestowed originally by Heaven, as was always held by the Confucianists. The bad came from the union of the soul with matter, and the existence of the passions. This explanation should be remembered before the Chinese doctrine, "that the nature of man is good," is condemned. If we say that the good principle, *sing*, "nature," or *le*, "reason," is the moral sense or conscience, and the evil principle original depravity, we have a coincidence with the Christian doctrine of which we should not lose sight on account of certain differences in nomenclature.

The tendencies of the Confucian morality are seen in the national system of education, in which the *moral* training of the child's mind is always put forward as the chief element. There is a universal system of self-supporting day-school education in that country. Every parent who has a few pence to spare in the month will educate his child. Teaching is the regular profession of the majority of the *literati*, that is, of the class who study for academical degrees. The course of instruction includes the reading of the Four Books, and the Five Classics, the former containing the opinions of Confucius and Mencius, and the latter the ancient books as collected and edited by Confucius. The word for religion in Chinese is *keaou*, and this is also the word for instruction. The idea of a religion is in that language a system of instruction. The highest character known in that country is that of an instructor. The greatness of Confucius did not consist in philosophical depth and originality, but in his being a moral teacher, the most sincere, earnest, comprehensive, and convincing that the Chinese have known. When the boy goes to school, he becomes a disciple of Confucius. If he is not educated, his nature will go wrong, and he will be a lawless subject and a disobedient son. The end of his education is to show him what virtue is, and to lead him to it. The true disciple of Confucius is the filial son, the loyal subject, and the kind and faithful husband. The Government regards the education of the people as essential to the welfare of the State. But it does not itself educate them by supplying free instruction to the poor. It appoints public examiners to confer degrees and other rewards on successful candidates for such distinctions, and in this way it stimulates and influences voluntary education. The Government decides what books shall form the subject of examination, and what school in philosophy and morals shall be counted orthodox. Its influence on the state of opinion in the country is therefore very great. More than this, the Government officers are chosen, according to the traditional theory, for their virtues as well as for their ability. The result of the Confucian education is supposed to be the formation of a highly virtuous character. The Emperor should choose his ministers from "the wise, the good, the consistent, and the upright"—words which have predominantly a moral rather than an intellectual meaning.

On the whole, the Confucian morality appears to agree in principle with Butler's system, while the chief energy of those who have taught it has been expended in the endeavour to give it practical effect on the individual, the family, and the nation.

What has the result been on the Chinese of the Confucian morality? It has not made them a moral people. Many of the social virtues are extensively practised among them, but they exhibit to the observer a lamentable want of moral strength. Commercial integrity and speaking the truth are far less common among them than in Christian countries. The standard of principle among them is kept low by the habits of the people. They do not appear to feel ashamed when the discovery is made that they have told an untruth. Falsehood is too often a favourite weapon of diplomacy in social life, and it is employed without remorse. There is a palpable absence of sensitiveness on this and other points which indicates the want of honourable principle in the national character. This renders the nation feeble in war and open to new temptations, such as, for example, the use of opium. Another cause of moral weakness among the Chinese is the practice of polygamy, an institution which operates as mischievously on them as on other Oriental nations. The state of opinion is such in that country, that in some cases the taking of a second wife during the lifetime of the first is regarded as a virtue. It is, for instance, the duty of a filial son to marry again if he is without children by his first wife, in order to have sons who may continue the sacrifices at the ancestral tomb. The chief evil attending domestic slavery in China is, that it directly promotes concubinage to a vast extent. Thus the Confucian morality, though good in theory, has not been successful in bringing the nation to a good moral condition.

Some modern writers have represented the influence of Buddhism on the moral character of nations as extremely beneficial. It must be confessed that there is a very good aim in much of the teaching of Shakyamuni Buddha. He says, in the "Book of Forty-two Sections:"—"That which causes the stupidity and delusion of man is love and the desires." "Man, having many faults, if he does not repent, but allows his heart to be at rest, will find sins rushing upon him like water to the sea. When vice has thus become more powerful, it is still harder than before to abandon it. If a bad man becomes sensible of his faults, abandons them, and acts virtuously, his sin will day by day diminish and be destroyed, till he obtains full enlightenment." The disciple of Buddha is forbidden to take part in any of the vices, and even in many of the lawful enjoyments, of life. He must not take wine, nor enter the married state, nor partake of animal food. He must exercise a strict watch over the tongue. Minute rules for self-government are given to aid in preventing the disciple from every kind of wrong-doing.

Klaproth, having in view these moral precepts, and their effects on the Asiatic world, speaks of Buddhism as being of all religions next to Christianity in elevating the human race. He says, "The wild nomads of Central Asia have been changed by it into amiable and virtuous men, and its beneficent influence has been felt even in Northern Siberia." It is a fact that Buddhism has been spreading during the last hundred years from Mongolia, where it has long prevailed, into Siberia. It is not to be wondered at that a literary traveller from Germany should be pleased to find Buddhism extending among the pagan hordes of Siberia. He would naturally be gratified to discover in those dreary regions the worship of personified ideas, and the doctrine of the non-existence of matter. Perhaps it is rather surprising that he did not place Buddhism on a higher level than Christianity, than that he should have viewed it only as second to it in point of excellence.

I feel compelled, however, to take a less favourable view than this sanguine traveller of the effects of Buddhism. So far from deserving to be compared with Christianity, it must be regarded as quite inferior to the system of Confucius in its moral influence.

Good has resulted, doubtless, from the prominent exhibition made by Buddhism of the danger and misery of vice, and the good coming from self-restraint. But much more benefit would have been derived if its system of prohibitions had rested on a better basis, and been supported by a different view of the future state. The crime of killing rests chiefly on the doctrine of metempsychosis, which ascribes the same immortal soul to animals that it does to man. Faithful Buddhists are told not to kill the least insect, lest in so doing they should cause death to some deceased relative or ancestor whose soul may possibly animate the insect. On this account the corresponding virtue is stated to be *fang sheng*, " to save life," constantly applied by the Buddhist priests and common people of China to the preservation of the lives of animals. The monks are vegetarians for the same reasons; they abstain from flesh, not only to bring the appetites into subjection, but just as much that they may not share in the slaughter of living beings. They construct reservoirs of water near the monasteries, in which fish, snakes, tortoises, and small shell-fish, brought by worshippers of Buddha, are placed to preserve them from death. Goats and other land animals are also given into the care of monks, and it is the custom at some monasteries, as at Teen-tung, near Ningpo, to feed the neighbouring birds with a few grains of rice just before the morning meal commences. I witnessed this upon one occasion. All the monks were seated at the tables in the refectory, perfectly silent, each with his bowl of rice and greens before him. One of them rose, after a sort of grace had been said, and brought to the door in his hand a few grains of rice. These he placed on a low stone pillar within sight of the birds that were waiting upon the roofs of the adjoining buildings, and knew how to act on the occasion. They flew down at once with great goodwill to receive their morning meal.

A morality which is so much connected with the fables of the metempsychosis, confounding men and animals as alike possessing immortal souls and a moral nature, should not be viewed as comparable to the Confucian, which bases its precepts on the consciousness of right and wrong bestowed by Heaven on all men. If the Confucianists do not say so much about the authority of God as we could wish, they speak at least of the authority of Heaven; and this is better than the atheism of the Buddhists. The Buddhist moral precepts, good as many of them are, would have more power, and the true character of sin be more felt by the people, if the authority of God were recognised by them as the great reason for acting well, the ground of moral obligation. The beneficent influence of the religion of Buddha would have been much greater, had it made the love and fear of God the first of all the virtues, and it might then have been brought more justifiably into comparison with Christianity. The sense of moral obligation cannot be strong in a system which consists very much of subtle intellectual abstractions, instead of strong convictions of the realities of life. In asserting the falsity of many things which the common consciousness of mankind declares to be truths—in subordinating God to Buddha, and denying that He is the creator and preserver of the world —and in sinking moral law to a position lower than the teachings of the human Buddha, this system loosens the hold of moral obligation upon man, and weakens the dominion of conscience.

We have in Buddhism some of the strangest facts that have ever been elicited in the history of the religions of the world. We have seen it attempting to subvert the faith of mankind in God, placing as a substitute on His throne a self-elevated, self-purified human sage called Buddha, and yet it could not prevent this personage from becoming dehumanised, clothed with divine attributes, and so coming to be worshipped as God by the multitude in all Buddhist countries. So far is this the case in Mongolia, that in the translation of the Bible by the Protestant missionaries into the language of that country, Buddha, or, as it is called, Borhan, is used for God. Now we see a fact analogous to this in the department of morals. The Buddhists, when they subverted the foundations of moral obligation by denying the authority of Divine law, put Buddha in its place. Just as Buddha in his personality took the place of God, so the Buddha of the heart was a sort of substitute for conscience. They say man's original nature, *sing*, is good. It is the inborn Buddha, which belongs to everything that has a conscious existence. It is pure and holy, but is overshadowed and shut out from view by the passions. Let every one search for it with introverted eye, and he will need no God or idol to adore, nor any law to control him. Let him uncover the veiled Buddha in his own heart. He will then become his own teacher and his own regenerator. In this language we see another sacrifice, a very acceptable one, to human pride. It elevates man by refusing to recognise the need of Divine agency in restoring men to a holy moral life, and yet it is a testimony to the existence of the inward light which God has placed in all human bosoms to guide them to what is right and good. The Buddhists, when they employ this phraseology, appeal to conscience after a certain indistinct manner. They go wrong, however, as the Confucianists also do, in identifying it with natural goodness; for they thus obscure its true character as the judge of right and wrong. To tell men that they are naturally good, is to assume in compliment to human nature a fact difficult to be proved, being contradicted by all history. And it has a bad effect on human character, as it is likely to induce men to look leniently on their own vices, and to regard them as originating from without and not from within. Whatever system weakens our sensitiveness to moral evil, must be so far wrong. The feebleness of the Buddhist appeal to conscience is further increased by its assigning the same essentially good nature to each member of the animal creation that it does to man.

We cannot, in China, see the whole effect of Buddhism as a moral system, because the national conscience of that country is much more Confucian than Buddhistic. The worshippers of Buddha and Poosa in that country retain the instructions on morality of their own sages; and to this Buddhism, than which there is not a more tolerant religion in the world, makes no objection. So also it is with Taouism. Both systems leave the people in possession of the convictions of duty produced by their Confucian education. But we notice among the Chinese certain popular customs and opinions that can scarcely be traced to any origin except Buddhism. Carefulness in avoiding the destruction of animal life is certainly, and the existence of many charitable institutions for the relief of the poor, the aged, and the diseased, is probably, to be ascribed to Buddhism. This religion has made the Chinese charitable, giving rise to almsgiving and many benevolent institutions. There is usually a tinge of Buddhist phraseology in the appeals made to the benevolent for the various charities and schemes for public convenience so common in that country. But the strong feeling, for which the Chinese are noted, of duty to parents, princes, and persons in superior station, they owe rather to their own national system.

Among the Taouists, the book that has the most influence of a moral kind upon the people is perhaps the "Kan-ying-peen," or Book on Retribution. In this treatise the punishments threatened for sin belong to the present life. They are losses, diseases, early death, and every sort of misfortune belonging to this world. The rewards of virtue are temporal blessings, and in certain cases immortality and transference to the abodes of the genii. But while the retribution of actions is Taouist, the actions themselves are characterised as right and wrong entirely by the Confucian standard.

Thus the most commanding position among the people is held by the system of the Confucianists. The introduction of Hindoo idolatry with a peculiar system of religion and philosophy has not lessened the power of the old orthodox morality in the country. The great struggle of Christianity must be with the religion that has the most power. To enter on a conflict with Buddhism and Taouism will be found an easier task by far than to displace Confucius from the faith of the Chinese as a faultless model, and the greatest and holiest of all moral teachers.

CHAPTER XI.

NOTIONS ON SIN AND REDEMPTION.

WHEN contemplating the introduction of Christianity into a country, it is important to know what opinions its inhabitants have upon sin and on the means of removing it. The consciousness of sin and the felt need of redemption undoubtedly belong to men who have no knowledge of religion except that which is derived from the light of nature. Some illustrations of the mode in which the Chinese feel and speak on these subjects will now be presented.

Sometimes there are answers given by the Chinese to the foreign inquirer of such a nature as to induce a doubt whether they have any sense of sin whatever. A respectable person will say, "I have no sins, and why should I need a Saviour? Your doctrine is good, but it is not important for me to attend to it. Why think of the future life? We know nothing about it. I discharge my duties. I am a filial son and a loyal citizen. I worship Heaven and Earth on the first and fifteenth of every month. I have nothing to reproach myself with."

I once held a conversation with an old man of seventy. I asked him, "Will you become a believer in our religion?" "No," he said, "I am too old. Here is my son; he is young and can earn money; I can do no work, and should be worth nothing to you." "You are greatly mistaken," he was told in reply, "in supposing that to believe in our religion has anything to do with earning money. It is for the forgiveness of sins that we advise you to believe in Jesus." His reply was, "I have no sins. I would not commit any sin. The money I owe to any one I give him. If I see a neighbour's child fall, I run and help him up." It was remarked to him, "Every one is a sinner; are you an exception?" To this he answered, "When my little girl had nothing to eat, and I possessed but fifteen cash (worth a penny), I spent them in buying food for my father."

Such an appeal as this to acts of kindness and filial piety formerly done would appear natural and perfectly satisfactory to large numbers of this man's countrymen. The tendency of the Confucian religion is to render those who believe in it unwilling to confess that sin is an element in their daily actions.

It would not be fair to Confucianism to say that it denies the existence of moral evil in the conduct of every man, for the Chinese sage said on one occasion that "he had never seen a truly good man." But he thought that men have the power to be virtuous in themselves, and that their nature leads them to virtue. He teaches that "by their nature they approach to goodness, but habit leads them away from it." By nature—*sing*—he meant the moral sense bestowed by God on every man. It is what we call conscience. A Confucianist writer would, however, rather describe it as a bias to virtue. Mencius, who is only second in authority to Confucius himself, tried to give greater distinctness to the doctrine of his predecessor by prefixing to the sentence above quoted the words, "Men originally have a virtuous nature."

In the moral code of the Confucian religion duties to God are little mentioned, while great stress is laid on duties to princes and parents. This circumstance could not but materially affect the extent and depth of the popular consciousness of sin in China. I remember a patient in a missionary hospital at Shanghai. He remained in one of the wards for several months on account of a wounded foot. He could not read, but he told many long stories respecting marvellous appearances of Buddha and other divinities. He remarked, when he heard the Divine nature

of Christ referred to, that Jesus must be a living Buddha
—the same designation that is applied to the Grand Lama
of Tibet, who is worshipped as an incarnation of Buddha.
He frequently expressed uneasiness of mind at not having
fulfilled his filial duty to his deceased father. He had
neglected to make provision for the customary funeral
rites. It was here that his consciousness of sin was
centred. The sphere of religious ideas in which this
man's thoughts revolved was Buddhist. But, though
he spoke of Buddha's divine power and providence, he
did not seem to feel himself a sinner against Buddha.
The worshipper of Buddha looks to him for protection and
instruction, but he does not pray to him for forgiveness, or
confess sin to him. He regards Buddha as a teacher and
Saviour, but not as a governor or a judge. His wounded
foot was proof to him of sin; but when asked what sin
it was of which he felt the conviction, his thoughts recurred
to the moral code of Confucius. He did what most of his
countrymen would have done in similar circumstances.
Instead of thinking of his transgression of God's law, he
recollected an omission of a duty to his parent. Filial
piety is the most strongly enforced of all virtues in his
native country. It has overshadowed the duty of piety
towards God, and the national conscience has become in
consequence comparatively insensible to sin as committed
against the Supreme Governor of the world.

All calamities, personal or national, in China are regarded as proofs of sin, especially such as are sudden and
overwhelming. A man struck by lightning is immediately condemned by the united voice of all who hear of
the catastrophe. He must have poisoned some one, or
have intended to do so, or he must have committed some
other great crime. If lightning strike a tree, the popular
remark made from one to another will be that there must
be a venomous snake concealed at its roots, and that on
this account the tree was singled out to be visited with the
retribution of Heaven. Blindness and other bodily cala-

mities are also ascribed to the operation of a retributory decree, the execution of which is superintended by the ruling power in heaven. The charge of personal blame is, however, often shifted from the present life to an imaginary one that preceded it. The Buddhist doctrine of metempsychosis is conveniently used to shelter the sufferer by any calamity from a charge of guilt made too direct to be pleasing to an uneasy conscience. He says to himself, "I must have committed some crime in a former state of existence." His misfortune does not permit him to deny his sin. It is evidence such as cannot be contradicted. But he finds in the doctrine of a former life the means of exculpating himself, so far as the present world is concerned.

The notion of duty in the Confucian system being the moral bond that connects man with man, instead of that which connects man with God, it comes to resemble the feeling of honour. The good man is called *kiun-tsze*, "the honourable man," while the bad man is termed *scaou-jin*, "the little man." Mean and dishonourable actions are said to be done by the latter, while all acts that imply self-respect and a sense of honour are attributed to the former. The law of virtue comes to be much more nearly identical with the law of honour than it can be in the Christian moral code, because so little is said by Confucius about our duties to God. Having no revelation of a future state to make use of in the inculcation of virtue, the Chinese system, as taught by native authors of the highest reputation, is led by necessity to appeal strongly to the natural sense of right and wrong implanted in man. Not claiming the inspired authority of special heavenly messages for the duties it enjoins, it rests upon the feeling of self-respect that men have. The man who always acts by this standard is the ideal of virtue. "He who makes use," says a Confucian author, "of reason and right to control the passions and the senses is an honourable man. And," he continues, "he who makes use of the passions and the senses to resist reason and right is a 'small man;'" that is, a bad man.

The moral standard being of this sort, sin becomes an act which robs a man of his self-respect, and offends his sense of right, instead of being regarded as a transgression of God's law.

There is another view of sin among the Chinese which has come to prevail extensively through the influence of Buddhism. To destroy animal life in any instance; to partake of animal food; the desecration of the written character, printed or manuscript, whether found on paper, porcelain, or carved wood, are considered to be sinful in a high degree. They are looked upon as great crimes, and it is thought that they will surely provoke severe punishment from the unseen fate that controls human actions. Such opinions diminish very much from the moral weight that attaches to the word *sin*, in Chinese *tsuy*. In common conversation the word is also used in such a way as to detract from its force. The phrase, "I have sinned against you," containing this word *tsuy*, is constantly employed in the sense of "I beg your pardon," or, "You greatly oblige me."

After this account of the limitations and misapplications of the notion of sin in the Confucian religion, it will not be expected that it can furnish a clear statement of any mode by which sin is to be taken away. The follower of that system says, as the Mohammedan does, sin will be forgiven on reformation, and that reformation is the sinner's own act. "To do wrong and not to correct the wrong, that is to do wrong," is a favourite quotation from the Chinese classics. If we do virtuously, say the disciples of Confucius, all our past faults will be forgiven. The work of self-reformation is that of men themselves. Let those who have sinned against Heaven not pray for pardon, or offer sacrifices to avert deserved punishment, but let them show, by their sincere desire to be virtuous, the genuineness of their repentance. Confucius said, when a man has sinned against Heaven, there is no need to pray. He meant that there was no advantage gained by the prayers and offerings, presented at the period in which he lived, to the spirit who presides over the north-west corner of the sky. He also said, on another occasion, "My praying has been long." This referred to the disposition he showed in his daily conduct to do what was good. If a man is virtuous and sincere, Heaven will be as much pleased with him as with the man who prays. Hence, if a man seek to act virtuously, he need not pray for forgiveness: he will be forgiven on the ground of the sincerity of his repentance. This is the common explanation of the passage, and it is authorised by Choo-foo-tsze. But some good scholars understand the expression used by Confucius as meaning that he really prayed, and that it was his daily habit.

The Buddhist notion of sin is what might be expected in a system where the presence and authority of a personal God are not felt, and where it is not perceived that the law which regulates human actions emanates immediately from Him. The ideas of sin and of misfortune are very much confounded. The sick man says of his disease, "It is my sin," instead of saying, "It is the punishment of my sin." The character ascribed to Buddha is that of a Saviour, but he saves from misfortune rather than from sin. When the Buddhists say, as they often do, "Great things can be transformed into small, and small into nothing," they mean either sin or the misfortunes that it brings; and they suppose that this will be effected by almsgiving and offerings to the idols.

The pity that Buddha feels for men is excited by the delusions and the sufferings in which he sees them involved, rather than by their guilt. He takes a misanthropic view of human life. He looks at it from the gloomiest possible point of observation. To live is to be wretched, and to die is wretchedness also, because death is but the introduction to a similar life for the same soul in a different body. He would rescue mankind altogether from the possibility of living and dying any more. The path to the Nirvana is the remedial scheme of Buddhism, and the Nirvana itself is its future state.

The most glowing terms are employed to describe the excellence of the Nirvana, yet when inquired into, it is found to be nothing but a philosophical abstraction, the boundary beyond which speculative thought found itself unable to pass. It is much too high a state for the common Buddhist priest to indulge the hope of arriving at it. One of them was once asked if he expected soon to escape from the metempsychosis and enter the Nirvana. He replied, "Living in this poor temple, how could I? To attain that happiness, I must dwell on a hill and meditate in solitude on the law of Buddha." "Why," he was again asked, "do you not make trial of that mode of life?" "I have not," he answered, "the 'root.'" He meant the intellectual germ or innate power or moral capacity from which the Buddhist mental development could proceed. His interrogator inquired of him further, "If you do not reach the Nirvana, how far on the path towards it do you hope to arrive?" "I can only hope," said he, "to become man again."

The feeling that the common Buddhist has of his condition is a humble one, if his expressions are to be trusted. He looks on himself and the rest of mankind as in a sunken state of degradation, from which few succeed in escaping. Life is described as a vast sea. Men are tossed upon the waves of this sea perpetually. There is a shore which, by Buddha's help, the tempest-driven soul may reach. On the rocks near large temples inscriptions are carved, addressing the visitor with such words as, "This is the shore," "You have but to turn back, and you are safe on this shore." Men are driven hither and thither on the waves of passion, and very few escape. Only an extremely small number attain to the Nirvana. The power to do so is a rare gift, as rare as the endowments of high genius.

But it is thought that much may be done by the monastic and hermit discipline to improve the condition of those who adopt it in the next life. A party of women and children will sometimes shut themselves in an apartment of a temple for a fixed time. Their employment is to repeat invocations to Buddha all day. It is Amitabha Buddha, who saves in the western heaven, that is prayed to on these occasions. They hope, after two or three days spent in reciting prayers, to have a better position secured to them in the next world, or else to enter the western paradise. The majority of Buddha's worshippers hope for nothing higher than to advance one or two steps in the scale of existence. They do not venture to anticipate absorption into the state of Nirvana, where human nature escapes at length from misery. They will have to wait through a long series of ages before that consummation.

The mode in which the disciplinary life of Buddhism, whether solitary or monastic, is supposed to benefit men is by the salutary restraint on the passions which it is said to exert. The passions are our enemies. The highest happiness of the soul is in tranquillity, and the agitation of the feelings is the cause of the diminution of our happiness. We should aim, therefore, at perfect rest; and this is sought after in the monastic institutions founded by Buddha.

The system, as it came from the hands of Shakyamuni, was more distinctly moral and less metaphysical than afterwards. Much was said by him and his first followers on the virtues and vices. They spoke of ten vices—three of the body, namely, killing, stealing, and adultery; four of the lips, slandering, reviling, lying, and words uttered with a vicious intention; and three of the mind, jealousy, hatred, and folly. These constitute, then, what is meant by the word *sin;* but that term loses very much of its significancy when applied to the desecration of printed or written paper, treading on an insect, or wasting rice-crumbs. To the lower class of Buddhists, this degenerated use of the word is that which most readily occurs. In the early history of this religion, moral duties were felt to be more important than they now are. Sometimes, even yet, a healthy state of mind in regard to moral distinctions is insisted on as superior to conformity with positive laws. When a missionary was urging that morality was above forms, and that dependence on those recommended by the Buddhists cannot secure salvation, one of the Chinese whom he was addressing expressed his entire assent to the statement, and illustrated his opinion by the story of a butcher. This man, although he followed a disreputable trade, to engage in which is highly criminal, was honest in his dealings, and fond of reading Buddhist books, burning incense, and prayer. He was taken to heaven by the great divinity Kwan-yin, who came in person at an appointed time and conducted him there. On the other hand, a priest, who had not an honest heart, was abandoned by the same divinity to become the prey of a tiger.

The forgiveness of sin is obtained, according to the Buddhist notion, by chanting books of prayers and leading an ascetic life. A common believer in this religion will reply, that the object of his invocations and prayers to Buddha is to avert misfortune, to obtain pardon for sins, and to lengthen life. But this belongs to the lower class of believers in Buddhism. The notion of pardon cannot assume any great importance where there is no God from whom to ask it. The idea of redemption in Buddhism is less that of procuring pardon than of conquering the sensual nature and obtaining perfect rest. It is altogether a subjective process. To help this process Buddha instituted monastic vows, and appointed a series of employments. The mode in which these are now operating in China may be illustrated by the following notes of an actual conversation. I once asked an aged priest at the head of a monastery if he had attained to the *true fruit*. (The result of meditation and discipline is termed *fruit*.) He replied, that he had not. He was again asked "Do you, with the 'Diamond Book of Transcendental Wisdom,' hold that all things having colour and form are empty and unreal, so that the objects surrounding us have no existence but in imagination?" His answer was, "It is difficult to say. Those who have attained the true fruit see all things to be delusive, but others cannot do so." This was an honest confession on the part of the aged monk. He did not himself believe, as his religion teaches, that matter is unreal, and that our senses are always deceiving us; but he thought that those who have risen into a state of exalted reverie are able to discern the truth of these propositions. I again asked him, "Are you the better for submitting to the tonsure and renouncing the world?" "No," said he; "it is good to be a monk, and it is also good to be a common man." "Then why," he was asked, "did you become a monk at all?" "To keep the heart at rest," he said, "so that it may not be ruffled by common affairs." "And have you attained that stage of advancement?" "No," was his response; "but there is a priest here who has done more than I have." He led me to see him. I saw him in his monkish costume, sitting on a board in the sunshine, his face turned towards a wall. I was informed that he never spoke. He had not done so for six or seven years, and was under a vow not to break silence again for the whole of his life. He constantly wore the same dress, and limited himself to the luxury of combing his long hair, which was never cut with razor or scissors, and washing his face. He ate like other priests, but scarcely ever left his apartment. He could read, but never took book in hand. His only employment was to mutter the prayers of his religion in a low voice. I wrote on a piece of paper a sentence, "Your vow not to speak is of no benefit to you." He looked on the paper, read it, and gave a faint smile. He refused to write any reply. I said to the septuagenarian priest who had led us in, "You can exhort men to repent of their sin, but he cannot." "Ah!" he replied, "I am not so good as he is." Last year (1858), I was told, the mute priest was seized in the street by one of the city magistrates as he passed accidentally, with his flags, gongs, and retainers. His hair hanging loose from his unshorn head gave him the appearance of a rebel, at the time when the city of Sung-keang, in which the incident occurred, was in excitement from the reported approach of an insurgent force. He would have been put to death as a "long-haired rebel," had not the neighbours who knew him explained to the mandarin what his real character was. Soon afterwards, I subsequently heard, he was found sitting on his board in the sunshine, dead. Such a poor imbecile as this is regarded by his fellow-Buddhists in China as having adopted an effectual method of rescuing himself from the corrupting and deluding influence of the world, and as having found a short road to high attainments in the path of Buddhist progress. His vow of silence is an example of the methods that suggest themselves to the Oriental mind by which the unbroken rest of the Nirvana may be as nearly as possible imitated, and the soul be freed from the dominion of that false and mischievous succession of sensations which come to us from an imaginary thing we call matter. Such is the Buddhist redemption; and the Buddha or the Poosa, who teaches men the fact of their delusion and the mode of escaping from it, is the Buddhist redeemer. Philosophy has attempted many great things, but it is only in Buddhism that it has attempted the salvation of the soul. In the absence of a Divine Saviour, manifested in a human form, philosophy undertook, by thought alone, to rescue men from the evils that involve them, and to frame methods of discipline and self-elevation that should harmonise with the denial of matter and of God. Buddhism is philosophy gone mad; for it is philosophy assuming the prerogatives which can only belong to a heavenly religion.

The aims of Taouism are less ambitious than those of the Buddhists. Its divinities are described as saving man from the calamities that belong to the present life, rather than as seeking to extricate him altogether from his connection with the world. It is far from denying the validity of the information given us by the senses, and the existence of matter. It tries to etherealise the body, and transmute it to a purer form, in order that it may become immortal, and capable of rising by its own energy to the celestial regions.

While Buddhism speaks much of the *false* and the *true*, saying that the knowledge of truth is gained when certain metaphysical dogmas are understood, and while Confucianism discourses on the *right* and the *wrong* in morals, the mind of the Taouist is rather occupied with the *gross* and the *pure*. It undertakes to subject man as a whole, soul and body, to a process of purification. All on earth is gross. All in heaven is pure. Those who employ a mode of discipline for themselves, similar to those used for the transmutation of gross substances into gold, and the restoration of the body in a state of disease to a state of health, will attain at last the power to rise from earth to heaven. The body will lose its grossness, the soul become more pure, and then the apotheosis will take place.

The idea of sin is the same in Taouism as in the system of Confucius. Its classification of the virtues, and the account it gives of retribution in the present life, are at one with what we find in Confucianism. These two systems have here borrowed from the same national beliefs. But there is this difference—Confucius is content with the reward of an approving conscience, while the other faith desires as rewards of virtue, longevity, riches, health, rank, and a numerous posterity.

Laou-keun, the founder of the Taouist religion, inculcated quietness and self-restraint. "Let all the passions be carefully controlled." "Strength and progress are found in rest." His followers interpreted this doctrine as requiring the hermit life; but they did not, like the Buddhists, think it necessary to take a vow of celibacy, or to have the head clean shaven, or to avoid the destruction of animal life.

The soul being merely a fine species of matter, the idea of salvation comes to be that of relief from all sufferings of body or mind. If the body can be made impregnable against the attacks of disease and death, it will then be like that of the immortals. In various ages there have been men who have sought the plant that confers immortality, and found it. Others have tried to discover by chemistry the process by which the baser metals are turned to gold. The principal agent in this process, being a universal elixir, can be applied to render the body immortal.

Beyond this low view of the method of rescue for man from the misery of his present state, the Taouists were scarcely able to rise at all till they began to borrow from Buddhism. The hermit life was a point of similarity which encouraged a general imitation of the system of that religion. They began to describe Laou-keun in much the same manner as Buddha is described, and they invented personages to correspond to Poosa. Rest and meditation are the means of redemption; and the human teacher is the redeemer. That from which man is redeemed is all that is gross and impure, whether belonging to the body or the soul.

Such a view of the results to which men have come in China, with the aid of three ancient and popular religious systems, on the great subjects of sin and redemption, is suited to awaken deep feelings of pity in the Christian's mind. And the nature of the Gospel, its adaptation to human wants, and the history of its past successes, will fill with sanguine hope the minds of those who seek to spread the doctrine of a Divine redemption by a Divine Saviour in that vast Empire.

CHAPTER XII.

NOTIONS ON IMMORTALITY AND FUTURE JUDGMENT.

THE notions of the Chinese people with regard to immortality and a judgment to come, it will be found on examination, are very unsatisfactory and indefinite. The knowledge of the future to be anticipated for the soul in the coming life is of the highest moral importance. It is not only an incentive to virtue to know that the good man will be happy hereafter, but it confirms the confidence of men in the principles of moral right to anticipate with certainty that the inequalities in the distribution of rewards and punishments noticed in the history of mankind will be made to disappear when the Divine government of this world shall come to be viewed as only a single scene in the universal Divine government, and the happiness and misery now distributed to men shall be seen to be only preliminary to a universal and perfectly just award.

The Chinese sage said so little on the subject of the unseen world, that the national tendency is towards unbelief in regard to the immortality of the soul. The unthinking accept the fables of Buddhism, but the reflecting too often profess entire want of faith. Confucius gave no distinct utterance to his disciples. He laid stress on duty and virtue, but said nothing of the rewards or penalties to be given for obedience or disobedience to what they enjoin.

Some in China hold that the souls of the good will go to a place of happiness, but not those of the common multitude. There are Confucianists who believe this, though it is properly a notion of the Taouists, and springs out of materialistic views of the soul. The materialist finds a heaven for the purified spirit of the good man in the fine ether which floats round the stars, far above the gross material world that constitutes our present abode; but he needs no hell for the wicked, whose souls he supposes to die with their bodies.

These opinions are indigenous in China, and they agree so closely with the peculiar philosophy that permeates the language and ideas of the people, that, although not strictly Confucian, they exercise great influence over many professed followers of Confucius. The immortality of the soul has not been discussed among them extensively, and it is common to take for granted that the soul is a certain small quantity of vapour capable of division into parts. The custom of calling to the soul, just after death, to come back, now prevalent among the people, is mentioned in very ancient books. It must have existed for more than 2000 years. The friends of the deceased go to the well, to the roof of the house, to the north-west corner, with other parts of the dwelling, and call to the spirit to return. "Death they call the breaking of the three-inch vapour." At the moment of death this portion of vapour, three inches long, separating from the organisation to which it belonged, escapes upward like a wreath of smoke, or a small light cloud, into the region of thin air.

There is also the notion of ghosts among the Chinese; and it would seem that these imagined appearances of deceased persons are to be regarded as thin material vehicles for the soul, as bodies constituted of a finer matter than those in which the soul previously resided. In this respect the popular notion is probably the same in China as in the West. Have the Chinese any conception, then, of the soul as immaterial? Have they the idea of spirit, of an immaterial being inhabiting the ghost-like appearance, as it inhabited the common human body, and capable of a separate existence? One would be inclined to reply in the negative to this question, and to say that it was the introduction of Hindoo thought that first made them acquainted with the doctrine of the immateriality of the soul, were it not for the meaning and use of certain terms in their language anterior to Buddhism. If a search were made in old Chinese books, classical and not classical, for passages to determine this question, they would satisfactorily show that the notion existed in the germ, although no direct discussion upon it had arisen. No one had come forward to affirm or deny it till the Buddhists began to attack the common Chinese belief that the souls of men separate into thin air at the time of their death.

The doctrine of the immateriality of the soul is necessary to that of the transmigration of souls. To spread their opinions among the Chinese, the advocates of Buddhism had to try what argument would do for the establishment of the doctrine of a future state. Several books were written with this object. The books themselves are lost, but their names remain in old catalogues, under the titles "Discussion on the Future Life," &c. The publication of such works early in the Christian era indicates the condition of native Chinese thinking on the nature and destiny of the soul. Although the books which take up the argument fully for the immateriality and immortality of the soul on the Buddhist side are lost, the traces which still remain in Chinese history of this controversy are clear enough to show that the Buddhists affirmed both these doctrines. Discussions were sometimes held in the presence of the Emperor between high officers of the Government for and against the Buddhist view. It was when the question of the persecution of Buddhism was brought forward for consideration in the imperial council that these recorded conversations took place. I have not now the opportunity of citing them, but the fact of their existence shows that the opposite view was the common one in China at the time.

The word used for soul in these early arguments on the immortality of man was *shin*. The term which is constantly used in antithesis to it is *hing,* "form." The possession of a perceptible form characterises material objects, and its absence, to the Chinese mind, defines that which is immaterial. This usage of the words exists in Chinese books earlier than the era of the introduction of Buddhism, and it has always remained. The sense, then, belonging to the term *shin* is a formless and invisible existence. Spiritual beings inhabiting nature, in heaven or on earth, powerful or weak, are, with the souls of men, included under this class. But whether the soul, or any of the innumerable unseen spirits called *shin,* be merely an attenuated form of matter, a kind of invisible gas, filling a certain space but not perceptible to the senses, or whether it be a substance entirely distinct from matter—viz., mind or spirit, had not, so far as we know, been considered in China. They had not gone further in their researches into the nature of the soul than to describe it as invisible substance.

If Confucianism had favoured speculation on this and kindred subjects, it must have adopted opinions antagonistic to materialism, because it is itself founded on the teachings of conscience and the immutable principles of morality. These would have led to a distinct preference for high views on the soul's immortality and immaterial nature. But Confucius was not speculative. He said there were four things of which he avoided the discussion: they were—supernatural appearances, feats of physical strength, disorderly conduct, and spirits (*shin*). Practical in his tendencies, he had no liking for the subtleties of metaphysics. Wishing to keep his footing firm on ground that he felt to be safe, he declined to discourse on death and its consequences.

The followers of the sage would willingly have copied the example of their teacher, and have left these points undiscussed, but they have not been allowed to remain on neutral ground. They have had to form some opinion on points where the Taouists and the Buddhists have succeeded in obtaining the assent of the multitude to their views. For example, if the modern Confucianist be asked, where is the soul of the sage, he will in very few cases answer that his soul perished when he died. He will prefer to say that the soul of Confucius is in heaven. The idea of a future state of happiness has become common among the mass of the people, and the disciple of Confucius, unconsciously almost, adopts the present belief, although in doing so he goes further than is warranted by the express teachings of the favourite sage of his country. If further questioned as to the details of the residence set apart for the good, he will either plead entire ignorance, which is the proper Confucian answer, or he will revert to the Taouist description of heaven.

The principal support in the Confucian religion to the statement that the Chinese know the fact of the future state, is found in the custom of sacrificing to ancestors. This existed before Confucius, from the earliest times in that country. It belonged, therefore, to the primitive Chinese religion, that from which the systems of Confucius and of Taou were both derived. Sacrifices were offered to deceased sages and the shades of ancestors, as they were to the spirit of Heaven and the spirits residing in the various parts of nature. The year after Confucius was dead, a funeral temple was erected to his honour. His disciple, Tsze-kung, stayed for six years at his tomb. In his temple were buried articles of dress that he had worn, with his musical instruments and books. Sacrifices were directed by royal authority to be offered to him. It was not till many years after that, an Emperor of the Han dynasty passing the spot, a bullock was slain to be presented to him as a sacrifice. It is now universal to offer a bullock, with other animals, to Confucius in every Chinese city. No priests are employed. It is an official act forming a part of the annual duties of the city magistrate and other resident officers.

This act of reverence to the *manes* of the national sage and to the souls of ancestors is described as a continuation of the respect paid to them while living. The fact that this worship is paid does not require them to be spoken of as divinities; but it may be taken as proof that the soul is considered still to have a certain sort of life after its separation from the body. Such a custom implies that they are believed to possess life, if not a high form of happiness. So far from dignifying their ancestors with divine attributes, or believing them to exercise a beneficent providence, as would be the case if they worshipped them as divine personages, they suppose them to be less happy than in their lifetime. Their happiness depends on the amount of honour that is paid to them by their worshippers. The wise and the virtuous are rewarded with the immortality of fame, the applause and imitation of subsequent generations, and with sacrifices in temples erected for their worship; but according to the strict Confucian doctrine they have no heaven, properly so called. The soul, if it does not return to its elements and become for ever dissipated, exists in a widowed and lonely state, hopeless and helpless. The time of its enjoyment as a conscious individual agent has passed. It is only during the period of union with the body that it can be called happy, except in receiving the approval and reverence of posterity.

The Christian reader who has proceeded thus far will feel that there is need for the Gospel to bring life and immortality to light in the land of Confucius. The system of that sage declines to speak at all of the future state, and it knows of no retribution except what comes in the present life or in the character given to the dead by posterity.

In the Buddhist view of the future state there are three phases. It will be convenient to notice them in the order of their origin.

The Hindoo national doctrine of the transmigration of souls forms the groundwork of Buddhism, as it does of other systems originated in India. According to this view, the present life of each living being is a state of retribution for the past and probation for the future. Neither the heaven nor the hell of the metempsychosis are eternal states. They are liable to change, and their inhabitants to death. In each of the thirty-six regions called heaven there is some ruling divinity and a multitude of subordinate persons. They are the Devas and Deva-Kings of popular Hindooism. Among them figure Brahma, Seeva, and Indra. The souls of men may pass into the paradise of any one of these gods and become either subordinate or chief. In course of time such a life must terminate, and another state will be entered on. It is higher or lower in the scale of honour and enjoyment in proportion to the merit of the individual soul. There is the more room for gradation in rewards and punishments, because there is in the present world the state of animals into which souls may pass, beside that of men. There are also two classes of beings, called Asura and Preta, between men and animals. The Pretas are much spoken of in China as "hungry ghosts." The three conditions of misery are those of hell, of animals, and of hungry ghosts. The other three, heaven, man, and Asura, are states of comparative enjoyment.

In the common notions of the Chinese at the present day, the state of the soul is determined at death by Yama, the Hindoo god of the dead. His Chinese name is Yen-lo-wang. Not much is said of him in the Buddhist sacred books, but his name is perpetually on the lips of the people when death and future judgment are mentioned. Among the very numerous Buddhist proper names transferred from Sanscrit, a few only have become popular. Of these Yen-lo-wang is one of the most familiar. He is believed to determine the mode and time of death, as well as the subsequent state of the soul. A common distich says, to express that death is inevitable:—

"Yen wang choo ting san keng sze
Twan puh lew jin taou woo keng."

"King Yama having decided that a man shall die at the third watch of the night, will certainly not allow him to live till the fifth."

This is the most common view of future judgment among the Chinese. The fate of men depends on the decisions of Yama, the king of death. But his reign is only within the lower sphere of existence, and he cannot control the man who, by the effort of his own wisdom and goodness, raises himself gradually higher till he passes out of the revolutions of the wheel of life and death, and enters the region of pure thought, where a much higher being, Buddha himself, presides.

The second phase to be considered in the Buddhist doctrine of the future state in China is that which has just been alluded to. The disciples of Buddha escape by his help from the six paths where the soul is exposed to a constant succession of lives and deaths, into a higher sphere where there is rest from change and from misery. The soul proceeds on the path to the Nirvana, and there becomes lost in absolute freedom from all sensations, passions, and thoughts. When Shakyamuni Buddha died, an old man surrounded by his disciples, he was said by them to have entered the Nirvana. This is a phrase used by the other Hindoo sects, as well as by the Buddhists, to denote the state aimed at both by philosophy and religion. It expresses the triumph of the soul over matter. The consciousness of existence is entirely lost in the Nirvana, and yet it is not annihilation. For that would be a negative idea, and the Nirvana is something neither positive nor negative, but the perfect absence of both. None but Buddha himself enters the Nirvana at death. Other beings have to wait till they become Buddha through abstraction of the thinking faculties from their activity by the various modes of discipline instituted for the purpose. They may have to pass through thousands of lives before they can attain this. The doctrine of a judgment to come forms no part of the notion of the Nirvana, because it does not admit of the authority, or even the existence, of a supreme governor and judge. The Nirvana, which amounts, in fact, to annihilation, is a fitting companion to the atheism which constitutes the prime error of the Buddhist creed.

The third phase of the Buddhist idea of the future state in China is the paradise of the western heaven. The doctrine of the Nirvana is much too abstruse to be popular. It does not come sufficiently near to popular wants to be the object of an ordinary man's ambition. Those who constitute the mass of Buddha's worshippers cannot enter into the idea of the Nirvana. They need something more gratifying to common human feelings. It was to satisfy this want that the fiction of the "Peaceful Land in the West" was framed. A Buddha was imagined distinct from the Buddha of history, Gautama or Shakyamuni. He was called Amitabha, "boundless age." All who repeat the invocation "Namo Amitabha Buddha," commonly read in China, "Nan woo o me to fuh" (Honour to Amitabha Buddha), are assured that they will be taken at death to the paradise of this personage, situated at an enormous distance to the westward of the visible universe. The souls of such worshippers will remain there for millions of years. Their employment will be to gaze upon the countenance of Amitabha, to hear the singing of beautiful birds, and to enjoy the magnificence of the gardens and lakes which adorn his abode.

Such is the heaven of charming sights and sounds which is promised as a reward to the faithful Buddhist. He can find in it something more attainable than the Nirvana. The ordinary worshipper may hope for it. It is secured by the help of Amitabha in answer to prayer.

The paradise of the western heaven is not known to the Buddhism of Birmah and Ceylon, but it is the most favourite article in the creed of the Buddhists of China and all the north parts of the vast region over which that religion has spread.

In the common phraseology of the Chinese, when it is said, as often occurs, of a man reputed virtuous, that he has "ascended to heaven," *shang teen*, it is the language of the

Taouists that is made use of. The books of that religion speak of many palaces among the stars, where the gods and the genii reside. To the majority of men they suppose death to be destruction of body and soul, but the virtuous few are rewarded with an abode in the paradise of the genii. The *tsing shin*, or soul, escapes at death to the region of stars, and enjoys there an immortality of happiness.

The historical founder of the religion, Laou-keun, is described as dwelling in the *tae tsing kung*, "the palace of exalted purity." The paradise inhabited by the first person in the Taouist trinity is called the metropolis of the pearl mountain, and its entrance, in imitation of the usual Oriental style in speaking of the abode of royalty, is "the golden door." The very common divinity, Yuh-te, subordinate to the trinity just alluded to, is enthroned in the "pure pearl palace."

The stars near the north pole are preferred in legends that speak of the abodes of the genii. Some of the stars receive names from the gods supposed to reside in them. Others take as their names the parts of a palace, as the "hall of heaven," "the celestial door," &c., given them doubtless in agreement with the notion that the stars are the dwelling-places of the divinities who rule the world. The stars were named before the Taouist nomenclature was formed, but the makers of that nomenclature, belonging to the early part of the Christian era, incorporated in it all the old popular notions respecting heaven and the gods which they found suitable to their purpose.

In their books the god of one of these stellar palaces is often described as addressing instructions on the doctrines of Taouism to a multitude of disciples. They are the genii who have escaped from mortality, and it is held out as the destiny of the good among mankind to become such genii and ascend to heaven at death.

In early Chinese fable, the Kwun-lun mountains in Tibet were a favourite region for the abodes of the genii. They are north of the Himalaya, are only second to them in elevation, and were sooner known to the Chinese. A female divinity, called Se-wang-moo, who plays a conspicuous part in the religious romance of that people, is believed to reside on one of the highest of these mountains. The heroes of Taouist mythology are often described as proceeding to that spot, and residing there as in a terrestrial paradise. The *seen jin*, or genii, are *teen seen*, "celestial immortals," or *te seen*, "terrestrial immortals." They all have ascribed to them wisdom, virtue, perpetual youth, and magical power. But there are degrees in these qualities. Those of inferior powers remain in some mountain paradise like that of Kwun-lun, while those of higher rank are transferred to the stars.

The Christian heart is grieved at the reflection that a wise and learned nation like the Chinese should be no better informed as to the future of the soul than these notices show them to be. But they prove at least that men, when left without the Bible, will find their way to some system or articles of belief, however incongruous and mistaken they may be, to satisfy the consciousness of a coming life natural to all men. Their possession of this consciousness is a preparation for Christianity, and they will learn one day to value the truth the more in proportion to the falseness and deficiencies of the beliefs which they will exchange for it.

CHAPTER XIII.

CHINESE OPINIONS OF CHRISTIANITY.

THE religious condition of the Chinese mind may be illustrated by the mode in which Christianity is received by it.

We cannot expect that the religion of the Bible should be accepted at once with a cordial and unquestioning faith by the people of a country like China. It must first be subjected to the criticisms that most readily occur to them. The nature of those criticisms depends on the state of opinion prevailing among such as use them. They have a certain standard by which they form a judgment on moral and religious subjects. The objections they bring against Christianity are, therefore, an index to their state in regard to morality and religion.

One of the commonest objections they mention against Christianity is, that it does not admit of the worship of ancestors. Not to worship their ancestors they regard as equivalent to an entire forgetting of filial duty. Confucius said that sacrifices to deceased parents should be offered in compliance with propriety and ancient custom. If this be neglected, as it must be by the convert to Christianity, it is viewed as a great crime. A person guilty of this is *puh heaou*, "unfilial," and nothing worse can be said of him by the malice of his greatest enemies. When the Emperor Yung-ching was bent on persecuting the Roman Catholic converts early in the eighteenth century, he was interceded with in vain by the Jesuit mathematicians whom he employed in the astronomical tribunal. He told them that the adoption of their religion was destructive of filial piety.

They defended themselves by reminding the Emperor that filial piety was expressly enjoined by Christianity as one of the most solemn and binding of human duties. They also stated that Christians were so far from forgetting deceased parents, that they carefully preserved portraits and other relics of them, and wore rings to keep them in memory. It did not, however, appear to the Emperor that anything could compensate for the want of sacrifices and religious worship, and he declined to revoke the edict of persecution.

The Jesuit missionaries wished to allow the converts to retain the practice of sacrificing to ancestors, as being a civil and not a religious observance. Missionaries of other orders held a different opinion. They viewed this practice as unquestionably religious, and they demanded that it should be entirely given up by all who professed to abandon heathenism. The Pope, to whom the dispute was referred, decided against the Jesuits, as he did on another point. For the missionaries of that order, when they pleaded with him for the adoption of the ancient terms Shang-te, Teen, and Heaven, as the equivalents of the word God, were unsuccessful, and the newly-invented term, Teen-choo, Lord of Heaven, the favourite with the other orders, was preferred by the Pope, and imposed authoritatively upon the missionaries and converts.

A recent Chinese author, in an attack upon Christianity, says, "The religion of the Lord of Heaven, in not permitting men to worship the tablets of their ancestors, nor to offer sacrifices to them, tends to lead away mankind from the respect they have been accustomed to pay to their parents and forefathers." He condemns the religion of the West as being like the systems of certain ancient Chinese philosophers that were condemned by contemporary Confucianists as not orthodox. Yang and Mih, the men to whose doctrines Christianity is compared, had advocated universal and undistinguishing rectitude and universal and undistinguishing love as the principles of their respective systems. The followers of Confucius had said that these doctrines were inconsistent with the duties of filial piety and loyalty, which require that greater respect and love should be rendered to some persons than to others. A Christian writer had said, "The follower of the Buddhist and the Taouist religions cuts himself off from the discharge of his duties to princes and parents, and he does not seem sensible of his duties towards Heaven. Even the disciples of Confucius are not without fault in this point." The Chinese critic grows angry at these words. He defends the Buddhists and Taouists by saying that they honour the "dragon tablet" in temples, so proving their loyalty. The practice to which he refers originated in times of persecution. The Buddhists were compelled to place a small tablet to the Emperor immediately in front of the principal image in their temples, so that the worshipper, in bowing to the image, bowed also to the Emperor. He also quotes a passage from a Buddhist work, saying that to honour a thousand Pratyeka Buddhas is not so good as to worship one's parents in the hall of filial piety. He proceeds to defend the Confucian system, and to bring coarse charges against Jesus, saying, among other things, that His crucifixion was because He had transgressed the laws of His country.

These and many similar remarks are found in the recent work, "Hae-kwoh-too-che," usually known as "Lin's Geography." The chief compiler and composer of this extensive production — a work in twenty-four volumes, and which has gone through five editions in a few years — was Wei-yuen, who did not long survive his more celebrated collaborateur, Lin-tseh-seu. Both were sincere enemies of England and the English, the one showing his antipathy in his acts as commissioner in the war of 1842, and the other in his writings since that time.

Another mode of assaulting Christianity, common among the Chinese literary class, is to express disbelief in its facts. I was visited several times by a scholar, very well informed in the books of his own country, named Chow-teen-ming. Many men of inquisitive minds visit the foreign missionaries at the seaport towns where they reside, hoping to gain from them some scientific information. He was one of such. He was introduced by a native friend as being conversant with the twenty-five histories, the great collection of the annals of the successive dynasties of the Chinese Empire. The conversation soon turned to the subject of Christianity. He said that the narrative of the death of Christ on the cross could not be earlier than the Ming dynasty; for it was then (in the sixteenth century) that the Roman Catholic missionaries entered the "Middle Kingdom," and first brought information of it. England, he said, was a new country, compared with China. Its history as a nation did not extend back more than a few centuries. We could not know the course of events so long ago as Christ was said to have lived, with any certainty. It was to him quite clear that the New Testament could not be so old as we said, for in that case the chief facts in the life of Christ must have become known in China much earlier. He was informed, in reply, that though the English nation had not been in existence more than a few centuries, we had an extensive body of old world literature transmitted in the ancient languages of Europe and Western Asia, and of an historical value fully equal to that of the classical literature of his own country. It was as old in time and as well supported by critical evidence. He professed assent, but with a look of incredulity on his countenance.

He was then asked if he had seen the Syrian inscription, which contained evidence that Christianity had been taught in China in the seventh century. This is an extremely interesting monument of the early spread of our religion in China through the labours of missionaries of the Nestorian Church. It was found accidentally by some workmen, two hundred years ago, at the city of Sengan-foo, in the north-west of China. Native scholars regard it as a most valuable specimen of the caligraphy and composition of the Tang dynasty, that to which it belongs; but they did not know how to explain its Christianity till the Jesuit missionaries came to their assistance. My friend said he had seen it, but he did not think that the religion of this monument was Christianity. The fact of Christ's death was not clearly mentioned, and he thought that the sentence in it which spoke of the division of the world into four parts in the form of a cross was not an allusion to Christ's death on the cross, but only to the four cardinal points of the horizon. Other passages in the inscription were then pointed out to him, which spoke of the trinity of Persons in the Divine nature, mentioned the Syrian name of God (Aloho), and the number twenty-seven in speaking of the sacred books evidently referring to the New Testament. Other allusions to the weekly Sabbath, to the birth of the Saviour under the denomination Messiah in the Roman empire of the far West, and to other facts of Christianity, made it certain that no other religion was described in the monument. It was thus shown that his statement, that Christianity was no earlier than the time when the Roman Catholic missionaries entered China, could not be sustained. It must be at least as old as A.D. 781, the date of the monument.

The advocate of Christianity in China finds this celebrated inscription very useful in meeting opponents like this man. To refer to the usual evidences, called the historical, is not conclusive to such persons, ignorant as they are of Judea and its history. In proving the genuineness of the Christian Scriptures, this monument is a most important stepping-stone to the era of primitive Christianity, and it has been much used for this object in works published by Catholic and Protestant missionaries in China.

The Jewish monuments at Kai-fung-foo help in China to sustain the genuineness of the Old Testament, just as the one now mentioned contributes to support that of the New. When this visitor asserted that we English were such modern people that we could not have books so old as theirs, I took a Hebrew Bible, and told him that the English were accustomed to do what the Chinese did not, to learn other languages besides their own; and that they read and preserved books with as much care in the ancient languages as in the modern, so that the late origin of the English nation could not affect the accuracy of their information on the books and events of 2000 or more years ago. Our Hebrew Bible was the same as that at Kai-fung-foo, except in containing not only the Books of Moses, but the remaining part of the Old Testament; the written symbols used in both were the same, and it was from them that our own alphabet was derived. A complaint was made to him that he should have rashly questioned the correctness of our testimony on the antiquity of our books. He said, "Do not be displeased. I do not wish to treat your holy religion with disrespect. We in this country belong to the religion of the holy sage Confucius, and how could I speak ill of another?" He was informed, in reply, that he should prove his regard for the morality of the national sage by "showing good feeling towards men from afar." To question the correctness of statements made by Catholics and Protestants in China for two hundred years past, respecting the origin of their religion, was to contradict this precept of the sage. He said that, as a literary man, he studied for himself questions such as this, upon the statements found in books, and endeavoured to sift them as best he could. We recommended him to learn foreign languages, and then he would be in a better position to criticise European literature.

The same opponent, in attacking our religion, referred to the difference, as he described it, in moral tone between the Old and the New Testaments. On hearing from men of education in heathen countries superficial opinions upon the comparative excellence of the Books of God, there is a strong feeling of revulsion awakened, but it is impossible to force upon them the authority of God's Word simply upon our testimony. They look at the book as ours, not as His. They must be brought by patient argument to admit that it is His, and they must be borne with while they read and judge. Nothing in the common course of things can lead an educated pagan to look on the Bible, when he first sees it, as other than a human book. This Chinese said he preferred the New Testament to the Old very much, and threw ridicule on some parts of the Old Testament. He was told that the wicked actions of men, when recorded in history, are as well adapted to promote virtue as their good actions. The aim of the writers in the Old Testament, in all they had transmitted in their works, was, to say the least, most unquestionably to advance the cause of piety and virtue. If he continued to regard it as a human composition, he must see in this fact their perfect justification in preserving the memory of wicked actions. But more than this, it was the glory of history to be faithful, and in the classical books of his own country the conduct of wicked men was related along with that of the good. Chinese moralists did not, however, consider these books unfavourable to virtue on that account. They were held up as models, and universally placed in the hands of youth for their moral training. It had been found, that of all books the Old and the New Testament were the most conducive to morality.

He did not like the high pretensions of Christianity as the only Divine religion. He thought that the authority of the Chinese classics was absolute for his countrymen and himself. When the conversation turned on the question whether the soul is single or divisible into two at death, he considered that its duality was certain, because it was stated in the classical books. "We have had these works," he said, "for three thousand years, and numberless productions of learned men in the interval from that time till now. Our Confucius was several centuries earlier than Jesus."

The lustre of learning and antiquity ought, in his opinion, to carry the day in favour of the religion of China. He was told, in reply, that the higher antiquity of Confucius would not constitute a sufficient claim to superiority, because Moses, the Jewish sage, was before him in time, and even before Wen and Woo, the two famous Chinese kings of the eleventh century B.C. "But," he retorted, "our wise Emperors Yaou and Shun were earlier than Moses." Our antiquity goes further yet, he was informed. The date of Yaou and Shun was not earlier than about 2300 years before Christ, but we have Adam, Enoch, and Noah, belonging to a still earlier period. He then proceeded, in a good-humoured manner, to show in another way, since he could not rival our antiquity, the superiority of the East over the West. He alluded to the fact that the art of writing was borrowed by us from Asia, our alphabet being derived originally from that used by the Hebrew nation.

Much of the opposition the Chinese feel to Christianity comes from national prejudice. They dislike the foreigner's religion because they dislike the foreigner himself. Many violent enemies of foreigners are found among the inferior officers of Yamuns. One such opponent I met in a temple at Shanghai, some years since. He began with asserting that our calendar was wrong. Our months did not coincide with the new and full moons, nor with the spring and neap tides. He was told that our calendar was formed so as to make the months agree with the motions of the sun rather than of the moon, for public convenience. He then said it was preposterous in us to exhort them to virtue, for they had books that taught morality much earlier and better than ours. All our science and learning, he said, was brought from the East. Laou-keun, the Taouist philosopher, had gone, as history recorded, to the West, and, no doubt, communicated the wisdom of China to the people among whom he travelled. Others had followed him. Knowledge had spread from China to all the surrounding nations, and it was in this way that we had become civilised. He insisted that our statements respecting Jesus were unreasonable. How could He govern the universe alone? He must have inferior divinities to assist Him. We denied their existence; but they must be needed in the superintendence of the world. Our Matthew, he said, for he had read some chapters of the Gospel of Matthew, was a Chinese spoken of in the "Three Kingdoms" (an historical romance of the second century of the Christian era), whose name was nearly like the word Matthew in sound. If any one became a believer in Jesus, he would throw away his character for filial piety, for he would not then be allowed to sacrifice to his ancestors. When reminded that this practice, if forbidden by God, must be given up, he replied that it was undoubtedly right, because it was complied with by the Emperor himself. This opponent was, as is clear from the account here given, not good at argument. He is an example of that unreasoning hostility which is often met with in China. Everything foreign is looked at through the spectacles of prejudice. An exclusive spirit marks the class of persons referred to, which leads them to regard as ridiculous all customs and opinions prevailing among the "barbarians."

A favourite mode of attacking Christianity is to represent it as derived partly from Buddhism and partly from the system of Confucius. "Why should you speak of heaven and hell?" an opponent will often say to the missionary; "we have that doctrine already. It is Buddhist, and it is nothing new to us." In fact, the Chinese have very minute descriptions of hell torments. The pictorial representations of them common among the people often reminded me of some of the plates in "Foxe's Book of Martyrs," and of Roman Catholic illustrated books for the use of the poor in Ireland. If descriptions containing variety and severity of torture were all that was requisite to constitute the doctrine of future punishments, the Chinese Buddhists have it among them in a very terrible form. This being the state of the case, and the missionary being compelled to use the Buddhist names for heaven and hell, objectors say that he is teaching them Buddhism. He then refers to the authority of Jesus as the Divine Revealer of the future state, and the certainty that marks His teaching as compared with the baseless statements of Hindoo mythology, a purely human and fictitious system, not capable of bearing a moment's careful scrutiny.

A Chinese work, published in the last century by imperial authority, criticises one or two Christian books. It is a catalogue *raisonné* of Chinese works in the Emperor's library, with descriptive notes on all such as appeared to call for criticism. Very few Christian books have been allowed to remain in the imperial library, the greater number having been burnt long since by order of Government. One or two, however, remain. The critic speaks of some by the celebrated Jesuits, Matthew Ricci and Adam Schaal. He says of the "Twenty-five Sentences," a tract by Ricci, published in Chinese about the time of James I., that much of it is stolen from the Buddhists, but that the style of its composition is not so good as theirs. He adds that in the West Buddhism was the only religion they had. The Europeans adopted its ideas, and put them forth in an altered form. When they entered China they saw the books of Confucius, and began to borrow from them not a little, in order to impart an air of literary elegance to what they gave out as their own. With this new help, he proceeds to say, they extended their system in new works, and began to boast that it was superior to the three religions of China.

The critic then gives his readers a description of a second work by Ricci, "The True Account of the Religion of God." As a supplement to this treatise, Ricci has collected passages from the Chinese classics which speak of the existence and providence of God. The critic says this was because the missionary felt conscious that he must not attack the religion of Confucius. Ricci also undertook to confute the Buddhists; but in the opinion of the imperial critic, his views differ very little from the Buddhist belief respecting heaven and hell, and the metempsychosis. He adds, that in regard to mankind being under a law of change, which compels us to live, to die, and afterwards to live again, and our also being under a law of retribution, which apportions happiness and misery to men according to their merit, there is little difference between the two religions. If the Christians did not believe in the metempsychosis, the forbidding to slay animal life, and the obligation of celibacy, it was because they wished to keep near the doctrine of Confucius. Some of the Christian books are, he says, like the liturgical works of the Buddhists, while others resemble those that treat of the contemplative life.

He concludes a long criticism on Catholic books by observing that the Europeans are profoundly versed in astronomy and calculation, and cunning in mechanical contrivances; but when they come to speak of morals and religion, they are very heretical. Their writings on these subjects did not deserve to be placed in the list of books forming the national literature. They had, however, been included in the catalogue of new works contained in the history of the Ming or last Chinese dynasty, made by command of the Tartar emperors. The compiler of that work had thought proper to class them among the books of the Taouist religion. In the new arrangement they were transferred to the class of books known as the miscellaneous division. So far the critic.

This style of remark on foreign books translated into Chinese is very significant. It shows in the true light the feeling that literary men in that country entertain respecting them. The Jesuit missionaries laboured hard in the production of good treatises on science and religion in the language of that country. Though their books on science are sought after and valued, those upon Christianity are scarcely considered worthy of a place in the national literature. Perhaps, however, their real influence is greater than Confucian writers are ready to admit. They may have helped, by their account of God, in His nature and attributes, to render the modern generation of scholars more willing to return to the doctrine of a personal God, and to abandon the notion, so prevalent before the Roman Catholics arrived, that He is nothing but an abstraction.

Wei-yuen, the author before referred to, compares Mohammedanism and Christianity, and thinks they have both derived many of their peculiarities from Brahmanism or Buddhism. He had been reading the translation of the Bible by the Protestant missionaries, and he believes that he finds there evidence of inconsistency and folly greater than existed in those two Hindoo religions. The prohibition of image-worship excites his indignation. Sacrifices to ancestors are forbidden, and yet the image of the mother of Jesus is adored by the Christians, and the cross is hung up in their dwellings. Why, he asks, do they transgress the law of their own religion?

The criticisms of this and other authors are very numerous. Some of them are extremely foolish, and prove nothing but the ignorance of those who made them. The Chinese easily fall into errors on this subject, and all others relating to foreign nations. There is nothing they so much need as the constant and widely-extended supply of intelligence on the world beyond them. It must be long before Christianity can become well understood by them. Missionary efforts must be greatly increased, and the agency of the press must be well worked, before they will be freed from many wild misconceptions. It is constantly said in China, that medicine in the form of pills is administered to all Christian converts; and that when a person is dying, his eyes are taken out by the priest. One writer sees in the works of healing performed by Jesus something similar to the cures effected by Hwato, a celebrated Chinese physician who lived in the third century, but entirely fails to notice that their object was to prove anything with regard to the character of Jesus Christ. It never occurred to him to consider what a miracle is for. He therefore refuses to rank Jesus with the sages who have limited themselves to moral teaching. In that country a far wider diffusion of knowledge respecting the facts and doctrines of Christianity is needed to put the natives in a position to judge of its claims as the only Divine religion.

CHAPTER XIV.

STATE OF ROMAN CATHOLIC MISSIONS.

THE state of Roman Catholic missions in China deserves to be studied by those who are interested in the spread of scriptural Christianity in that country. These missions have met with great success. Abbé Huc, in his work on Christianity in China, has given an interesting account of their commencement and progress to the reign of Kanghe. Many persons of rank became converts, and chapels and churches multiplied fast in the cities and villages. When times of persecution arrived and court favour was withdrawn, doctors of literature and masters of arts ceased to tread in the steps of Seu-kwang-ke and other Christian converts holding high office in the State. At present the work of the missions lies much with the humbler classes. There are indeed men of property among the converts still, but they are not known beyond the community to which they belong. In days of persecution, during the present century, there have been not a few among these men who have courageously endured banishment to Western Tartary, or loss of property, for the sake of their religious belief.

The introduction of the Protestant religion has induced the European Catholic missionaries, who are about three hundred in number, to give certain precautionary directions to their converts! They have told them that the religion of the English is only three hundred years old; that their own is the true and ancient form of Christianity; and that salvation is only to be found within the pale of the Catholic Church. Catholic converts frequently meet Protestant missionaries, and state to them that their religion began with King Henry VIII. of England. He commenced it because he was not allowed by the Pope to divorce his wife. Such is the account of Protestant Christianity which has been industriously disseminated far and wide among the converts in the province of Keangnan, with the state of whom I have had the opportunity of becoming best acquainted.

Among the converts sometimes met with are inquiring men, fond of reading. Such a person came on one occasion to seek an interview with a missionary, who had recently arrived in his boat, in one of the interior cities in that province. He stated, in the conversation that then ensued, that he had read many Buddhist and Taouist books, although the "spiritual fathers" recommended the converts not to do so. He did not like this restriction, and, feeling confidence in himself that he could distinguish the true from the false, he did not fear to read them. He was asked his opinion on the Buddhist doctrine, that all things are mere emptiness, and exist only in imagination. He had evidently read Buddhist statements of this sort with the impression that they are metaphorical and not to be taken literally, for he answered that it was quite correct to hold that all in the world is vanity and a dream. He then inquired if it was true that a king of England separated from the Church of Rome because he was not permitted to marry as he pleased. He was informed that the king did so, but it was on a different account that the people separated. The reason of their separating was, that they had become convinced from the Scriptures that they ought to do so. He then asked when our English religion really began, and was told that there had been a Christian Church in Britain from the second century, and that it was then and for long after quite independent of Rome and the Pope. He replied, that he could not see how this could be, his information being entirely different. He was also surprised to learn that celibacy for all priests was only required for the first time in the Romish Church in the eleventh century. He had read the books of the early Jesuit missionaries, Ricci, Jules Aloni, and others, but not any of the writings of the Apostles. No translation of the Scriptures has ever been published in China by the Catholics.

Although a professed Christian, he appeared to believe in many Buddhist legends. He regarded Kwan-yin as a real personage, the daughter of a certain king, as stated in one of the fictitious accounts of that divinity. The missionary, seeing that he was to a considerable extent a believer in Buddhism, advised him not to read the books of that system, but ineffectually; for he said he felt no danger, and wished, for curiosity's sake, to examine various religious systems.

In the province of Keangsoo there are about 75,000 converts.[1] A great portion of these are villagers. A small chapel is erected in villages and hamlets, usually in a retired situation. Service is held here on Lord's-day mornings. After this service, the poor are allowed by a dispensation from the Pope to work in the fields or at their other employments. Those whose worldly circumstances are good abstain from work on the Lord's-day. Foreign priests visit these village stations four or five times in a year. In their absence the service is conducted by natives. When these Roman Catholic villagers are asked who it is that forgives sins, they will frequently reply, the priest. If the inquiry be made through whom it is that they expect to be saved in heaven, some will say, through the aid of Mary; others, through the merits of Jesus Christ. They are taught to repeat the creed and a small catechism composed in a plain, unadorned style. On the walls of the chapels are hung fourteen pictures representing the sufferings of our Lord, after the usual manner of Roman Catholic edifices. The altar is ornamented with artificial flowers and such-like appendages. Sometimes the relics of a martyr are preserved in the altar. There is often a

[1] In 1858.

school in connection with these village chapels. The ordinary converts residing at the country stations are generally civil to foreign visitors, but if native ordained priests happen to be there, they are very hostile in their manner to those whom they find to be Protestants. They are able to speak a little Latin, taught them at Macao or at some of the seminaries for training native priests in the interior of the country, and they resort to that medium of expressing their ideas when they do not wish the neighbours to hear what is said in conversation. When engaged in discussion on questions of theological controversy, they usually prefer the Latin language.

In North China, when the converts in any heathen village raise half the money themselves for a church, the European priests find the other half, and a church is accordingly built.

The Catholics have not a few well-conducted schools in China. That at Seu-kia-wei is well known to those who have visited Shanghai. It is seven miles from that place. Many of the pupils are taught the art of moulding images in clay, sculpture, &c. It caused us some painful reflections to see them forming images of Joseph and Mary and other Scripture personages, in the same way that idol-makers in the neighbouring towns were moulding Buddhas and gods of war and riches, destined too to be honoured in much the same manner. With such exceptions as this, we could not help admiring the arrangements of the school, which appeared to be large and efficient. There is a handsome modern chapel in connection with it.

Another school that I saw with a friend at Ningpo was one of great interest. It was a school for deserted children of the female sex. There were seventy of them at the time enjoying its privileges. The buildings were new and very extensive. They were in an open situation outside the south gate of the city. Seven French Sisters of Mercy conducted the school. They received us most kindly, and permitted us to inspect the whole establishment. They appeared to be much attached to the children, whose apartments were well supplied with crucifixes and pictures of the Virgin. The sisters wore their regular costume of black serge, which looked very uncomfortable and unsuited to the season, the hot weather not having terminated at the time of our visit. They showed us the graves of some of their companions in the adjacent garden. They informed us that they did not employ native schoolmasters or schoolmistresses to instruct the children in reading, but they learned the Chinese written character themselves, and then taught their scholars. This is a proof of no little resolution and energy on the part of the sisters, for the acquirement of the art of reading Chinese is difficult, and it is the custom in Protestant and Catholic schools for boys to obtain native aid in teaching the pupils to read the native books. The sisters proved to us their competence by reading some passages in a simple Chinese style from the Christian class-books used in the school. Attached to the establishment is a free dispensary for the neighbouring poor.

To assist in the training seminaries for native priests is one of the most important duties of the Catholic missionaries. A large number only can meet the wants of their numerous stations, scattered through all the eighteen provinces of the Empire. Most of the pupils in the seminaries are received when very young. The consequence often is, that on growing up they are unwilling to submit to the restraints which the life of a priest would impose on them. I knew one who after receiving his education wished to marry, and not to become a priest. The European missionary in charge of the seminary frustrated his hopes by inducing his intended wife to enter a nunnery. He left the Catholics after this, and entered the employment of Protestant missionaries as a teacher of the language. For this occupation his knowledge of Latin was of some advantage. He still continued to pray to Mary, although he professed attachment to Protestant views in most respects.

He was asked why he did not give up the worship of the Virgin; to this he replied, that he could not abandon it without a great sacrifice of feeling, having been always accustomed to it. "But," he was informed, "every being except God is forbidden to be worshipped." "In honouring the mother," he said, "I honour the Son." "You may honour her," said the missionary, "but you should not pray to her. She cannot hear prayers and answer them, as God can, and as Jesus can." In answer to this he related an anecdote, which led him, as he stated, to place great trust in Mary:—When at the seminary he had been accused of a crime, of which the real perpetrator was one of his fellow-pupils. He prayed to Mary that the true criminal might be discovered in seven days, and his own reputation vindicated. The prayer was answered within the necessary time, and he felt such confidence ever after in the efficacy of prayers to the Virgin, that he could not think of omitting them in his morning and evening devotions. It was suggested to him that he ought to refer the interference on his behalf that had occurred to the providence of God, not to that of the Virgin. We were never told in Scripture to pray to her, nor could we expect her to answer prayer. He replied, that in this instance his prayer, which had been remarkably answered, was addressed to Mary and not to God. "So," said the missionary, "may the sailor say of his prayer to *Teen-how*, the 'heavenly queen.' He supposes that goddess to preside over the sea, and he supplicates her protection from storms. To her he ascribes his safety, though he ought to refer it to the providence of God." "But," he replied, "Mary is the mother of Jesus, and has intercessory power with God, which Teen-how-shing-moo, 'the holy mother, queen of heaven,' has not. Jesus honoured His mother," he added, "on the cross, and we must honour her also." His attention was drawn to the second commandment, which forbade the worship of all images; but he would not admit the inconsistency of the worship of Mary's image with this commandment, because the kind of worship offered to her was different from that offered to God.

The numbers of the native Catholic community in China were kept up previously to the last fifteen years by teaching within the community itself. Few converts, comparatively, were made from the surrounding heathen. The successive persecutions instituted by the Government checked the aggressive efforts of the missions, and chilled the zeal of those who were contemplating the adoption of the Catholic faith. As the missionaries arrived from Europe, they were conveyed secretly into the interior, under the care of converts, and passed their time afterwards entirely in the society of the members of the community. Strangers were not permitted to know of their presence. The boatmen or chair-bearers who conducted them from place to place were native Christians. So also were their servants at the residences provided for them. On their reaching any station to perform their official duties, information was quickly communicated to all the residents who regarded them as their spiritual guides, and they then assembled to receive their blessing. It was and is indispensable on their entering the presence of the European priest, that they should perform a prostration before him. No one outside of the community was allowed to see the foreign priest till he had gone through a course of instruction under the native catechists and priests. When a heathen was ready for baptism he might have an interview with the "spiritual father from the Western Ocean," but not usually sooner. This circumspection was rendered necessary by the state of the laws in China, which did not then permit the entrance of foreigners into the interior of the country. Very irksome was the restraint under which foreign priests were placed, for it was not considered safe for them to be noticed by any eyes except those of trusted friends. Sometimes when a rumour was spread of their presence in a walled city, they were conveyed in a sedan chair out of the gate, and brought in again by the gate on the opposite side of the city. This was done to induce the belief that they had taken their departure. They usually, however, avoided cities altogether, and remained in the country, where accommodations were provided for them under the superintendence of the converts. They were liable to ejection at any moment from their temporary lodging-place, should suspicion be excited and inquiry be made for them. Huc speaks, in his "Travels in Tartary and Tibet," of the enjoyment occasioned to him and his companion by their sense of freedom when they had passed beyond the Great Wall into Tartary, because there they could allow themselves to be seen without fear of capture. In these circumstances the gathering-in of new converts was necessarily left to the zeal and efficiency of the native converts.

I had a discussion on one occasion with a shopkeeper who was on the point of becoming a Roman Catholic. He was strongly prejudiced against Protestantism. He insisted, that in propagating a religion it was essential to have a visible earthly chief from whom to receive orders. Our system was defective, because it was a system without a head. It was stated to him that Christ was our Head, and that we did not need any man to wield supreme power in our religion, just as in the religion of Confucius it was not found requisite to have any person at the head of it. As to his assertion that our religion could not be spread without submission to some visible head, he should recollect that the religions of Buddha and Confucius were able to subsist in China in the same circumstances. He then inquired what authority we had to preach. He was informed that men are miserable, and in need of the Gospel to render them happy. Any one that knew the Gospel might preach it, and how could it be wrong to try to save men? He remarked, that if men undertook this office they ought at least to be self-denying enough to refrain from marriage. A passage was pointed out to him in the Gospel of Matthew, which showed that the Apostle Peter had a wife;

but he observed that he could not know the book to be correct. He was recommended to take it and examine it for himself; and he might ask his priest if it was a book to be trusted. He declined to do this, and insisted that Protestants were in the wrong.

A few days after this, at a town not far from the scene of this discussion, I had an unexpected opportunity of ascertaining the strength of the Romanists in country places in the province of Keangsoo. The Shanghai river, before it reaches that city, at twenty miles south of it, bends to the westward. Our boat, after proceeding up the stream fifteen miles beyond this point, turned up a broad canal which entered it by its right bank. In that great alluvial plain canals are very numerous. They need no locks or sluices, the land being level, and if their course be followed, towns having a large population are found on the banks of all of them. They are the market-towns for the produce of the neighbouring country, consisting of wheat, rice, cotton, beans, indigo, and other articles. On arriving at one of them, at a short distance from the junction of the canal with the river, we went ashore with Testaments and tracts for distribution among the respectable inhabitants of the town. While thus employed, a French priest unexpectedly made his appearance, calling himself Père ——. One or two native Romanists had noticed our arrival, and proceeded to report the fact to this priest. After a few words of ceremony, he asked us why we came there. He was informed that we wished to teach the heathen inhabitants of the town the truths of Christianity and the folly and wickedness of their superstition. He replied, that he had resided there for many years, and it was not right of us to interfere with his labours. In answer to our inquiries, he stated that there were about 200 Christians under his care, while there were 7000 or 8000 inhabitants in the town. We then stated, that the pagan proportion of the population being so large, there was great need of the public preaching of the Gospel there, and we understood that he and his fellow-missionaries did not teach in public. Could it be wrong for the doctrine of salvation to be proclaimed there? He said that this was not wrong; but what authority had we to teach at all? He was reminded of the Saviour's commission to His disciples, "Go ye into all the world and preach the Gospel to every creature." A crowd of interested listeners had collected around us, while this dialogue proceeded in the dialect of the place. The priest, observing the attention which they paid to it, turned to them and said, "I have long been residing here; you can trust me. Do not listen to a new doctrine which comes to you without authority. You should not believe in the teaching of these new-comers." He was requested not to be angry with us for trying to do good to the heathen. He then complained that a passage occurred in a book published by Protestant missionaries which spoke disparagingly of the Roman Catholic faith. He was, however, unable to state in what book he had seen it, or what had been said. The passage had been shown to him several years before, and he had forgotten the particulars. I expressed regret that his memory did not serve him better, and offered him what books I had for examination, that he might convince himself there was nothing in them derogatory to the Catholic religion. He declined this, and soon afterwards retired.

The Catholic missionaries find themselves in a position of difficulty from their not having the same literary standing that distinguished their predecessors in China in the sixteenth and seventeenth centuries. Perhaps it is thought that there is no need for new efforts in science, since the Chinese Government has ceased to employ Jesuits to superintend the preparation of the calendar and to calculate eclipses and the places of the heavenly bodies. At any rate, the modern missionaries write no new works on science or religion, but content themselves with the use of the old ones. Fully occupied with pastoral work, they seem to devote little attention to literature, so that they fail to obtain that place in public estimation that was held by many of the Jesuits whose names illustrate the early annals of the Catholic mission in China. It would be an advantage to them in more ways than one if they had among them men of learning and literary ability. The Chinese are very reluctant to read what is not composed in an elegant style, and it is important to meet the taste of the readers, as well as can be done, by putting into their hands such works as will not offend their sense of literary propriety. A good knowledge of the written language is needed to give facility in conversation with the educated, and in preparing new works. The old scientific treatises of their predecessors are based on obsolete theories, and need to be superseded by newer and better. They taught the Ptolemaic system of the universe, instead of that of Copernicus and Newton. The natural philosophy promulgated by Ricci supposed the four elements—fire, air, earth, and water—to be the original principles of all natural objects. Great changes have occurred in the mathematical sciences since the translations of the early Jesuit missionaries were published in China. With their present want of attention to these things, the Romanist missionaries cannot acquire the *status* that they would otherwise have, and fail to exert an influence on that large class of persons in China who know anything of the student life.

Under the new treaty now in force, according to which foreigners have the right of visiting whatever part of the country they please, as might have been expected, new energy has been infused into the Catholic missions. The missionaries have been able to abandon their strict incognito, and adopt new measures for increasing the number of their converts. Permission is enjoyed to travel and reside in all parts of the country, and this permission is practically so interpreted as to render legal the longer or shorter stay which the Romanist missionaries make in rotation at the stations under their charge.

They will scarcely attempt again to obtain power at court and among the literary class in China. They succeeded remarkably at first by this policy. But it was dangerous to trust to court favour. They felt the reaction to be very severe when honour and power were exchanged for the storm of persecution. Their scientific attainments kept them in their places in the imperial tribunal of astronomy till 1822. The last Jesuits employed at Peking were then sent from that city to Macao, and they were desired to return home, the services of foreign astronomers being no longer required by the Son of Heaven. Report says that the last three Jesuits who received the emoluments of office as servants of the Chinese Emperor, wanted the power to make themselves valued as men of scientific ability.

This is another instance of the results of the worldly policy of the Jesuits. Their first splendid successes have almost invariably been followed by ignominious failure.

They have prospered better in the more spiritual part of their work in China. While the scientific treatises written by the early Jesuits are becoming useless on account of their obsolete and erroneous principles, the converts they made among the poor have transmitted to their descendants a faith more or less enlightened in the Catholic form of Christianity. At the present time there are many instructed and zealous members of their community, mixed, as might be expected, with not a few nominal Christians of a much inferior kind.

CHAPTER XV.

MOHAMMEDANS, JEWS, AND WOO-WEI BUDDHISTS.

THE number of Mohammedans in China is much larger than that of the Catholics, or any other of the smaller religious communities in that country. They have been there during a very long period, for some of them arrived within a century after the era of Mahomet. But it was principally in the Sung and Ming dynasties, A.D. 1000 to A.D. 1600, that the colonies of these religionists entered China.

They are most numerous in the North of China, where in some parts they form a third of the population. Their mosques are called *tsing-chin-sze*, " pure and true temple." The name of their sect is Hwei-hwei, which is derived from Ouigour. They call God Choo, " Lord," or Chin-choo, "true Lord." In race they are predominantly Turkish and Persian.

Their avoidance of pork keeps them distinct from the other Chinese, and the habit they have in some northern cities of placing the words Hwei-hwei, " Mohammedan," or Kiau-mun, " religious sect," on their shop signs and over their doors, is an indication that they wish to be exclusive, and not to be regarded as one with the rest of the nation. This spirit of exclusiveness, and the opposition they always express to the idolatry prevailing among their neighbours, has not prevented them from entering into the service of the Government. The road to office is not in China closed to adherents of particular religions. There is no Test Act there. Roman Catholics as well as Mohammedans have held high office in China. But there are many duties to be performed by those who occupy most Government offices which would be an effectual bar to the acceptance of such offices by a conscientious Christian. The sacrifices to Confucius, the worship of the State gods, and many public acts which are encouragements to idolatry, direct and indirect, cannot be omitted by the resident officers in a Chinese city. Yet it is difficult in China to resist the temptation to imitate the tolerant and latitudinarian spirit of the Confucian system. The Chinese love, not uniformity, but conformity. Sects that have when they entered China been very exclusive, have gradually adopted the plausible liberality of the followers of Confucius, who may conform to the customs of other religions without at all compromising their consistency. Conscientiousness has no high value among them. It is not reckoned so good as the politeness that admits the excellences of other systems.

The mosques are erected in the Chinese style of architecture, mixed with Western peculiarities. The principal hall for preaching and praying is provided with a pulpit, and has five naves or aisles, separated by three rows of pillars. It is ornamented with Arabic and Chinese inscriptions painted on monumental boards. Behind it is the chamber for holding the sacred books. Service is performed every Friday at two o'clock.

Not much use is made of translations among them. The Koran is read in Arabic, with which the native Moollahs are familiar. This language, as well as Persian, is studied in the schools attached to the mosques. The knowledge of the principal features of their religion is obtained by Chinese readers from treatises of greater or less extent in the language of the country.

They keep up the practice of circumcision. This is made indispensable to admission to their religion. But they are certainly not so attentive to daily prayer as other Mohammedans. I have met with many of them who altogether neglect this habit.

They speak of Jesus under the name Urh-sah; but they

will not allow that He is more than one of the 48,000 prophets, or of the six great prophets, that preceded Mahomet. Of course they deny His divinity. Wei-yuen, a Chinese author already cited, in giving an account of the Mohammedan religion, says that Adam, the first man, receiving the commands of the true Lord, transmitted them to Seth; Seth to Noah; Noah to Ibrahim; Ibrahim to Ishmael; Ishmael to David; and David to Urh-sah. Urh-sah died, and with him the line of tradition was broken. The orthodox faith was lost. Heresies sprang into vigorous life. But after 600 years Mahomet was born. He alone stands in the highest rank, while Noah, Abraham, Moses, David, and Jesus occupy the second class. When Mahomet was born, the words "Prophet of Heaven" were seen inscribed on his breast. He wrought many miracles, but his greatest work was to correct and republish the inspired revelation from the true Lord, which had been corrupted during the long period of time between Jesus and Mahomet.

The Chinese Mohammedans appear to be very much cut off from their co-religionists, and none now make the pilgrimage to Mecca. Yet the same Chinese author says that every believer in this religion is bound to do so. To whatever country he may belong, he must, once at least in the course of his life, make the journey to worship at the Prophet's tomb, and touch the sacred stone.

He condemns the Mohammedans for borrowing from the Buddhists, a fault of which they have not been more guilty than the Christians, whom he charges with the same crime. The Mohammedans, he says, are like the followers of Confucius in worshipping God; but they have copied their prayers and their abstinence from different kinds of food, their notions upon retribution in a future life, almsgiving, and such-like unimportant teachings, from the Buddhists. They were added as supplemental to doctrines of a higher class, and they certainly, so he thinks, do no harm to mankind.

He points out what he considers faults and inconsistencies in Mahomet. He had given his daughter to his elder brother's son in marriage. This appears to the Chinese to be unnatural and sinful. It has been the invariable custom in China, since a thousand years before the birth of our Saviour, to abstain from intermarriage with a family having the same surname, even though there should be no relationship. The Mohammedans compare the prophets to a tree. They are the stem, branches, leaves, and flowers, while Mahomet is the fruit. He then ought to be perfect in wisdom and in virtue. We do not find this to be true, says the Chinese critic. When he went into the market-place of Medina and saw slayers of oxen there, he asked them why they did not change their trade. "Because," they replied, "we have no other means to gain a living." "Slay sheep," said he, "instead of oxen." They did as he advised them, and thus acting, they resembled an ancient king of Tse, who was so affected by the sight of an ox trembling at the prospect of death, that he ordered the animal to be spared and a sheep slain instead. Mencius, the well-known Chinese sage, was a witness of this incident, and condemned the king. Our Chinese author concludes that Mahomet, not being able to perceive that the life of sheep was equally valuable with that of oxen, could not be perfect in wisdom.

The little colony of Jews at Kai-fung-foo is fast declining, and has no influence in the country. They have almost forgotten their national traditions. I had opportunities some years since at Shanghai of conversing with three individuals of this community. One of them was an educated man, a literary graduate, who would be well acquainted with the state of opinion among his fellow-religionists. It appeared by his statements that the knowledge of a future state, and of the prophecies respecting the Messiah, have almost died out among them. It was not without reason, therefore, that the Jews of England and

America have recently attempted to open a communication with them for the purpose of educating some of their youths in Europe, inquiring into their condition, and, if possible, improving it. They number in all only 200 individuals, and are the solitary remnant of the Jewish colonies in China. The last among them that could read Hebrew died nearly a century ago. They evince no wish to recover the knowledge of that language, nor do they seem to have any idea of a future revival of their condition, which could occur only in the case that the Emperor may be induced to command their synagogue, called, after the Mohammedan style, "the temple of the pure and true," to be rebuilt at the public expense.

The Jews have conformed not a little to the opinions of the Chinese, as is shown by the inscriptions on their tablets, as well as by the melancholy fact that they have no notion, except a Chinese one, of a future state. For God they use the word *teen*, "heaven," without making any effort to keep the distinction between the material firmament and the Ruler of heaven prominent before the minds of their people. They say on one of their monumental inscriptions:—"Although between us and the doctrine of Confucius there are differences of no great importance, yet the object of the establishment of our religion and theirs is the same. They are intended to inculcate reverence for Heaven, veneration for ancestors, loyalty to the prince, and piety to parents, the five human relations and the five constant virtues." The whole of this phraseology is Chinese, instead of being Jewish. This says little for the independence and confident faith in the Divine origin of their religion that ought to distinguish the posterity of Abraham.

One or two things they retain of their national characteristics, namely, reverence for the *law* and the seventh-day Sabbath. They had, till their synagogue was destroyed, an autumn festival, when they walked in procession round the hall of the synagogue, taking the rolls of the law with them. It was called the festival for the circulation of the law. They had till recently twelve copies of the Pentateuch; but with some of these they parted, and they were brought to England a few years since. They do not appear to be very ancient copies. They have also many single sections of the law, and books containing the genealogy of their families. They were originally a large colony of seventy families, and they had communication with their brethren in Persia and in other cities of China. It was apparently in the Han dynasty, according to the opinion of some, B.C. 200 to A.D. 220, that they first entered China, but they had new accessions from Persia at a much later period.

The Mohammedans in China regard the Jews as almost a sect of their own religion. Their abstinence from pork, and the peculiarity of their origin and their religious belief, lead to this. The Jews distinguish themselves by the name Teaou-kin-keaou, "the sect of those that pluck out the sinew," and also by the colour of their turban or distinctive cap; at least, the Mohammedans say that their own turban is white, while that of the Jews is blue. Yet the Mohammedans in Peking wear a blue cap at their religious services. The common costume of both sects in China is the national Chinese dress; so that this distinction is only obvious in the religious attire of the Moollah and others of the two sects when they appear in their appropriate costume.

The Mohammedans are most numerous in the north and west and at Canton. During the long siege of Shanghai by an imperial army a few years since, I conversed with some Mohammedans from the province of Sze-chuen, the most westerly part of China. They insisted that the Christian religion was like their own. When they enter the Chinese army they are, of course, allowed to retain their own religious views and the practice with regard to diet to which they are accustomed. They feel a unity with us on the subject of opposition to idolatry, the worship of the one true God, and the doctrines of repentance and future retribution.

To judge from those I have met in the south, the Mohammedans of China are less bigoted than those of other lands. This is the natural result of their living in a latitudinarian country, and it renders the prospect of their conversion to Christianity more promising than that of the followers of Islam elsewhere.

One of the most interesting among the minor sects in China is that called the Woo-wei-keaou. It is an offshoot from Buddhism. The words Woo-wei mean "non-action." These words are in China a favourite philosophical phrase, used by all schools of a contemplative or mystic tendency. The Taouists, who spoke of the Eternal Reason which underlies all existences, held that it could be understood and the perfection of our nature reached only by rest, by stillness physical and mental, by abstaining from external methods of improvement, and by disbelief in their efficacy. This they called Woo-wei, "to do nothing." The esoteric Buddhists made use of the same term. They said that the worship in temples, the use of idols and particular vestments and ceremonies, was useless: real progress would be made much more effectually by the abstraction of the mind from outward things, and the turning of the soul inwards on itself. This was the principle of Tamo or Bodhidharma, and his followers, the founder of the esoteric sects of Chinese Buddhism.

The sect we are now describing was originated by men whose thoughts also led them in this direction. They were mystics who avoided the common idolatry of the country because they regarded it as mischievous. They say that the universe is a great temple. The fragrance of flowers is the incense of Nature to Buddha. The singing of birds is music spontaneously performed to the honour of Buddha. The roaring of the sea and the rushing sound of the winds is the voice of prayer and praise ascending to the same divinity. There is no need of an idol. Heaven and earth are the image of Buddha, present always and everywhere. This description reminds us of such passages in our poets as—

> " 'Tis a cathedral boundless as our wonder,
> Whose quenchless lamps the sun and moon supply;
> Its quire the winds and waves, its organ thunder,
> Its dome the sky."

This sect does not figure in the national literature. Its name is not mentioned in books; and the treatises of its founders and their disciples are not known beyond the boundaries of the community that regards them with religious faith. It does not excite the attention of the literary class in the country, like the Buddhist and Taouist religions, or like Mohammedanism and Christianity. Its professors are humble in station, possessing little mental culture, mild in manner, and decided in their religious convictions.

This sect has grown up and spread itself during the last three centuries in the eastern provinces of China. Its founders were persecuted as revolutionists in the province of Shantung, and some of them were crucified by the local authorities.

I was conversing on one occasion at Shanghai with a knot of Chinese on some of the doctrines of Christianity, when a follower of this religion interposed a question:— "Is it not a sin to eat animal food? It is wrong to take life." Instead of meeting him with a direct answer, I inquired of him why fowls and swine were created, if not to serve as food for mankind. He did not assent to the doctrine that these animals were created to be eaten, for his sect is strictly vegetarian; but the rest of the bystanders expressed their approval of it. He then asked if eating beef was not unquestionably a great sin, because oxen plough the soil. He was reminded that if it is ungrateful to use oxen that plough for food, there are very large numbers of them that do not plough, and these cannot be shielded from death on this ground. Besides, he was told, Confucius has oxen offered to him in sacrifice, and he also ate beef; so that, though it is a common notion in China that beef should not be used for food, it was not supported by the example of the man whom his countrymen venerate as the wisest of their sages. He was then asked if he worshipped images. "No," he said, "we adore the Buddha of empty space." "Why," we inquired, "should you pay your homage to him? He is not in the position of emperor or father to you. Why do you not worship God, who is both your emperor and your father?" He asked, in reply, for information as to how God should be adored. He was told, by feeling reverence for Him and addressing Him in prayer. He then remarked that the sect to which he belonged had two leaders who were put to death by crucifixion. This, he said, was a point of resemblance between their religion and our own. He was informed that the death of Jesus differed from that of others who had been crucified, in the circumstance that it was borne voluntarily for the salvation of others. It is the habit of the Chinese of all religions to seek out resemblances between their system and that of others, and when they have discovered such resemblances, they proceed to assert that the principles of the two systems are identical.

In the halls used for worship by this sect there is a tablet set up, dedicated to heaven, earth, prince, parent, and teacher. Small loaves of bread, or balls of glutinous rice, are placed before this tablet, and also cups of tea; and the names *Bread-religion* and *Tea-religion*, by which this sect is also known, have thus arisen.

I once asked a believer in the Woo-wei-keaou how he performed his religious duties. He said he would feel no objection to show us. He then took his seat on a stool in a cross-legged attitude. At first he sat tranquil, with his eyes closed; but gradually he became extremely excited, though without speaking. His chest heaved, his breathing became violent, his eyes shot fire—he seemed to be the subject of demoniacal possession. I stood expecting some oracular utterance from him; but after remaining in this excited mood for some minutes, he suddenly brought it to a termination, left the stool on which he had been sitting, and resumed conversation as rationally as before. The bystanders said that this man was able to cause his soul to go out of his body and return when he pleased. This was their explanation of the phenomenon we had witnessed.

The simple sincerity of the followers of this religion has attracted the attention of European missionaries. They exhibit more depth and reality in their convictions than is common in other sects in China. This, added to their firm protest against idolatry, has led to their being regarded with interest by foreigners, and to some efforts to instruct them in Christianity. Among the Protestant converts are some of these men, but they have not all been persuaded to give up their vegetarian habits. They had been so long accustomed to a vegetable diet that animal food was extremely distasteful to them. They were informed that Christianity laid down no law as to food, and that they might continue to be vegetarians, if they desired it, so that they did not retain their old opinions that to partake of other fare was sinful, and a vegetable diet both meritorious and the only lawful one.

The books of this sect are in the form of dialogue or of narrative. The principal speakers and actors are the three founders. They are written after the common Buddhist model. The teacher enters into discussion with his disciples, or with some opponents of the doctrines professed by him, and the doctrines to be communicated are brought forward in a conversational form.

The late origin of this sect, and its extensive propagation among the villages of Eastern China, shows that there are still some remains of life in Buddhism. In the orthodox Buddhism there is the appearance of unreality and want of earnest faith in the majority of the monks. They adopt the peculiar garb and discipline of their sect merely as a profession, to gain a living by. When they enter on the monkish life, they of course abandon their secular occupations. For an hour or two in the day they are engaged in chanting their sacred books, and are idle for the rest of their time, except when called to perform services for the dead or on occasion of the great festivals. Such men contrast unfavourably with believers in a religion like the Woo-wei-keaou, who continue their respective crafts, wear the common dress of the country, and show strong faith in their religious creed.

The ruling classes in China, however, refuse to give them credit for religious earnestness, and have never ceased to represent them as a political sect. They were persecuted as such by the last native Chinese dynasty, and they are still described as a secret political society in the Sacred Edict, where the people are warned by the Emperor against false and dangerous sects.

CHAPTER XVI.

THE TAIPING INSURRECTION.

IN bringing these chapters to a close, some reference to the recent Christian insurrection in China cannot be omitted. When that remarkable movement commenced twenty-four years ago, the Western world was astonished to hear that Christianity was the adopted creed of a powerful rebel party that was waging war in China against the reigning Tartar dynasty. Credible accounts were received, of the most interesting kind, of the existence of a body of mountaineers and others in the hilly districts near Canton, who met for prayer to "the Heavenly Father" in the name of Jesus, read Christian books, and made strenuous exertions to propagate their opinions. Attacked by persecution, they met in lonely places, but afterwards took up arms to defend themselves.

There is no reason to doubt the truth of these accounts. The informant from whom Mr. Hamberg derived the materials of his narrative, the best history published of the early part of the movement, appeared to be a sincere and simple-minded Christian. He was a cousin of Tae-ping-wang, the rebel leader, and spoke the same dialect, the Hakka, used in parts of Canton province, and also in Kwangse. Several missionaries knew him during many months, and felt convinced that he was a speaker of the truth. According to his testimony, there can be no reasonable doubt that this insurrection began in strong religious impressions derived from reading the Scriptures and tracts published by Protestant missionaries and Protestant native converts.

In the mind of Tae-ping-wang and his first followers, a fanatic element very early united itself to the religious element. This led them into excesses from which they would probably have been preserved if missionaries had had access to them. They felt the power of Christian truth. They were impressed deeply by the doctrine of the atonement, the divine mission of Christ, the sin of idolatry, &c. But they were without guidance in comprehending the use of the Old Testament in Christian times. They wanted sober and enlightened explanations, such as would have prevented their deducing from the books of Moses that sacrifices are to be offered to the Trinity, that a war-spirit is needed to put down idolatry, and is a proper accompaniment of Christianity, and that the polygamy of patriarchal times is a model for imitation now.

The good that would have resulted from sincere faith—such it must have been—in our Bible and the religion it teaches, was very much counteracted and overborne by the unhappy intrusion of that enthusiasm which led Tae-ping-wang not only to draw these conclusions from the Old Testament, but to believe himself inspired. This led him to regard himself as the divinely-appointed Emperor of China, and changed into a fierce warrior one who would otherwise have been a zealous preacher of Christianity. There was no hope after he took this step that he would submit to have his opinions criticised and corrected, even if Christian missionaries could have obtained the opportunity of conversing with him. He was at the head of an army that reverenced him as honoured with revelations from God, and as specially commissioned to occupy the throne of a new dynasty in China. He would not now become the humble disciple of foreigners. He, and such of his followers as were animated by the same fanaticism as himself, would rather have died than give up the objectionable articles of their creed. The same fanatic energy that gave them their first successes and nerved them to accomplish their triumphant march to Nanking, kept them faithful to their adopted religious belief to the last.

Although many critics of Chinese matters have preferred to call these men blasphemers and impostors, their preference has come from a view of the subject much more difficult to support than that here given. That Tae-ping-wang should have put forward pretensions to be the brother of Jesus Christ is much to be deplored. It was caused by fanaticism and want of proper instruction. It should be considered that he was just emerging from heathenism, and it could not fail to be difficult for him to transfer himself completely into the Christian sphere of thought. Whether he may fairly incur the charge of wilful blasphemy on his assuming such titles as those which are found in the rebel proclamations, is not easy to say. How was it with Mahomet in his claim to a divine mission?

To read the books written by him is to become convinced that he was sincere, so far as he knew it, in the acceptance of Christianity. In the work called the "Three Character Classic," he describes the creation of the world by God, and sketches the history of the Israelites. He then proceeds to relate the mission of Jesus, the Son of God, into the world, His death on the cross for the salvation of mankind, His resurrection and ascension, with His parting injunction to the twelve Apostles to propagate His doctrine and the book containing it through the whole world. He further states, that in the earliest ages the worship of God was practised by the Chinese as in foreign countries, and condemns the emperors who had helped to introduce the Taouist and Buddhist superstitions among the people whom they governed. It was Tsin-she-hwang who, a little more than two centuries before Christ, was ensnared by the belief that then began to prevail in the existence of genii and of a method by which immortality for the body may be attained. He was imitated by Han-woo-te. Ming-te, their successor on the throne of China, was as assiduous in the encouragement of the Buddhist religion as they had been in promoting the Taouist. He reserves his severest censure for Hwei-te, of a much later period, the eleventh century of our era. This monarch had given the ancient Chinese name Shang-te to a Taouist divinity Yuh-hwang. "Now," he says, "Shang-te, God, is the Great Father of the whole world. His name is most honourable, and it has been in use a long series of years. Who is Hwei-te that he should dare to change it?" He then adds that a deserved retribution overtook him for the part he took in spreading the practice of idolatry. It was on this account that he was captured by the Tartars, his foes, and, with his son, died in imprisonment.

Although the book does not close without those fanatical pretensions that show themselves in so many places in the writings of this man, there is enough to make plain that he understood something of the Christian doctrine of God, and of the salvation of mankind through the death of Christ, as also that he had become sensible of the mischief flowing from the introduction of idolatrous religion into China.

In judging of the sincerity of these insurgents, who baptized one another in the name of the Trinity, and called themselves Christians, it ought to be remembered that the greater part of their adherents did not belong to the original nucleus of earnest, religious, or fanatical men through whose enthusiastic courage Tae-ping-wang won so many battles and took so many cities. Multitudes afterwards joined them of a far inferior mould of character, some impressed by force, others invited by hopes of plunder. The Christianity of such men was non-existent, and they were not fair examples of those who began the movement, nor were they such good soldiers. Many of the first adherents of this party had died. Those whose hair had not been shaven for seven years, who were the private friends of the chief at the beginning, who joined him in religious meetings and marched with him to the field, before he shut himself up in seclusion within the walls of his palace, and knew him intimately, had mostly disappeared. The character of the rebel army became on this account necessarily much less religious than it was, although they still maintained imperfectly the forms of Christian worship and the observance of a Sabbath.

The Christian insurgents in China never had the confidence of any part of the nation. Their religious character was one reason of the unpopularity of their cause. If they had been crafty impostors, they would have chosen some other watchword than that of Christianity. Instead of fighting in the name of Shang-te (God) and of Yay-soo (Jesus), they would have waged war in the name of their ancestors, or they would have inscribed on their banners the titles of some of the national gods. But they chose for their religion one that must of necessity be extremely distasteful to most of their countrymen. Nothing could be further removed from the sympathies of the influential part of native society than a course like this. Their books were constantly spoken of as *yaou shoo*, "goblin books;" and they themselves were, as might be expected, never honoured with any more respectful appellations than thieves and robbers. Their profession of Christianity did not obtain for them any better reputation among those who give the tone to society, and have influence and property. With the adoption of a religious creed coming from a foreign source, and introduced by the barbarians themselves at Canton within a few years back, they resigned in the estimation of their countrymen all title to be considered patriots. This party had by the Chinese never been regarded as patriotic, and nowhere was there exhibited the intention or desire to co-operate with them in effecting a revolution, except on the part of those who had nothing in character or property to lose by it.

The power of this party, then, did not consist in any sympathy felt with them, beyond the actual limits of the districts that they occupied. Their courage was admitted to be superior to that of the imperialist soldiers. Their discipline is favourably spoken of by some of those natives who witnessed it for its rigour and for its moral tone. The fact that they had a sort of Christian worship did not win them favour with the general population.

Now that this insurrection has disappeared by the destruction of the actors in it, it may be asked what have been its results? It shows that there is a susceptibility in the Chinese mind to receive Christian doctrine for which we were before far from giving them credit.

They are, as a nation, usually represented as having only sordid aims in life, and as almost incapable of feeling reverence for God or curiosity respecting the future state. We see, by the history of this insurrection, that there are many among the Chinese who are prepared to receive these and other religious tenets in the spirit of an earnest and practical faith. They have shown themselves capable, to a degree unexpected by the rest of mankind, of a religious enthusiasm ardent enough to increase their bravery as fighting men, and make them capable of submitting to a self-denying discipline, such as cannot be very agreeable to a people trained in national habits like those of the ordinary Chinese. They are too slothful and sensual to consent to such a discipline with much satisfaction, were they not affected by an enthusiasm to which they have not been accustomed. There is hope, then, that the Chinese as a nation may take up the religion of the Bible with strong faith, and propagate it by their own exertions.

We also see in this movement the effect of the distribution in that country of Bibles and Christian tracts. A reading population, such as there exists, can receive the knowledge of Christianity in this way without the presence of the living teacher. They have reprinted some Christian treatises with slight alterations, and composed others modelled on those prepared by foreigners. One of the most important of their publications is an elaborate treatise by the late Dr. Medhurst, on the Attributes of God, composed at Batavia more than twenty years ago.

The fact that they published many parts of the Scriptures is a striking one, and is strange to account for on any hypothesis but that those who did so were sincere believers in the book. No political prophet could have foretold that a body of revolutionists in China would have spread their opinions by the printing and circulation of Christian books. We never expect to hear of Hindoos or Malays, when commencing a warlike movement, adopting Christianity and resolving to propagate it. To show that the effect of these books, and of the religion they teach, has been something more than ordinary on the moral condition of these people, I shall detail an interview with a former follower of Tae-ping-wang, who was met by myself and others at Shanghai. His name was Wang-fung-tsing. He had come into the city to join the rebel force that then held it; but he soon left them, dissatisfied with the state of affairs prevailing among his new friends. He conversed with me in one of the Protestant chapels, and told us that he had been baptized by Dr. Gutzlaff, seven years before. A convert at Hongkong had taken him in hand to instruct him in Christianity, had supplied him with a little money, and recommended him to unite himself to Dr. Gutzlaff's Christian Union. He became a member of that body till the death of its founder. He then proceeded, by the advice of his old friend, the convert, in search of other members of the Christian Union, who had then joined Tae-ping-wang, and were engaged in organising an armed opposition against the Government. He joined them in time to be with the Taiping army on its march through the interior provinces to the important city of Woochang-foo. Favoured by a shower of snow, they took possession of that city, with the two adjoining ones, Hanyang and Hankow, and then descended the Yang-tsze-keang to Nanking. From this point he returned to Hongkong, and afterwards found his way to Shanghai. He told us, in answer to inquiries, that there is the administration of baptism in the Taiping army to men and women, old and young, by sprinkling.

They have the Lord's Supper every month, and not upon the Sabbath-day. At this ceremony they use wine made from grapes—a curious circumstance, grape wine scarcely ever being seen in China[1]—showing the anxiety of these Christians to maintain as exactly as they know how the creed and practice of Christianity. They admit new applicants to baptism after not more than a day's instruction. Twenty-four elders, or *chang-laou*, have assigned to them the office of preaching. There are also priests who superintend the sacrifices. The practice of offering sacrifices they have unquestionably adopted from reading the Old Testament without guidance as to what parts of it are and what are not intended for imitation by Christians. He told us that he met several men who had been baptized by Dr. Gutzlaff, holding posts of influence in the Taiping official staff. He denied, when asked, that he smoked opium, saying that it was forbidden strictly in the regulations of Tae-ping-wang. When the question was repeated, he replied, "How could I tell a lie, who am a disciple of Jesus?"

The effect of this interview was to strengthen our impressions of the extent to which the imitation of Christian practices was carried by these people, and also of the height of the moral standard that they set for themselves. The ordinary Chinese do not assume this high tone in vindication of their veracity.

But a prolonged state of war is most prejudicial to morality, and the greater part of the Tae-ping-wang forces, recruited as they are indiscriminately from the population of the regions through which they pass, of course do not share any earnest faith in religious doctrines to which they are obliged to conform, but which they do not really understand or believe.

This movement in favour of Christianity, originated and

---

[1] We learn from Mr. Lockhart, who took part in the interview here described, that wine is made from grapes in some of the interior provinces, but not near Canton, from which part the rebels came.

carried on by the Chinese themselves, was injured by the political aims which were combined with it. It was the error of half-enlightened minds to believe themselves called to overthrow, by force of arms, the Government that persecuted them and the idolatry which Christianity had taught them was a sin against God. Many of their countrymen have wondered at their crusade against images. When describing the mode of operation pursued by the adherents of Tae-ping-wang, they praised them for their discipline, and their avoidance of petty thefts and other excesses commonly practised by the soldiers in the pay of the Government; "but," they added, "they show an extraordinary hostility to the idols. They kill *poosa*." They showed no mercy to the images of the gods. We could have excused their iconoclastic tendencies if they had not also undertaken to accomplish a political revolution. By this course they have done harm to the cause of Christianity in China, and have given its enemies an opportunity to misrepresent it. We will hope that when the Chinese shall again take up our religion in an earnest manner, they will eschew other aims, and receive it as a spiritual kingdom, and not in the spirit of Fifth Monarchy Men. In this case the enthusiasm they have shown will be again exhibited, and will produce the happiest results. China is not so incapable of change as is thought by most persons. Her population is not so exclusively devoted to a gross and sensual life as to be proof against impressions of a religious nature. That the Chinese are capable of warmer religious feelings than was thought possible has been proved. There is, then, encouragement to be derived from the story of the Christian insurrection by those who are interested in missionary labours in China.

There need be no fear for the ultimate success of Protestant missions there, when we have had so recent an example of the effect of the distribution of books. The first agents of Protestant societies who went to China to teach Christianity met with very little apparent fruit of their labours. Few converts joined them. Much opposition was excited against them. They sowed the seed of truth in a hard soil, in the time of wintry winds and unkindly influences. Now, however, it has been shown that effects have followed which they had not anticipated. Not only have their books been widely circulated by the machinery they themselves organised, but for several years past a native Chinese party, in the midst of anarchy and internecine war, have been diffusing Christian truths in an extensive series of publications which they have widely scattered through the country. The Christian atonement has been in this way made known over regions much broader in extent than could be reached by the agencies set on foot by European missionaries. After making all the necessary deductions for imperfect instruction, the mingling of Christianity with political designs, &c., there still remains good reason to hope that not a few of the Kwangse insurgents may deservedly be called Christians. At any rate, when they die by the sword, if such is to be their fate, there will be many sincere, brave, and stalwart upholders of what they believe to be Christianity, who will meet death with an unflinching courage worthy of the name, and by the hands of far worse men than themselves.

The converts under the immediate care of the Protestant missionaries differ widely in character from the men we have been considering. Remaining where they received instruction, and where they became professed Christians, they are under no temptation to adopt revolutionary views or to imbibe the terrible war-spirit to which fanaticism has so often given birth. They are learning that calm, enlightened, and domestic Christianity which spreads its silent influence in private life, converting first individuals, then families, then whole villages and larger communities. Christianity must in China be national to be powerful. It must take hold on the hearts of the people, and they must teach it every man to his brother, before our Protestant missions there can be said to have gained their object.

But while these evangelistic operations are so recent, it is far better that the native congregations of Christians should remain under the supervision of the foreign missionaries than that the converts should be left entirely to themselves. That they have among them the elements of self-support, and possess a vitality that must ensure progress, is shown by the considerable number of catechists and preachers that have, in consequence of a few years' training on the part of the missionaries, become their helpers in teaching the doctrine of salvation. The Protestant converts were in 1859 still not many more than 1000.[1] These were the remaining fruits of sixteen years' labour by about a hundred missionaries at the five treaty ports. While few in numbers, it is better for them not to be thrown entirely on their own resources. They might fall into error, as did the Kwangse Christians, who began so well and so zealously with reading the Scriptures and prayer-meetings. It was in an evil hour that they decided to take up arms. There was no one to tell them that our religion is peaceful, and that the weapons of our warfare are not carnal. The zeal of these men, which, untempered by an enlightened prudence, led them to the brink of destruction, would have wrought wonders for the spread of Christianity if rightly directed. Among the lessons we may learn by their history is this, that in prosecuting the task of evangelising China, there needs to be careful instruction added to the possession of the Word of God. The Bible needs an expositor, and zeal needs a wise regulating prudence. We may still hope for those Chinese who shall incline to receive the Gospel, that the intelligence of the national mind will in due time give them knowledge, and that the enthusiasm exhibited in their religious history will give them zeal. When these qualities are combined they will produce a development of Chinese Christianity such as will bear a proportion to the very pro-

[1] At the present time (1877) the converts are about ten times as numerous as when the first edition of this book was published.

minent position that China holds among the nations of the East. As great as they have been in the arts and in literature, in education and in politics, so great may we expect them to become in the exhibition of an intelligent practical Christianity, when, in God's providence, and by His gracious influence upon their hearts, they come to accept it.

The preceding examination of the religious state of the Chinese has shown that that in which they are deficient is not so much a system of morality as in clear and correct notions on God, redemption, and immortality. Only Divine revelation can meet this want, and Christianity, the religion of the Bible, must therefore eventually become the religion of China. In this instance the light of Scripture prophecy blends with the pre-intimations afforded by reason. They alike forbid us to doubt that Christian missions in that country can fail to be ultimately successful. But what is the probability that large masses of the population will soon become Christian? Is any lengthened period likely to intervene before our religion shall come to be in any sense national? The difficulty of answering these questions suggests the words of the world's Redeemer, "It is not for you to know the times and the seasons, which the Father hath put in His own power."

Yet, certainly, the great political and social changes recently begun are in favour of Christianity. It is now a tolerated religion. Foreigners may teach it, while natives may profess it. The two idolatrous religions prevalent in the country are sufficiently worn out and weak to render the victory of Christianity not very difficult. If the followers of Confucius are self-sufficient and proud, their want of faith in Buddhism, and the circumstance that their own religion fails to satisfy the spiritual wants of man, favour the hope that they will accept Christianity. The universal use of one written language and of the art of printing are an immeasurable advantage to missionary operations, which ought not to be omitted in enumerating the circumstances favourable to the spread of Christianity.

CHAPTER XVII.

JOURNEY TO WOO-TAI-SHAN IN 1872 COMMENCED— PEKING TO LUNG-TSIUEN-KWAN.

THE excitement connected with the Emperor's marriage had been intense, and had arrived at a climax the night before our departure for Woo-tai-shan, when the bridal procession took place. The Chinese Government expects on such an occasion from the metropolitan population not joy but reverence. The Emperor and Empress are to be regarded as a sort of divinities, and as the most distant approach to familiarity is to be avoided, no one is allowed to be in the streets, perfect silence is maintained, and orders are even issued that none must look from the houses lining the route while the procession is passing. If a light were to be seen in any house it would call down instant punishment on the householder. Yet multitudes were looking out from the darkness of their dwellings on the street everywhere illuminated by red paper lanterns. For Peking society was agitated to the centre. Who would like to miss seeing this the most striking of all processions?

Singularly the new Empress's grandfather, Sai-shanga, has reappeared on this occasion as if from the grave. Many years ago he had been appointed generalissimo to conquer the Taiping rebels. Having failed, he was proscribed and deprived of all his influence and official duties. He was long supposed to be dead. Now unexpectedly he has returned to notice in connection with his granddaughter's elevation.

Since then the imperial husband and wife are both

dead, and China has entered on a new period of infant sovereignty.

We left Peking October 16, 1872, at half-past ten A.M., having been delayed by the shoeing of the mules. Only their front feet are shod. Five packed mules constituted our cavalcade with a pony. We were three in number, one American and two English missionaries, with a native catechist and a servant. Two muleteers, speaking the Siuen-hwa dialect, which is much the same as that of Shanse, completed our number.

At this time we may expect in North China uninterruptedly fine weather. We can be more sure of the absence of rain than in an English October. What seem to be rain clouds pass away, and week after week goes by with unchanging sunshine. October is eminently a month for tourists in this part of the world.

Our train passed along the 120 feet wide streets of Peking to avoid jostling the crowds which throng some of the narrower thoroughfares. Going by the gate called Hata-men we took an inclined road to Choo-she-kow, in the centre of the Chinese city, and from that point proceeded westward to the execution ground and the gate known as Chang-ye-men. These five miles of continuous traffic before leaving the city give a considerable impression of the activity of life and trade in this metropolis.

We were pleased to notice proof of a good cotton harvest in several long trains of camels, bearing two-hundredweight bags of cotton from Pau-ting-foo, which met us on the way. Four days distant from Peking, this large cotton region forms a most valuable element in the wealth of the province, and supplies the population of North Chihle and Shanse with blue cotton gowns in summer and wadded clothing in winter. What an advantage to grow cotton at home, the inhabitants having so much need of it in the cold winters, when they need not only their long gowns and jackets, but their stockings, trousers, shoes, teapot covers, door curtains, coverlids, cushions, mattresses, and chair and cart covers!

We wonder what they did formerly without cotton, for they have only had it a few centuries. When we remember the skins of innumerable flocks of sheep and goats scattered over the plains of Mongolia and the mountains of each of the northern provinces of China, we see how it was. But they have more comfortable clothing now, and a much larger population to clothe, than in those old times.

Leaving the Chang-ye-men, we found ourselves upon the busy stone street which for twenty *le*, or seven miles, conducts the traveller towards the bridge Loo-kow-chiau. It is at certain seasons of the year the scene of immense traffic. The coal supplied to Peking from Fang-shan and Ta-an-shan come this way, as also lime from Hwei-chang, and all the traffic of the west and south-west. Sometimes it presents to the eye an almost continuous stream of camels, mules, and donkeys. Many a slip do they make on the worn stones of this causeway. When a stone sinks below its neighbours, nothing is done to replace it or to fill the vacancy. To repair an imperial road or ruin without an imperial order would be regarded as presumption and as a punishable offence. So the holes in the road are stumbled over in all weathers by each new train of loaded animals, as they have been for very many summers and winters, and no one ventures to murmur. Year after year, while new generations slowly succeed the old, the mischief goes on increasing. Good vegetable gardens flank the causeway.

A handsome *pai-low*, or public archway, forms a terminus to this stone road. Three miles more of travelling over a waste tract, which was at some distant time perhaps desolated and changed to a wilderness by a flood of the rivers now at hand, bring the traveller to the bridge. We noticed that there are 280 stone lions on the parapets of the bridge, and that there were elephants pushing with their trunks and tusks at the ends of the parapets to keep the fabric firm. Chinese symbolism loves to make the stronger animals subservient to man, and to represent them as laying aside entirely their natural fierceness under his renovating influence. The bridge crosses what is now a broad and rapid stream. The water coming from the hills is abundant and very muddy. The swelling tide rushing down the river channel looks as if it could do mischief. It might, if larger, break its banks. We were soon to see with our own eyes what it can do.

It was late, and we stopped for the night at the busy town, Chang-sin-tien. Taking our lodging in an inn, a stroll from the night's quarters brought us to the locality injured by last year's inundation on the east of the town, which lies north and south. There was here a good strip of land, consisting, till the summer of 1871, of rice fields. The river, a mile to the north, supplied water for the cultivation. The outbreak of the river occurred just at this point, and the rice lying low, the whole of it was covered by a broad swollen stream which rushed on to the south-west. It laid a deposit of stones and sand over the rice fields to the depth of three and four feet. This deposit is a mile wide at the point we visited, and proceeds for eight miles farther, having completely destroyed farming operations all the way till it reaches another river. In the summer of the previous year I saw the river soon after it broke through, a mile and a quarter below the bridge. We walked along the sands to the spot. The land we then saw under the rushing current, strewn with the remains of trees and cottages, was the same which we were now examining. The villagers who conversed with us looked unhappy. One had lost a hundred *mow*, or seventeen acres, of good land, and had thirty *mow* remaining. Another who lives a few miles to the south told me the next day that he had lost fifty *mow*, worth to him as many taels of silver per annum. Of course he looked the picture of sorrow. This frightful devastation leads the

Chinese, who are witnesses and victims of it, to pray to Heaven and the gods for their protection.

At the gate of Chang-sin-tien was posted a proclamation from the military authorities, warning the people that at the review of artillery near the bridge conducted by great officers sent from Peking each year, they are not to raise the prices of vegetables on account of the arrival of the soldiers, nor are they to pick up cannon-balls or make disturbances.

Our inn was very full of mule sedans and baggage animals. Fresh from Peking, and not having taken a journey for a long interval, everything diverted us. The inscriptions on our sleeping-room walls, written by passing travellers, were of the usual style. They were such as *Ki sheng mau tien yue, jen tsi pan chiau shwang* ("Cockcrow is heard in the straw-thatched inn in the moonlight; footsteps are seen on the wooden bridge in the frost"). These two lines are very popular, and deserve to be so. They are evidently by some true poet. The words are few and excellently chosen. They make up a pair of pictures, one of the interior, the other of the exterior, of the traveller's lodging-place, remarkable for their brevity and effectiveness. The bad verses made by scribblers it is best to say nothing about. They would disfigure the narrative as much as they do the walls of mine host's furnished apartments.

October 17th.—To-day we were detained by rain, which does sometimes fall in October. Left at eleven A.M., and reached Lieu-le-ho in the evening. This is an important place, as being the point from which the lime and coal of the western hills are conveyed to Tientsin. On the way to it our road began to pierce hills of *loess*, that dry, fine, uniform brown dust which distinguishes North China and forms the basis of its soil, as also that of Southern Mongolia and Manchooria for several thousands of miles. It is found on both sides of the Tai-hang mountain range, across which we go into Shanse. If only found inside the mountains, it might be called a lake deposit, but it lines the mountains on their eastern slopes just as much, and covers over in many places hills of granite and limestone in such a fashion that Richthoven's hypothesis of dust-storm agency seems the best. In positions on the plain, such as we saw to-day, where unstratified masses of *loess* form uniform heaps of a fine mould eminently suitable for agriculture, Pumpelly's hypothesis of lake and river deposit seems inapplicable. The proper place for that hypothesis would seem to be the beds of old lakes, such as the valleys and plains of Shanse. The vertical cleavage of which Richthoven speaks occurs everywhere in the regions occupied by this formation.

We crossed the Tsing-ho, which comes out of the hills near Loo-kow-chiau, and noticed that it followed the line of road for some miles on the left. There is a bridge similar to that already mentioned, having elephants and lions on its parapet, at Liang-hiang, a city with a pagoda. The crops are good on the plain. The autumn wheat is springing, and there is a large quantity of it sown. Before reaching Lieu-le-ho we travelled along a broad stone causeway for nearly a mile. The large collection of water from brooks and hidden springs at Lieu-le-ho is the cause of this. Some of the rivers, as the Tsing-ho and Hwun-ho, flow down valleys among the mountains, and so reach the plain. Others rise from springs not far from the foot of the mountain range. (The same is true of some of the streams in the south part and beyond it.) The boats at Lieu-le-ho take upwards of four hundredweight of coal or lime. They bring back wheat and other cereals. The town has five hundred houses.

October 18th.—Went on to Cho-chow to breakfast. When nearing that city we ferried over the Ku-ma-ho, a river which this year is very full. It comes from Kwang-chang, north-west of Yu-chow, and running eastward it passes the western imperial tombs on the north and proceeds to Cho-chow. A busy scene. Crowds of passengers filled the ferryboats. On them also were placed the burdens of the mules, which were coaxed to walk across through the water. A large party of soldiers, armed with foreign rifles and bayonets, passed at the same time. They were, they said, searching the roads for bandits. They carry their rifles each of them horizontally on their shoulders and a banner in the other hand. A red-balled officer was in charge of this detachment, or was travelling with them. Sellers of new dates and pastry were plying their trade on the river banks. Now and then a foolish donkey would fall behind his companions and hesitate to cross the river with them. The half-naked pilots had then the task of persuading the beast to proceed.

Fish abounds at Cho-chow. We had the celebrated Le-yu (carp) for breakfast. A short walk from the ferry brought us to a handsome bridge, at the north end of which is a lofty open arch spanning the way. Its inscriptions state that the bridge and causeway are 2000 feet in length. It was erected by a public-spirited magistrate within the last half-century. The wall and gates of Cho-chow are imposing. Within the north gate are two pagodas of the Sung dynasty. The northern can be ascended by a staircase in the very thick and substantial walls. They are five stories high. The south pagoda has a carving of Buddha in relief on each face.

As we passed on to Sung-lin-tien, six miles, and Kan-pei-tien, fifteen miles, we noticed on the road indications that we were in a country of old traditions. Who in China has not heard the story of Lieu-pei, who, in A.D. 221, succeeded in making himself Emperor of Western China by the aid of Choo-ko-liang, the wisest of counsellors, and Kwan-yun-chang, the most loyal of heroes? It was a pleasure to the emperors and *literati* of the Sung dynasty to exalt these men to a higher place in history than they had held before. They made of one a model of an emperor who, belonging to the Han imperial family, showed in the struggle for power patience, sagacity, and perseverance. The Manchoo dynasty has followed them in investing Kwan-te with honours, and encouraging his worship as god of war and the embodiment of loyal and military virtues. A monument on the roadside informs the traveller that the adjoining village is the home of Lieu-pei. Another indicates the former home of Chang-fei, his faithful friend and follower. It is the ancient Leu-sang, "the mulberry of the tower." The village of Chang-fei close by is also marked by a monument. Near it was the well from which the same old worthy drew water. So says tradition.

Arriving at Sung-lin-tien, six miles from Cho-chow, we struck the Yu-chow road from the west. At fifteen miles we reached Kau-pei-tien. Here we were among the last of the cotton crops, interspersed with fields of young wheat. The cotton plants are kept short by the growers that the yield of cotton may be increased. They are only eighteen inches high.

Saturday, October 19*th.*—This morning we left the city of Ting-ling on our right. It has a small well-built wall. South of it was a monument to Tan-tae-tsi of the contending states (Chan-kwo), B.C. 300. He belonged to the Yen kingdom, in the modern province of Chihle. He publicly invited able men to his service, and at the locality indicated by the monument entertained a hero, King-ke, in a tower called Hwang (yellow) kin (cloth, *i.e.*, as here meant, *turban*) tai (tower). This hero undertook to assassinate the prince of Tsin, father of the Emperor, who burned the books. He wished thus to show his loyalty to the prince of Yen. While approaching with drawn sword to carry out his fell design he was attacked and slain by the servants of the King of Tsin.

We now passed the Ku-ma-ho, a river which flows from Kwang-chang, east of the Tsi-king-kwan, cuts the Great Wall, leaves the imperial western cemetery on the south, and proceeds by Lai-shui and Ting-ling, south of Cho-chow, to the lakes. We crossed it at Peiho, thirteen miles from

Cho-chow. The water was here too deep to allow the mules to take over their burdens, which were intrusted to the ferrymen. The mules as they crossed were nearly swimming on account of the great depth of the water caused by the late floods. After breakfasting at Ku-cheng, a small town chiefly noteworthy for its inns, which are numerous, a little north of An-su, the city where we were expecting to stay during Sunday, we arrived at Pai-ta-tsun, a village with a handsome pagoda belonging to it. An-su is a busy town with a northern suburb a mile long, and having many monuments in honour of the most respected inhabitants. The Catholics have a school and mission twenty-three Chinese miles west from the city. They are spoken of as having a staff of bishop and clergy, schools for children of varying ages, church, and houses used as residences.

Sunday, October 20th.—My companions went out to distribute books and speak to the people. Having an ailment which prevented walking, I stayed in the inn to receive visitors. Soon there came some representatives of very good families. I spoke of the Christian religion and of the motion of the earth. After explaining the roundness of the earth and its diurnal and annual revolution, I asked them if they believed in it. The more talkative hesitated; the quietest said, "Yes, we do." On asking if they had heard of "Cheng-cha-pi-ki," a work in three volumes published by the Emperor's first envoy to Europe, Pin-chun, now deceased, they replied that they had not. A work like this, elegantly written in prose and poetry, fails to reach far in Chinese society. The Chinese conductors of the book trade do nothing to push the circulation of new works. A few hundred copies are sold in Peking; that is all. A few years hence it may be reprinted by some rich antiquarian in a distant city. None of my visitors had heard of the motion of the earth. Our teaching permeates slowly among the reading class through the general poverty of the people, the deadness of trade, the want of newspapers, the stagnation of ideas, and the absence of rapid and regular traffic. The innkeeper also came to ask for books, and told me the position of my visitors.

We found an odious peculiarity in An-su. Singing girls with guitars infest the quarters of travellers, and seem to be an institution in all the inns. They enter the doors of rooms uninvited, and if complaint is made to mine host, he laughs, and says it is impossible to prevent it. He is probably bribed to display this indifference. All the evening we heard their singing in the rooms in our vicinity with the guitar accompaniment. The singing was not good. It is merely a pretence by which to gain admittance to the inns. They say, "I wish to go and sing," and then enter with the air of professionals. In one of the most famous dramatised tales a Chinese girl, distinguished for filial piety and other virtues, begs her way to the capital in search of her lost husband with her guitar. On arriving she finds him distinguished for his scholarship, a Chwang-yuen, a court favourite, and his fortune made. This very popular story has surrounded with much respectability the notion of a girl singing with a guitar. But in the present day it is a sort of badge of the unprincipled to sing to the guitar.

Monday, October 21st.—To-day we arrived at mid-day at Pau-ting-foo after first crossing the Tsau river, we taking a boat and the mules fording with their loads. Long before reaching the city we heard distant firing. This was at the Kin-tai, "golden tower," a review ground on the south-west of the city, the usual position for the military drill of cities. When cities are large and have available space within the walls, the exercise ground is inside. The walls of Pau-ting are only four English miles in circuit. It is small for its rank as chief city of the province, and will probably soon be reduced to the rank of an ordinary department. The governor-general since the Tientsin massacre has been ordered to remain nine months of the year at that far larger and more influential emporium.

A few years more may show the Government that even for the winter the residence of the governor-general at Pau-ting is not needed. Tientsin will then become the capital of the province. As we passed through Pau-ting the wall was under repair. We met an American friend in an inn. He was on his way from Kalgan and Yu-chow to Tientsin, and had come by Kwang-chang and Foo-too-yu to the north-west.

Leaving this city, we changed our route to westward. As in the morning, the land appeared very productive. In addition to the cultivation of cotton, wheat, and other cereals, the people spin and weave. They also make new paper out of old, an art which is much practised all over this province. We stopped for the night at Pei-poo, and here we were said to be 500 *le* (160 miles) from Woo-tai. This is the ordinary route of Lamas from Peking, and along the road may occasionally be seen more than usually devout pilgrims prostrating themselves on the ground all the way to the sacred mountain. Their idea is this: Woo-tai is the favoured region of the Buddhas and of Manjoosere, its great Bodhisattwa. To bow down and fall at full length before the images is meritorious. To do this all along the road must be far more meritorious. The pilgrim says to himself:—" I will make a vow. I will therefore prostrate myself at every third step. Though the distance is long, I shall arrive in a month, two months, or three, and I can walk back without prostrations on my return." It is only the Mongols that do this. We do not hear of the Chinese making this sort of painful pilgrimage. The Mongols are willing on account of their reverence for Woo-tai-shan and a wish to conform to a fashion that has grown up among them. The Chinese, however, have their cages of spiked nails, in which they stay three months without once coming out, and unless that imprisonment is easier to endure, we have in it an equivalent.

We came on to Wan-hien to breakfast. It is a small city, with no people within the walls. Soon after we passed Ma-ri-shan, a hill standing alone in the plain with temple and pagoda upon it. It is shaped like a horse's ear, and is therefore called Ma-ri-shan. Beyond it, to the west ten *le*, is Tang-hien, the residence of the Emperor Yau before he came to the throne. Near it flows the Tang river. From the river and country he is called Tang-yau. His mother lived at a neighbouring hill. But are we in these days to respect any old traditions? The merciless critics of ancient China are not willing to leave anything remaining of that curious fabric of grandeur and dry details which the Chinese call early history. The temple where Tang-yau is worshipped at present is farther south on the Koo-kwan route, and we shall not be near it.

At Tang-hien we found the people collected from all the country round at a fair. The street was crowded. There were at least three thousand buyers, sellers, and lookers-on, clad chiefly in wadded cotton jackets and leather or cotton trousers. Announcing our books for sale at the usual unremunerative prices, we were beset with eager purchasers, and at dusk we closed our account with a heap of cash amounting to a dollar and a half, which represents a very large number of separate selling transactions. That night, probably, in every village round, our books would be read by the flickering flame of the little oil lamp, with its tiny wick of rush pith, which has served the Chinese for so many ages. In out-of-the-way places candles are not to be had. After not many years, perhaps, the people here will all be using petroleum brought by railway from West China, where it abounds. It will be burned probably in iron lamps made by Shanse artisans following American models, and sold at a shilling a piece, a price which the people may be far better able to give then than now. If, however, they have to wait fifty years for such an improvement, it is very lamentable, and so much the worse for the people, who now certainly have very dark houses at night, except at a wedding, when candles made of mutton-fat brighten the scene.

We had a reminder that many Lamas pass this way in Tibetan inscriptions on the walls of the inn.

We have been travelling on limestone at Wan-hien, and apparently sandstone at Tang-hien. We began to meet stoneware jars going on carts to Pau-ting-foo. They sell at 1300 cash each, or a little more than a dollar. They stand in houses to hold water, and are called *shui-kang*.

Wednesday, October 23d.—Left Tang-hien at three A.M., and reached Ta-yang-tien at nine, forty *le* distant. The road is agreeably interspersed with pretty villages. The poplar grows abundantly, and forms a very graceful feature in the scenery. The brown soil is relieved by its tapering form and white bark, which is remarkably contrasted with its dark green leaves. Here may be seen houses of stone built up like fortresses. There, a team of heavy drays laden with cotton, corn, or large *kangs* of stoneware. Here a boy looks down from a bank forty feet high with mingled curiosity and fear, as he notices strange people with light eyes and large beards riding past. Who they are he knows not. He registers it in his memory as an unexplained wonder. We have now entered the hilly country. Clear streams of mountain water, tasting slightly of lime, pass over a sandstone bottom. Fine beds of cabbages swelling into a globular shape are now seen. They are not like the oblong Shantung cabbage called *hwang-ya*, "yellow bud," but like our home cabbages. They abound in Shanse. Date trees, their leaves all dropped, good beans, sweet potatoes, and the Chinese yam, frequently meet the eye; with, here and there, an old barn partly ruined and open to the weather, but secured against storms by large bundles of straw and *kau-liang* stalks stuffed into holes, evidently adapted to induce the observant traveller to moralise on the faults of the lazy owner.

Our mules, walking at a rate not exceeding three miles an hour, enjoy the approach of the hilly country, for they are accustomed to climb, to plant the foot carefully between stones, to turn round at a sharp angle, to go up steep paths, to wade through rivers, and occasionally to be a little tricky and upset their riders. If in dusty soil the mule puts his forefeet down and kneels, let the rider know that he is bent on having a roll in that soft bed; and if he can get him up again without losing his seat on the animal's back, let him do so.

We crossed the Tang-ho river soon after leaving Ta-yang-tien. It flows through the Great Wall at Tau-ma-kwan to Ho-kien-foo, a prefecture to the south-east. There was a wooden plank bridge placed just below the junction of the river with the Siau-tsing-ho, a stream whose valley we now entered and ascended for several miles, crossing the river in various places, the water not reaching above half-way up the mules' legs. Leaving this valley, we mounted by successive terraces a tract of high country, presenting to our view everywhere nothing but broad and well-cultivated surfaces of *loess*. At length at Ke-yu we reached the bed of another stream, the Sha-ho, the third river we have seen to-day. The first was the Tang-ho, deep and rapid, rushing swiftly over stones and sand, which we saw but once. The second was the Siau-tsing-ho, which we crossed six times while travelling as many miles. At each ford there is a plank bridge for foot passengers, among whom are many Lamas on pilgrimage. The planks are placed loose on strong piles, that they may be easily removed at the swelling of the river in summer and at its freezing in winter. The piles and planks are all removed when a flood is expected. The eight miles of high *loess* country which we passed before reaching the Sha-ho may be referred to as illustrating the probable origin of that formation. It appears to me to be an immense sandhill eight miles wide, lying between two rivers, and formed, as sandhills are, by wind. The winds of a few years (thirty, a hundred, or two hundred, we cannot tell how many) suffice to heap up sandhills round the walls of Peking, between the buttresses, to the height of ten, twenty, or more feet. The wall of the Temple of Heaven, where it has an open exposure, affords examples. In the country a clump of trees or a village will be found affording sufficient shelter for the rapid formation of sand heaps of considerable size. So I believe the ancient dust which forms the *loess* formation, and the excellent agricultural qualities of which have been described by Richthoven, was blown against the barrier consisting of the mountain range, Taihang-shan, at the roots of which we now were. The result, after an immense lapse of years, was such heaps of that formation as we crossed to-day. Since then the rivers have been quietly undermining both the *loess* heaps and the sandstone, limestone, or granite on which they rest, and have carried away vast quantities of earth and stone to the plains on the east. Richthoven seems to have seized on the right idea for explaining how hills of this kind were formed.

In the Sha-ho valley we found what we had been expecting to see—the manufactory for large water-jars. It is at a place called Wa-le, or "tile village." Here we saw the process. The clay is called *kan-tsi-too*, and is found close by. The kiln is cut in a *loess* hill which stands isolated in the valley. At the bottom of the kiln, which is excavated at the east end of the hill, is a long large furnace. Over it is spread a network of iron bars, and on this rests a pile of new jars, large and small, to the height of fifteen feet. The jars are placed carefully one over another in readiness to be fired. Next to the firing-house on the west were storehouses for jars kept in stock. These storerooms are cut deep into the *loess*, and their roofs and side walls are supported by wooden framework on the principle adopted in coal mines. Next was the potter's room, where two men sit, the potter and his assistant. The potter sits on a low stool with a large round flat stone before him, which revolves from right to left horizontally. He places his lump of softened clay, of a dark colour, well kneaded, on the flat stone. Inserting his fist in the lump, while the stone revolves, a sort of flower-pot shape is given to it. He gradually enlarges the hollow made by his fist till it becomes the interior of a two feet high and eight inches wide jar. The quantity of clay needed for a jar of a required size is previously known. He also uses in moulding a flat oblong piece of wood and also a round piece. By these he completes the moulding of the jar, which shows gutters parallel with the base, which are not ornamented, and can scarcely be intended for any use. The wheel is turned by the agency of another man who is placed a few feet distant, and draws a handle in and out horizontally. This turns a wheel near the ground, round which is wrapped a band of hemp. The band turns the potter's wheel on which is placed the moulding board. The jar was made in about five minutes, and a hundred can be made in a day. Large quantities stood in the vicinity ready for sale. Jars spoiled in making are used in building cottages. We saw several huts whose walls were thus constructed. The working wheel is called the waterwheel, *shui-lun;* the other is the dry wheel, *kan-lun.* The boy who drives is the *chiau kan lun tsi tih.* This word *chiau* is the same that is used in turning a capstan on canals.

Coal is brought twenty *le* down a valley which debouches at Wa-le near the pottery. It is anthracite, and not equal to that of the mines near Peking. We passed the night at Ke-yu.

Thursday, October 24th — Wang-kwai.—This morning we saw signs of the inundation of last summer. Many trees lay on the sands of the Sha-ho, up which we were now travelling westward towards the pass Lung-tsinen-kwan. Willows, poplars, and date trees abound in this valley. The people are beginning to carry away the fallen trees, some of which are dead and others still green.

We were glad to find that vaccinators come to these mountain valleys in the spring. They charge 400 cash for girls and 800 for boys. The people will allow their little girls to take small-pox rather than pay as much for them as for boys. A curious fact this, indicating a contempt for girls, which, though highly discreditable, is felt by the parents. In the village where we made the inquiry, about four hundred are vaccinated every spring. The fee for each is ninepence on the average. How much better taken care of are our own poor in England, who get vaccination for nothing, and will be fined if they neglect it!

We were told that *ying-tai* or *tsoo-po-tsi*, known among us as goitre, occurs 200 *le* to the north of these valleys near Kwang-chang, but is very rare in this part, perhaps because the country here is open and the valleys wide. The great width of our valley is also a preservative against sudden floods. We noticed *loess* lying in many places in a thick deposit on sandstone or limestone. The road led us over several hills consisting of these three formations.

Friday, October 25th.—We slept last night at Foo-ping, a city built on the banks of the Sha-ho. We went in by a small gate, and reached an inn, where, as we lay, we could hear the rushing sound of the river a few rods away. At places like this the traveller must expect very small rooms and close quarters. One would not suppose that in a poor inn in a far-off place the people would care much for the rules of politeness, but wherever the Chinaman goes he takes these rules with him. As I took a cup of tea carelessly from the inn boy with my hand over it, he checked me, saying good-naturedly that a cup of tea should always be taken with both hands placed beneath, otherwise there is a want of respect. How many times do we offend unconsciously the native notion of what ceremony requires, when an inn waiter in a little mountain town is piqued at the want of respect shown in an act such as this!

In the plains meals are paid for according to what is asked for by the dish. Each dish is charged. But among the mountains there is a fixed rate for a meal, the same for men and for animals. The rate is 140 cash, or about threepence, for each person or animal. This includes lodging. The mules receive straw but no corn from the inn. The owner is expected to bring corn with him. The food supplied for men is of a homely kind. No other can be provided, so that travellers having a dainty palate had better not go or carry a cook with them.

Silver begins to be 10 per cent. dearer. A tael only brings 1500 copper cash, instead of 1650. The scale used subtracts 8 per cent. per tael on the weight, and the number given for a hundred is 99. In this way it will be found that the custom in regard to exchange goes against the traveller in every particular. In Peking we receive 98 for a hundred. In Cho-chow and Ansi we had only 96. We use the market scale, while the people prefer the old smooth scale or Lau-kwang-kwang. One thing we were saved from on the route we took. There was no counting of 660 to the thousand. The system of counting 165 one *tiau*, 325 two *tiau*, and so on, is said to have been introduced by Chang-si-kwei of the Tang dynasty, subjugator of Corea. In South China 1000 copper cash count as a thousand. In the north 500, and in some places 660, are a thousand. The system of calling 660 a thousand exists south and east of Peking, but not to the west.

Noon, at Lu-ying-poo.—We came on forty *le* to this place. There is a large inn here. Bituminous coal is used, and is brought from a place forty *le* east of Woo-tai city. Four hundred cash a pecul is paid for it here. The prosperity of the inn, which appeared evident from extensive building operations going on at present, depends on the traffic along the road, which consists of cotton bales and cotton cloth going to Shanse, and wool, water, and tobacco coming back again. It is on the trade route between Pau-ting-foo and the north part of Shanse, including Kwei-hwa-cheng. Coal is here called *shi-tan*, "stone charcoal." Ironware comes from Yu-hia, 300 *le* distant. Leaving the Sha-ho after following it ten *le*, we went up the valley of another stream, the Wan-nien-chiau-ho, which flows down its channel rapidly through boulders, pebbles, and sand.

In the evening we were at Lung-tsiuen-kwan. There is a fort below the pass, and it is here that customs are collected. As we entered the collectors asked us to pay duty. They spoke in a bold and noisy tone. I said to an old man who showed the most violence of demeanour, "Do not be violent. We are going to an inn to stay the night. Come there and look at our passports." They then ceased to be noisy, and never appeared at the inn. Some more sagacious person perhaps told them that to demand duty from foreigners is irregular.

We found evidence to-day that, though we had stopped a Sunday on the road and were travelling very slowly, we were going faster than many Chinese would do, for a party came up to us at noon that had passed us a day from Peking. Seventy *le* (twenty-three miles) a day contented them. A dissolute young man in a mule sedan was chief of the cavalcade. He seemed to have been made an invalid by a vicious life. As we stayed both a day at An-su and half a day at another town, we had gained one day in six as compared with the Chinese travellers; yet we were impatient and they were contented. The first point with the Chinese is not to be made uncomfortable; with the Anglo-Saxon the object is not to be slow.

Our course now lay up a valley with vast granite boulders. It reminded us of the Nan-kow Pass near Peking. The water has immense force when increased by its depth. The hydraulic pressure thus caused works great destruction. We saw its effects in the Siau-tsing-ho. An idol shrine, image, table, and offerings had been placed under a steep cliff. Helpless as Dagon the idols looked on the sand, leaving in their original station on a ledge of the rock no trace to show where they were formerly, except some rude painting made by devotees on the cliff.

A cross inscribed on walls and stones excited our curiosity. It is for the protection of the harvest. The villagers form a club for mutual aid against robbery. A watch is kept by the members in succession. If a thief is caught, he is brought before the club for punishment. A mark, such as the character +, is inscribed on the walls of enclosed lands guaranteed by the club. If any villager refuses to join the society, his land is not marked, and he has no guarantee against robbery.

We were now beneath the Great Wall in a little fort. Here we passed a night in an inn. In the morning we were detained till gun-fire, which takes place at dawn. The gates are not opened till then.

Saturday, October 26th.—Breakfast at Shi-tsui at eleven. This morning we went through the pass called Lung-tsiuen-kwan, which is very steep and high. On the top of the hill we found oatmeal and potatoes ready boiled for travellers. They are excellent after a steep walk up the hill.

Foo-ping is in the province of Chihle. At Lung-tsiuen-kwan we left that province and entered the department of Tai-yuen-foo in Shanse. The wall separating Shanse and Chihle dates from the time of the contending states, Chan-kwo, B.C. 300. When the Chau kingdom separated itself from the Yen kingdom by a wall, Shanse was Chau, and Chihle was Yen. Afterwards, in the time of Tsin-shi-hwang, B.C. 220, of Sui-yang-te, A.D. 500, and of the Ming dynasty, particularly when extensions and repairs of the various boundary walls were made, this branch would receive attention. Such strength as it has now is owing to the exertions of the Ming dynasty to keep itself in security against the Mongols. Tsin-shi-hwang was the greatest builder among many builders who lived before him and after him. Like them, he found that mountain barriers formed the natural boundary of their country, and like them he thought it best to fortify the passes. The forts and gates at the passes were the essential idea. The ancient rulers of China thought, however, as the Romans thought in Britain, that a continuous wall to connect these forts should be built to impart an air of greater strength and security. Tsin-shi-hwang only extended further the ideas of earlier rulers when he ordered Meng-kwa to build a wall all the way from Shan-hai-kwan, on the sea-coast, to the western end of Shense, west of the Yellow River. Lung-tsiuen-kwan is not so important as Tsi-king-kwan and Ku-yung-kwan farther to the north. When armies have invaded the province of Chihle, they have come by Ku-yung-kwan on the Kalgan road in three cases out of ten, and by Tsi-king-kwan near the imperial tombs in seven cases out of ten. This is partly caused by the easier travelling on the road which leads from Kwang-chang (and Yu-chow higher up) down the valley of the Ku-ma-ho to Tsi-king-kwan. Once past that fort, and a rapid descent down a good road brings the traveller to the productive plains of Yu-chow and Pau-ting-foo.

The country now known as the Pau-ting-foo department was a battle-field for two centuries between the Tang and early Sung dynasties. Chen-ting-foo was the middle capital of the Kie-tan kingdom at a still earlier time. North China under that Tartar dynasty had then three capitals, one of them in Mongolia.

At Lung-tsiuen-kwan we were probably 1000 feet higher than at Pa-ta-ling, the top of the Nan-kow Pass. It is twenty *le* from the fort to the top of the pass. At Nan-kow the distance is forty-five. The steep rises much more rapidly at Lung-tsiuen-kwan.

A steep mountain, or any mountain at all remarkable, is supposed to have a special local spirit, who acts as guardian. The Chinese Government provides for maintaining certain sacrifices to the deities of mountains on a large scale for the Empire. But among the people the same religious belief exists, and leads them to worship the spirits of certain mountains in small shrines or temples on the roadside. In one such shrine on the way up to the top of the pass were placed five small tablets of wood. On the middle one was inscribed the "tablet of the spirit of the mountain." On the left were a tablet to the spirits of the five roads, and another to the spirit of local fever. On the right side were a tablet to the Tsiang-kiun named Peh, and to the spirits of water, grass, and corn. Tsiang-kiun is a military title corresponding to our "general."

Near this temple was another to a divinity, Liow-wang, who is in these regions prayed to for rain. Both shrines were newly repaired and gaudily painted.

Not far away, and lower down the mountain, was a temple to Kwan-yin, who was called on the inscribed tablets, Ling-ying-fo, "the efficacious, prayer-answering Buddha." On both sides of the road were numerous tablets set up by admiring devotees. Here follow sundry specimens of the sentences inscribed on them:—*Kwang-kio*, "wide perception;" *Me-yew*, "secret aid;" *Hwa yu man feng*, "Flowers fall like rain over the whole mountain;" *Tsi hang poo too*, "The ship of mercy universally saving;" *Woo-poo-ying*, "Never-failing efficacy;" *Kiow-koo*, "Saves from misery;" *Nan hai ta shi*, "Great teacher of the Southern Sea."

CHAPTER XVIII.

JOURNEY TO WOO-TAI-SHAN CONTINUED—FROM LUNG-TSIUEN-KWAN TO WOO-TAI.

AFTER crossing the Tai-hang-ling, the summit of which separates the provinces of Chihle and Shanse, we soon passed a Lama monastery called Arshan-bolog, "the temple of the fountain of the genii." It was originally an ordinary Buddhist temple in the hands of Chinese priests or *hoshangs*, and was founded in the reign of Wan-leih. When the Emperor Kanghe, of the Tartar dynasty, passed this way on the road to Woo-tai to worship there the images adored by the Lamas, he observed that the idols in this temple were broken and neglected. He was angry at the priests and gave it in charge to Lamas. There are now twelve Lamas there, who all came from Eastern Mongolia. This incident and the handsome style of the buildings show how great was the attachment of that Emperor to the Buddhist religion. Yet at one period in his life he was, say the Jesuits, nearly converted to Christianity. He was probably a man open to impressions, easily wrought upon, but not capable of being induced to abandon the traditional etiquette of emperors by adopting the religion of the scholars from the Western Ocean.

The descent was slow and slightly inclined. We soon came to another handsome temple occupied by more than a hundred Lamas, who rushed out with great eagerness to see us. The temple is called Tai-loo-sze, "temple of the foot of the terraces," *i.e.*, of Woo-tai. Twelve of the Lamas are Mongol and the rest Chinese.

The valley leading to Shi-tsui goes south-west and continues its descent to Woo-tai city. We were to take a turn in a nearly opposite direction at Shi-tsui conducting us up the valley of a stream which fifty miles to the north flows past the monasteries of Woo-tai.

We met a crowd of travellers at Shi-tsui. The inn was large and a good meal was provided. Among other things there were sweet cakes made of flour, sugar, and a little sesamum oil. They taste something like shortbread. Hear this, ye Scotchmen; you can still enjoy in China the luxuries of home. There was also a dish of celery. The market was busy and the buyers and lookers-on numerous. A merchant came forward and said, "I have read your books." To the answer, "What book?" he replied, "The Old Testament." Of this he had completed the perusal of two volumes (in all there are three). He showed himself to be tolerably familiar with Genesis. He had received the book from a friend who had obtained it from a Bible Society's colporteur. I gave him other books.

We noticed in passing forward up the long Woo-tai valley the special customs of the people. As we are now high above the zone of wheat cultivation, oats are extremely common. A flail is used to thresh with. Two men stand opposite to each other, each with a flail, and beat the oats right lustily. The part held in the hand is round, while the flying stick is constructed of plaited willow forming an oblong flat piece of basketwork. The oatmeal is usually eaten in the form of macaroni or as porridge in a rice bowl.

We passed an overshot mill which was at work pressing oil. The stream, which, to increase and steady its force, is collected in a dam, is directed upon a large vertical wooden wheel. Round its circle are several small troughs which the stream fills with water. The weight of the water turns the wheel. A horizontal wheel is attached which revolves by means of cogs. The axle of this horizontal wheel is an upright shaft, which goes through the floor of a room above, and there turns the stone which presses out the oil.

North of the mill, advancing up the valley of the little stream which joins the Siau-tsing-ho at Woo-tai city, we found it necessary to ford the little river frequently. Many of the Lama pilgrims are pedestrians, and for them trees are laid across the stream. Mules ford by crossing the water, which is broad and shallow. The bridges consist of two, three, or four trees, sometimes slightly flattened with a hatchet, but oftener they are left in their original round shape. Travellers are expected to have good nerves and not to grow giddy on slight occasions. The soles of Chinese shoes, being of cloth, are good for stepping along a prostrate tree laid across a stream.

We passed several monasteries as darkness came on and afterwards. We were now near the Nan-tai, the southernmost of the five mountain peaks which make up Woo-tai. It was too dark to make inquiries. We proceeded steadily onward till we reached the town of Tai-hwai. Here, at a quarter to seven P.M., we arrived, and found an inn belonging to a monastery, where lodging was given to us. A visitor, who was a Mongol Lama, came in to see us while our evening meal was preparing. He belonged to the Harchin tribe. He took tea willingly, offered his snuff bottle, and professed friendship. This we reciprocated, and stated our belief in the common brotherhood of mankind. To this he cordially assented, for Buddhism, as held either by Lamas or Hoshangs, teaches its votaries to look on universal brotherhood as a great truth. He was elegant in manner, and wished to consider himself as our friend in future. He could not read Mongol nor expound Tibetan, and is therefore without depth.

Sunday, October 27th—Tai-hwai-kiai.—A cold frosty morning. I went out to look at our surroundings. A few Lamas were stirring at an early hour, and were rapidly moving along the street in the cold air. Round the town smoke began to rise from the various monasteries. Traffic was proceeding north, west, and south from our little town along the valleys that lie in those directions. Half a mile to the north stands Poo-sa-ting on an eminence, the residence of the chief Lama, and the richest and largest Lamasery. Beyond it towers up above its neighbour summits the North Tai.

Over the south gate of the little town of Tai-hwai there is a small temple to Hormosda Tingri and Dara-ehe. Both are known to Chinese Buddhism, but in China it is not usual to place Yu-hwang-shang-te (Hormosda) in a temple as guardian of a city gate. We were now in Lama-land, and must expect to see arrangements peculiar to Lama Buddhism. Hormosda was in this case just a Chinese Yu-hwang. He faced south. Dara-ehe is the Mu-fo (mother Buddha) of the Chinese, and Ehe Borhan of the Mongols.[1] She has a Bodhisattwa's diadem, or, as the Mongols call it, a *tidem*. On all of its five leaves there was a picture of Buddha. On each side of her is seen a tall branch of flowers, in this instance the lotus, reaching to her head. On her forehead is a spot or small elevation which the attendant Lamas told us sends forth a hair which, when Dara-ehe wishes, goes out for thousands of miles in an instant. This is an instance of the magical miracle in which the Buddhist imagination indulges itself without limit. For what object is the hair extended? To show the power of the goddess, in order that the worshippers may be filled with reverence for her. We conversed for some time with three or four Lamas in a court beside this temple, who kindly entertained us with tea. We discoursed on their religion and ours. They received our books gladly.

I afterwards walked to the Shoo-siang-si, a monastery standing on the north-west of the town and south-west from Poo-sa-ting. A party of Mongol women, youths, and men were just entering, pilgrims visiting each principal shrine in rotation that they might prostrate themselves in each. Such in the Middle Ages was a great part of Christian worship even in England. They proceeded to the great hall of Manjoosere, patron deity of Woo-tai. Here

[1] She belongs to the Sivaistic element in Buddhism.

he is seen as a large gilt figure seated on an immense lion. The lion is many coloured. The name *Shoo-siang* means image of Manjoosere or Wen-shoo. Round the image just mentioned is a representation of Tien-tai, constructed of moulded figures, Buddhist personages, trees, &c., occupying three sides of the hall. It is erected on a high dais of brickwork and reaches to the ceiling. The object is to give in successive landscapes, amid rockwork and marine scenery, the history of the celebrated Buddhist establishments at Tien-tai in the province of Che-kiang.

Lohans appear here to the number of five hundred. Some of them appear floating on the waves of the Southern Sea, others are seen on clouds and mountains. Near a temple of Yu-hwang appears Tamo the Indian patriarch, Bodhidharma, with his pupil Sheng-kwang, standing before him. The pupil, a Chinese Buddhist, holds in his right hand his own left arm, which he has just cut off near the shoulder as a sign of his devotion and dominion over the body. This is said to have taken place in the fifth century. Beyond this group sits the Buddhist sage Chi-chay, with Lohans near him and four Yakshas raging round him, who fail to disturb his tranquillity. Among native Buddhist authors his writings have been perhaps the most extensive in influence. The priest who showed me these things was very frank and communicative. Two other Chinese priests led me into a room to take tea. The room showed signs of comfortable living and also of some literary industry. A manuscript on the table contained a collection of tracts on the doctrine which is "not dark," meaning Buddhism. When I told them of our religion, the abandonment of monasticism, heart-worship instead of image-worship, and the history of Jesus, they assented. Buddhism is an extremely tolerant religion.

October 28th.—The Hoshangs in Woo-tai are almost all Shanse men. Natives of the south could not, they say, live in so cold a region as Woo-tai; nor could Northern Buddhists live in the south.

The Lamas at Woo-tai are, if Mongols, almost exclusively from Eastern Mongolia, indicating the importance of that region in regard to wealth and population. We are surprised at the large number of Lamas who can read the Mongol writing. In Peking they can usually read only the Tibetan character. Here they receive our books cheerfully. Yet it is probable that in Peking if the number of the Mongols who can read were told it would not be small. They are more reticent and retiring there than here, because in that city a foreign costume is no rarity.

On the east side of the valley from Shoo-siang-si is a monastery called Kwang-an-si. It has been recently repaired and decorated. Red and green paint and yellow silk and satin have been used in profusion. Hollow brass images, life-size, were very abundant and seemed quite new. We visited three *tiens* or chapels all richly fitted. Tibetan pictures of the favourite mythological scenes and personages of the Lama religion hung on the walls. Outside these chapels were stone and slate tablets commemorating the work of restoration and chronicling the gifts of Mongol princes. Among them were the names of the Kalka-hans or chief princes, and several southern Wangs or princes.

October 29th.—We, Mr. Wheler and I, went up a path on the eastern ascent leading to a monastery from which a fine view is obtained of the whole valley, here presenting a beautiful and busy scene. Large droves of camels are seen grazing over the valley. The bazaar close to Poo-sa-ting is full of life. Mongols are constantly here buying from the Chinese shopkeepers. The great monastery Poo-sa-ting stretches its immense length along a conspicuous hill just above. In the same group were some Tibetan monasteries where more than a hundred Lamas from Eastern and Western Tibet permanently reside. A boy Lama of ten years went with us as *compagnon de voyage.* We were amused at his tricks. When we spoke to Lamas he stayed at a distance too far for recognition by them. He was afraid not of us but of them. He talked freely enough in their absence.

To the north of Poo-sa-ting, a mile or more up the valley, we visited the monastery of the Seven Buddhas. The Buddhas here referred to are six legendary and one historical—that is, Shakyamuni himself and the six who are said to have preceded him. They are placed from west to east in the order of time.

Here we also saw a large figure of Ochirwani with three eyes and five skulls on his head. He held in his hand a *radjra*, apparently a short sceptre, but really a symbol of magical power. It is believed to be thrown by the genius of the thunderstorm, and is therefore sometimes called a thunderbolt. This *radjra* is the characteristic of the image. In Mongol this Sanscrit word has become *ochir*, and hence the word Ochirwani. Behind the skulls are five wheels and five flames. He is one of the Hindoo Devas, and is regarded as having unconquerable strength, which is symbolised by the *radjra*, in Chinese *kin-kang*, "diamond," "what cannot be broken." He belongs to the same class as the four great heavenly kings found in the entrance hall of Chinese monasteries.

Behind Ochirwani was Shakyamuni, with Manjoosere and Samantabhadra beside him. Near them was a picture of Aryabolo, otherwise known as goddess of mercy.

We went in the afternoon to the chief Lama's temple, the Poo-sa-ting, built on the flat top of a hill about 400 feet high. There is a flight of 109 broad stone steps at the south end. A well-clad Lama at the gate informed us that the chief Lama was employed in preparing for the *cham-harail*, or sacred dance, and could not see visitors. He lives in the south-east part of the monastery. We proceeded along the whole range of buildings to the north. At the back of the halls of the images were long ranges of lodging-rooms for Lamas, forming quite a little town, for a crowd of them congregates here as at Yung-ho-kung in Peking. Many Mongol women are seen in this part, probably all belonging to pilgrim parties, who find quarters in rooms provided for them. Many ranges of buildings have upper and lower verandahs. Elsewhere are seen Tibetan houses with their small square windows in the upper part of a strong high wall. Among the pilgrims and resident Lamas there was great eagerness for our Mongol catechism and tracts.

Returning to the chief entrance, we found that the secretary and other chief attendants of the Jasah Lama, as the abbot is called (*jasah* means governing), were prepared to receive us in their apartments in front of his residence. Our entertainers were Tibetans, speaking fluently both Chinese and Mongol. They treated us to tea with milk, the *soo-tai-chay* of the Mongols. An elderly man with a long beard named Pan, and another, both from Lassa, had a good deal of conversation with us. They will soon return to their country. They knew well that India, the land south of the Ghoorka country, belongs to England, but did not seem to be aware of Huc and Gabet's visit to Tibet. The room was arranged as a Chinese room, with heated dais or *kang*, and cupboards opposite. It was kept warm further by a charcoal or coke fire without smell, and standing on a brass bason. A kettle is here kept hot for tea. The hot air ascending turns a praying wheel which is suspended for the purpose from the ceiling. We intrusted to our entertainers books for the abbot, namely, the Old and New Testament in Mongol, with catechism and tracts. He sent us in return by the hands of Pan Lama two bundles of Tibetan incense with several sentences of complimentary expressions, such as, were we comfortable in our inn, had we a pleasant journey, and how long we would stay. The incense is in bundles of twelve sticks, twenty inches long.

The Poo-sa-ting was formerly called Chen-yung-yuen, "temple of the true face," which dated from the fourth century. The Tartar Emperor of the day, Hiau-wen-te, caused twelve temples to be erected round the monastery of the Han Emperor Ming-te, then in existence, and sent officers periodically to worship Buddha there. This gives an antiquity to the Poo-sa-ting of fourteen hundred years, if we do not take a change in name to be a disturbance of its identity. Nothing is now known respecting the locality of the other eleven temples, or of the original monastery erected in the Han dynasty, whose name was Ta-fow-ling-tsiow-si.

Ashoka, monarch of all India, a little before the time of Alexander the Great, is said to have caused the spirits and demons of the air, the Kwei-shen, to erect 84,000 pagodas in all countries to receive the relics of Buddha. Among them was one at Woo-tai. Formerly there was some building which connected itself with this tradition. We did not learn anything of it. Three of the 84,000 relics were in China. I have seen one in the province of Che-kiang, in a temple near Ningpo. I wished to see another at Woo-tai, but was not successful.

At the doors of houses where Lamas live it is usual to write lucky sentences in the Chinese fashion. They are translated into Mongol from Chinese. Here follow some specimens:—

"May your age be the same as that of the pines in the southern mountains."

"May your happiness abound as the waters of the Eastern Sea."

> "Nasu anu umun agola ne narasun adeli
> Boy in anu jagon dalai ne usu metu."

The Chinese reads:—

> "Foo joo tung hai chang liow shui,
> Show pe nan shan poo lau sung."

Sentences of this kind keep poetical sentiments before the eye, and they may thus have a softening and refining effect on the mind, but they aid superstition as being founded on the doctrine of luck, and promoting its hold on the people.

An old and young Lama came to our inn, the latter a boy of fifteen. He had been at Woo-tai four years.

They live in the temple of Hormosda Tingri, a short way down the southern valley. The boy is from the Ordos country and has seen there the tomb of Genghis Khan. Agriculture is practised in the Ordos country, but not by members of his family. His brother attends to sheep and horses in preference. I gave him a book to learn to read from. The old Lama said he would find some schoolmaster or *bakshi* to instruct him. We learned from these Lamas that we had passed the Ehen-omai[1] in coming to Tai-hwai on Saturday evening. It is an exhibition in a cave, near which is a temple, twenty Chinese miles south of the town.

This morning (Tuesday) went to the temple of the Ubegun Manjoosere west of Poo-sa-ting. It is a mile up the side of a mountain. The image is that of an old man, one form assumed by Manjoosere, having a white beard three inches long. He is placed in a small shrine. Heaps of small silk kerchiefs on his hands and knees, placed there by enthusiastic worshippers, prevented the figure from being well seen. Round the hall from floor to ceiling were ten thousand figures of Manjoosere, indicating the multiform shapes he assumes in his efforts to save men. In the great hall behind, Manjoosere appears again in company with Samantabhadra and Kwan-yin. He there wears the crown of a Bodhisattwa over the oyster-shell cap of a Buddha, and with no beard. All these personages are supposed to assume various metamorphoses. Manjoosere carries a bow in his left hand and a sceptre in his right. In colour he may be red, white, black, green, or yellow. He very commonly has in his left hand a flower. When he is painted with eight hands, they hold a small umbrella, a thunderbolt, a wheel, and other things. If not seated on a lion he sits on a lotus dais with bare feet crossed, the soles turned up. He appears frequently, so it is believed, to the inhabitants of the valley, taking the shape of a blind man, a shepherd, a Lama, or some other personage. Once he appeared as a poor girl who left her

[1] Womb of Buddha's mother.

hair to be buried at the spot now known as Wen-shoo-fa-ta, "the tomb of Manjoosere's hair." It is on the Chung-tai, "central terrace." In the reign of Wan-leih (sixteenth century) this tomb was repaired and the hair seen. It was of a golden hue and emitted a many-coloured light. In the twelfth century a shepherd named Chau-kang-pe saw a strange priest enter the Na-la-yen cave on the Tung-tai and leave an umbrella there. He erected a tomb in which to bury it. Not far from this tomb a woman with white hair was seen once washing her rice bowl. A monk named Ming-sin asked her whence she came. She replied, "I have come from Chung-tai begging food." Then in a moment she disappeared, and nothing was seen but a remarkable light illuminating the grove and the valley. A girl belonging to the adjoining city of Tai-chow refused to be married, and ran away to a spot called the "Cliff of Mercy," also at the Tung-tai. Here she ate the leaves of a certain plant and drank dew. Her father and mother came and tried to compel her to go home and be married. She then threw herself from the cliff, but when in mid-air she took wing and fled into the upper regions.

Woo-tai is a large place. The valleys, caves, springs, rocks, brooks, tombs, gardens, images, are numberless. A legend is attached to most of them, and the marvellous things said to have been seen and done are all produced by the magic power of Manjoosere, the patron god of the mountain. The fountain where the silver-haired old woman appeared is known as the Wen-shoo-se-po-che, "the fountain where Manjoosere washed his rice bowl." It is his presence that causes this whole region to appear to the inhabitants to be instinct with legend. The maid that would not marry was a metamorphosis of Manjoosere.

The five colours are distributed among the five mountains, and the flowers that grow on the Nan-tai are said to have the same five colours. These flowers are dried to make medicine of, and visitors to Woo-tai purchase little packets to bring away with them. They make a little tea by infusing them in hot water, and think that they do them good. If the partaker does not perceive any benefit to his own health by these medicines, he consoles himself with the reflection that others are more successful in obtaining powerful aid from Manjoosere, by which their bodily ailments are cured. This was the way in which the matter was represented to me by a Liang Lama, a friend of mine at the Yung-ho-kung, who had himself brought some packets of medicine with him from Woo-tai.

The view of the sacred valley from the temple of the Aged Manjooscre is very fine. Just in front is the Poo-sa-ting. Up the north valley several other monasteries are seen. Beside them winds the road which leads up the Hwa-yen-ling. The pass of this name crosses a shoulder of the North Tai and East Tai. Up the steep the road is seen to bend circuitously. Next day we were to leave Woo-tai by this route. To the south lay the little town of Tai-hwai, where our inn was, and in the near neighbourhood of Poo-sa-ting was a cluster of monasteries, the Mongol bazaar, and a collection of buildings looking like a small town, where the animals belonging to travellers and to the monasteries are taken care of. These groups of buildings lent variety to the valley, which, on account of the brown appearance of the stunted autumn grass, needed this relief where it was not pierced by a silvery rushing brook which flows from the north down the valley till hidden by the hills of the southern landscape. To the west the view looks towards the North Tai; to the east the East Tai is visible.

We went on to the Dara-ehin-sum, "the temple of the mother Buddha." The worship of this divinity was introduced in the Tang dynasty, when Sivaism entered the Buddhist religion. The Hindoos, who from that time forward came to China and Tibet, seem to have been all propagators of Sivaistic Buddhism. It was from the seventh to the fifteenth century, anterior to Lamaism, and subsequent to the contemplative school, the *chan-men*, that this form of the Buddhist religion flourished. The festival of the hungry ghosts, the magical movements of the hands, the use of iron and bronze mirrors, with Sanscrit charms, and an image of the Buddha mother upon them, belong to this age. We were now to see a temple specially devoted to the honour of Dara-ehe. There were two image halls. The first represented the twenty-one metamorphoses of Dara, all in sitting shape, arms and chest bare. The long right arm touches the lotus-flower dais on which she sits. A large *hau-kwang* (literally "hairy glory," in allusion to the parallel hair-like rays which are represented upon it) forms a back screen for her body, and a coloured circle for her head. She assumes at pleasure the favourite five colours. Her head-dress is usually that of five tufts with a top-knot; but in this hall she wore the Poosa crown of six leaves. On her left is in every instance a standing flower. Behind her were the three Buddhas, past, present, and future. They hold the place of honour, while Dara-ehe is most prominent. New images, when introduced into the temples of Northern Buddhism, could not push out the older ones. They could only be placed in front of them or near them.

In the other principal hall was Buddha, and in an anteroom Tsung-kaba, the founder of Lamaism, who lived only four hundred years ago. His form is repeated in several large pictures. The stools and cushions for daily worship were all arranged here, this being the hall for morning and evening prayer.

A Lama, whom I met at Kalgan five years ago, presented himself at this temple. He says that he has led here a moderately happy life for four years. When I saw him formerly he was employed by an American missionary at Kalgan as teacher of the Mongol language. I think he looks back with satisfaction to his more varied and interesting life at that place.

The observance of the sacred dance, "Cham[1] harail," at

---

[1] *Cham*, a Tibetan word, "to dance."

Woo-tai, a masquerade of Hindoo gods going in procession, is after the model employed at Yung-ho-kung in Peking. At Poo-sa-ting there are first ten days of chanting, from the 6th to the 15th. The dance and masquerade are on the last two days. The books used are the Kongso. The performers are about sixty in number, and they practise their parts for two months beforehand.

The Lama from Kalgan told me that at Woo-tai it is the custom for boy Lamas to wear red. When young men they put on *tsi*, or purple-brown clothing; when old they wear yellow. He thinks there are two thousand Mongol Lamas in Woo-tai; others think there are not more than seven hundred. Statistics are difficult to procure on account of the floating character of the population. Lamas are fond of wandering, and, if of frugal habits, can easily obtain a hospitable reception in temples. They flock in crowds to Woo-tai, and prostrate themselves at the various shrines with great apparent fervour. Of Buddhist priests, Chinese by birth, there are several hundreds. Then there are also many Chinese Lamas. The fashion is, when the Chinese become Lamas, for them to chant Tibetan prayers, and to have in their temples the same images and costumes which are customary in Tibet.

I gave the Kalgan Lama at his request a Mongol Testament. He wished it for some friend. He is himself greatly injured by opium smoking.

Lamas coming on pilgrimage swell the number of resident Mongols greatly. So also the Mongol laity are very fond of visiting Woo-tai, especially women, to worship the images. We noticed some of them at the pagoda south of Poo-sa-ting. This pagoda is in appearance like that within the Ping-tseh-men of Peking. It constitutes a striking object on entering the Woo-tai valley from the south. It has at its base an impression of the soles of Buddha's feet cut in a block of marble and facing outwards. His hands, also cut in the marble, are seen near. More than three hundred praying wheels are attached to

The Best Recent Fiction

THE MACMILLAN COMPANY, Publishers
64-66 FIFTH AVENUE, NEW YORK

A MAN'S WORLD. By Albert Edwards.

Cloth, 12mo, $1.25 net.

The intimate story of a man's life, that is what *A Man's World* is. Arnold Whitman, Mr. Edwards's hero, is a sort of Probation Officer in the "Tombs," and as such is brought into relation with a certain stratum of New York City life of which the ordinary person knows little. It is while thus employed that he meets Nina, a woman of the streets, around whom the interest of the book centers. Nina has a soul, but it is undiscovered, and it is of its birth, of the development of a noble woman from one of the lowest, that the author writes with amazing strength and absolute frankness.

THE IMPEACHMENT OF PRESIDENT ISRAELS. By Frank B. Copley.

Illustrated. Cloth, 12mo, $1.00 net.

This is the story of the impeachment of David Israels, President of the United States, as told by his private secretary. Instead of preparing for war to avenge the killing of four American sailors, President Israels persisted in proposals for peace, finally sending a fleet to Constantinople, to celebrate some Turkish anniversary, which act brought upon him the terrible stigma. All this, it might be explained, has yet to take place, for Israels is a future president. The effect of reality is well kept up by Mr. Copley, who incidentally introduces some very wholesome truths, notably that the way to realize universal peace is to refuse even to consider the possibility of war, that moral suasion is more forceful than physical threats and that a war resulting from mob panic and hate is only folly and wickedness.

MY LOVE AND I. By Martin Redfield.

Decorated cloth, 12mo, $1.35 net.

This is not an ordinary love story. It reads, on the contrary, more like an intimate confession of a man's life. Married to a woman whom he idolizes, Martin Redfield tells in his own words of his sad awakening, of the other woman who came into his life, and of how he dealt with the problem which confronted him. At all events the book is a decided departure from stories which have dealt with the triangle before. Besides Martin and his love, there is intimately interwoven with it the story of Blake and Mary. An idealist, a poet, able only to earn a bare living, he forms a striking contrast to Martin, a practical man and a popular novelist.

tan are improvised by the use of movable furniture in a short space of time in front of temples, to be used for as many days as required. According to the Lama notion the *hoto-mandal*[1] represents the city where each divinity sits in state in Buddha's land. Sometimes the *hoto-mandal* supports offerings in front of the image of Buddha.

The pilgrims are also conducted to see each marvel in the various temples. At the back of the large Dagoba is a revolving library, turned by two men, entering at the floor beneath it. It is sixty feet high and has eight sides. The Chinese copy of the Ganjur is inside it. The visitor sees the whole vast wheel turning slowly from east to west. All praying wheels should turn in the direction in which the sun moves. There was before the time of the Taipings a revolving library like this in the Ling-yin monastery at Hangchow; I saw it about twenty years ago. There is also one at the Yung-ho-kung in Peking.

The Mongol women are fond of buying. They appear in the shops discussing with the bazaar men the prices of articles. Almost everything they can need in tents is to be purchased here. The head-dresses of the women vary with their tribe. Pearls, coral, and silver are very profusely used by them, and often cover the whole head. Their black hair is put up in large rings, one, two, or more in number, and varying in position according to the recognised usage of their tribes.

The Mongol women are very kind to strangers, and give the impression to travellers on their grassy wilds that they are less selfish than the Chinese. They part readily with milk and cheese, and will rise in the middle of the night to give up their bed to some footsore wayfarer. They keep a light burning in their tents, which serves a double purpose. It is an offering to the household gods and a waymark to travellers. The traveller pushes the tent door aside, enters, stirs the fire, and makes his meal while

---

[1] In Sanscrit, *man* is "to worship;" *mandari*, "a town," "a temple." *Hoto*, in Mongol, is a "city."

the inmates are in bed in the interior of the tent. In this abounding hospitality the Mongol women are animated partly by natural kindness of disposition, partly by religious motives. Being very fervent Buddhists, they believe that good actions are meritorious, and will be the means of bringing upon them and on their families great happiness.

The Mongol women rejoice in fast riding, and may be seen on their ponies with their husbands on their native plateaux riding neck to neck without ever showing signs of a desire to fall behind.

Each tent has its little images. They are Shakyamuni Borhan, founder of Buddhism, Geser Han, champion of Buddhism, Galin Ejin, god of fire, the spirit who presides over cookery and the safety of the home.

Their devotion to their religion renders them very willing to give up their sons to be Lamas, and also induces them to make long pilgrimages to Peking and Woo-tai in order to worship the sacred images and relics of their divinities.

The richest monastery in Woo-tai is the Hung-tsiuen-si. It has a copper temple among its curiosities. The Poo-sa-ting is also very rich. It has landed estates supposed to bring into the treasury several tens of thousands of taels annually. The lands of the monasteries are in Shanse, but also in Pau-ting-foo, Chen-ting-foo, &c., belonging to the metropolitan province. A large sum is conferred each winter by the Emperor on the Tibetan chiefs of the monastery during their visit to Peking, where they appear at the New Year festivities.

The daily life of most Lamas must be regarded as monotonous. Their duties are chiefly reading prayers. Some are engaged in instructing young Lamas, taking care of buildings and property, arranging for special days of worship, and study of their own department of Buddhist theology. More than half the houses in Tai-hwai belong to them. The proprietorship of our inn was in a monastery, to which belonged a Lama who was constantly riding about on a pony, engaged in matters connected with property. I saw one Lama printing a book of prayers from cut blocks, probably brought from Peking. The innkeeper who entertained us told me there are a thousand Mongol Lamas and two thousand Chinese Lamas and Hoshangs in Woo-tai. We saw many of them repeating prayers *memoriter* with beads in their hands. They appeared to have the outward form of devotion. But our arrival disturbed their equanimity not a little. In a temple where there are about a hundred Tibetans we saw two of the same nation prostrating themselves with zeal. Another still more zealous entered, who, not content with striking his forehead, laid his whole body flat on the ground. He went very near the image in order to do this. He repeated this act of humility, and then turned round to look at us as we stood at a side door. A minute afterwards he came across the hall to feel our clothing with a smile on his face. While feeling the foreign garments with his fingers he still continued his recitation of prayers or charms. We were surprised at the little real devotion manifested in the behaviour of this outwardly zealous Lama.

Woo-tai is a favourite place for burial. On the hillsides the graves are exceedingly numerous. Cemeteries in the plain, in the vicinity of the monasteries, are also not rare. To be buried in so sacred a spot is considered great good fortune. The Gegens of the Yung-ho-kung monastery in Peking are brought here to find a final resting-place. White tombs, enclosing an urn which contains the ashes of the departed, are everywhere seen.

Should the follower of Confucius go to Woo-tai, he will find his favourite sage occupying a comparatively insignificant position. In the temple over the north gate of Taihwai there is an image of the great sage. It is very small, and stands beside a larger one of Wen-chang, god of literature. On the south side is Chen-woo, who is a legendary protector of the faithful Taouist from pestilence and other calamities.

The Ming emperors went frequently to Woo-tai; the present line less frequently. But Kanghe interested himself greatly in this seat of Buddhism. The imperial lodge where he resided is still there, but in a ruinous state. The description of Woo-tai in four volumes, which he caused to be written, is in full sympathy with Buddhism, and says not a syllable in condemnation of it. The object kept in view in maintaining the monasteries is, that prayers may be offered by the monks for the prosperity of the Emperor and the State.

CHAPTER XIX.

JOURNEY FROM WOO-TAI-SHAN TO PEKING BY WAY OF TSZE-KING-KWAN.

October 30th, 1872.—Rose at cockcrow and left the "clear and cool Woo-tai." Our course lay by the north valley and up the winding Hwa-yen-ling. The view became very fine as we ascended. Poo-sa-ting kept in view all the way up to the top. From that point the North and East Tai may be easily reached. The ascent is gradual, and is uniformly over a brown grassy sod all the way. Much snow was lying on the north face of the various mountains. There is ice there which does not melt in the hottest summer on the side of Chung-tai. On the top above it is a white pagoda. On Pei-tai the view is of overwhelming grandeur, as Mr. Gilmour told us, who ascended it yesterday, from the accumulation of peaks of more or less altitude all round. Next to Heng-shan the North Tai is the highest peak in this part of Shanse, and in fact through the province. Hence the large number of visible peaks, presenting the appearance of a vast waving sea of mountains, which impresses the observer at the top of the North Tai. Like it in grandeur is the scene from the East Tai, where at sunrise the sea can be seen far away on the east. The five mountains are called terraces because they are flat on the top. According to the theory of Pumpelly the valleys are all cut out gradually by the action of water from the plateau, which anciently extended far to the southward of its present limits. The Chung-tai, Pei-tai, and Tung-tai are linked in one; and perhaps also the Se-tai and Nan-tai. The only deep valley is probably that by which we entered this sacred seat of Buddhism.

The height of Woo-tai-shan is 10,000 feet, according to Richthoven. The monasteries must then be 7000 or 8000 feet. The same traveller says that oats are cultivated to within 2000 feet of the summit. In support of this estimate it should be remembered that snow and ice remain near the top of the mountain on the north side all the year round. It seems therefore just to reach the snow-line. The top of the Pei-tai is a flat space about four *le* square. The ascent to the top from the valley of the monasteries is forty *le* in length. The lesser Woo-tai-shan on the north-east is also stated to be 10,000 feet high.[1]

The mass of mountains called Woo-tai-shan are five hundred *le* in circuit. The Poo-to river, rising at Ta-ying and winding south and east past Woo-tai city into the province of Chihle, forms their west and south boundary. On the north the Confucian mountain, Heng-shan, over-tops them in altitude; on the east the Tai-hang chain, marked by the south extension of the Great Wall, forms the natural limit.

The north, south, east, and west branches are all connected with the Chung-tai as their centre. Such is the native idea. The Nan-tai is the most beautiful, having a southern slope, which nourishes a sufficient number of flowers and shrubs to lead to its being called Kin-siou-feng, "the embroidered mountain."

The top of the South Nan-tai is a *le* in circuit, and convex in shape; that of Tung-tai is three *le*, and that of Se-tai two *le* in circuit. Perhaps as the Chinese accounts make the circuits of the five mountain summits exactly one, two, three, four, and five *le*, they are open to question. Nature does not shape the dimensions of her mountain-tops quite so methodically as this.

---

[1] Mr. William Hancock lately ascended this mountain, and estimates the height to be, as here said, about 10,000 feet. He found snow congealed into ice at about 8000 feet on the north side in autumn weather.

One may easily imagine an enthusiastic Buddhist looking on Woo-tai with pride from this pass. "This," he would say, "is the 'cool and clear mountain,' where for nearly two thousand years our monks have never ceased to recite their prayers. It is one of the three most noteworthy Buddhist mountains. But neither Ngo-mei in Sze-chwen, nor Poo-to in the Eastern Ocean, can compare with it in the number of its monasteries, monks, and pilgrims. Here emperors order prayers to be made for their mothers and for the people. Kanghe himself was a frequent pilgrim at these shrines, commemorating his visits by monumental inscriptions at the chief temples. It is a fit spot for the professors of that religion which teaches purity of conduct and mercy to all living beings, which aims at ascetic self-denial and encourages sage meditation, which leads men to virtue, and calls them away from the companionship of vice. Well may those find a rest here who struggle after a pure life, far from the dusty world, where care, vice, and distraction perpetually reign. On that southern eminence our Manjoosere has on many occasions specially appeared, in the hope of persuading men to almsgiving and benevolence, to a victory over the animal nature by the monastic life, to the patient endurance of insults and wrong, to quiet meditation and lofty aspirations after superhuman wisdom."

Kanghe, when he visited the mountain, thought in this way about it. Though a Confucianist, he looked complacently on this nest of monasteries high up among the clouds. Such men have a habit of believing in two religions at once. His father is said to have died a Buddhist.

The panegyric on the ascetic life expressed in the preceding paragraph is all extracted from his edicts. Yet neither he nor his father ever thought seriously of becoming a Hoshang or a Lama, or of retiring like Charles V. to some monastery as a refuge in old age.

When the Mongol Lama arrives at the same spot, his feelings will perhaps be different. By the sight of Woo-tai his mind is filled with indistinct conceptions of the greatness of Borhan. Woo-tai is a chosen seat of Borhan, and therefore he must prostrate himself when at last he comes in sight of it. This he will do amid the wide scene of mountain ranges which meet the eye, while the north wind blows cold on his back. He will prostrate himself before the sacred valley as a holy place, to see which is both a great happiness and a great merit. To him, as to the Mongol laity, Borhan is the possessor of boundless power and mercy. If he be religiously disposed, he goes to Woo-tai as to a spot where, by the fulfilment of vows, the offering of gifts, and the reciting of prayers and charms, he may obtain any desired form of happiness.

And what do those Mongol women expect as the result of their pilgrimage? You meet them in the bazaar trafficking with the bazaar-keepers, going the round of the temples to worship, pushing the praying wheels, or mounted on camels on their way home. They must each have an object. Probably it is some special matter, some trouble of their own, from which the mighty Borhan will free them for the asking, or it is an impulse which leads them to make this journey with an indefinite notion that it will be good for them, or it is doing as others do, in accordance with a custom which to them has the obligation of a law, or it is a wish to visit a mountain where Buddha has made every inch of ground sacred by his presence, where the images, the priests, the worship, the temples, the tombs, are all more holy than elsewhere.

As we went down the pass in order to strike the plain of the Poo-to river, we saw Heng-shan on the north-west, a mountain very striking for its lofty horizontal line. To judge from its appearance, as we saw it, it might have a very broad flat surface at the top. The shepherds whom we met said it was higher than Woo-tai. Annual worship is offered here by officers whom the Emperor deputes to keep up an old practice. The worship of mountains was an element in the ancient Persian religion before the introduction of the Magian system, and it is described in Herodotus.

Our course was down a rapid descent. In the evening we were at the bottom, sixty *le* from Woo-tai, and just on the edge of the plain, at a village called Tung-shan-te, "foot of the east hill." Here we were two hundred and forty *le* (eighty miles) from Tai-tung and forty from the town called Ta-ying. Both are to the north. Wolves are spoken of as being very fierce here; two or three persons in the village are said to have been not long since bitten by them. Wheat begins to be grown a little way out on the plain. The plain here is in fact a broad valley.

Thursday, October 31*st.*—This morning we left our quarters at six, and crossed the plain in a north-easterly direction to Ta-ying. A great road passes down it leading to Tai-chow and other cities, and bearing south-west. The river which runs through this valley is the Poo-to, which rises near Ta-ying and pursues its windings by Tai-chow to the south-west, afterwards bending round to the south-east and entering the province of Chihle near Chen-ting-foo.

The *loess* formation here begins again, and occurs across the valley, forming hills which stand isolated, and also clothing the hollows of the mountains at their base.

Being on a great road, we met many muleteers bringing loads from Peking. Some knew our muleteers and greeted them. One as a mark of friendship gave my driver two newly-baked cakes, which, without a word of needless comment, were duly accepted and enjoyed.

At Ta-ying it was market-day. A crowd of people pressed into our inn. As soon as we had arrived, a military officer from Ping-hing-kwan heard of us, and came to our inn to see who we were. I went out to meet him. A rather stern man on a horse stood in the inn-yard surrounded by the crowd and his underlings. After the first questions, I asked him for protection from the crowd, that would not allow us leisure to have our breakfast. He said it was natural that the crowd in a new place should wish to see us. He would himself like to look at any *ping-ku* [1] we might have with us. He referred to our passports, which would be proof of our right to be here. I produced mine, which he read on his horse and returned to me. I said my two companions also had similar documents. He replied that one was enough for him to inspect; he had while riding past just come in to see who we were. Here the catechist began to speak, when he said, "Oh, it is you that have brought these people here." This he said in a not very agreeable tone. I therefore called to the catechist that he should bring some books to give to the officer; they were graciously accepted, and given to a follower to carry. The officer then turned his horse towards the inn gate, and ordered his attendants to drive all the intruders out of the yard. On his leaving immediately after, it might have been supposed that the attendants would make some attempt to expel the crowd; but nothing was further from their ideas; they made no effort of the kind. The burden of controlling the crowd must fall on us, and we adopted the simple plan of selling books. We were too crowded in the inn. It was necessary for us to go into the street, each with a pile of books, to draw away a part of the idle onlookers. The innkeeper and his satellites would then be able to prosecute their duties. In the street selling the books was preferable to giving, because the crowd was thus prevented from disorderly snatching. At a market or a fair it is essential to sell our Christian books if we would secure order.

When you meet a small knot of Chinese alone, they will not, as a rule, buy books, but they will take them thankfully if given. In a crowd, however, the laws of the human mind make a man willing to part with a sum of money for his book. He is excited. One man excites another. Example is infectious. If a man sees one buy he wishes also to buy. The Chinese become different in a

---

[1] Both words mean "hold in the hand;" hence "evidence," "proof."

crowd to what they are when alone; they become eager to buy what in other circumstances they would not care for—in very many cases I saw them borrowing money rather than not buy. The excitement is too great for them.

A Buddhist priest carefully examined a copy of Mark's Gospel. He thought much of it and decided to buy. Having no money, he went to a shop to borrow some. Coming back, he noticed that Acts was thicker than Mark, and wished to exchange. Although his money was two cash short, he was allowed on the ground of benefit of clergy.

Another, after buying Luke, notices that it is labelled volume three. He wishes to change it for a Testament, as being a complete book, but is anxious not to pay more money. The unreasonableness of this is pointed out to him. He presses the exchange on the ground that Luke is imperfect. At last he brings the extra money and receives the Testament.

One poor man with a sickly-looking face came to ask for medicine to cure him of opium. He was told that we had none, but here was a book exhorting the victims of opium to abandon the habit, and containing a good recipe. "That," said he, "is the book I want." Others, hearing that this book is for sale for four small coins, seize it with avidity and carry it away exulting. The misery produced by opium is a lasting and everywhere present evil. Much opium is grown on the hills in this part of Shanse.

We came on in the afternoon thirty more *le* to Ping-hing-kwan, a pass in the inner Great Wall. We first came to a fort. It is on a *loess* hill with large fissures in it seventy or eighty feet deep. Some of the party went up the hill, and others proceeded by a path at the bottom of one of the fissures; consequently they speedily became separated by a considerable difference in altitude. We were for some time in a difficulty to find each other. One calamity will soon follow another. The petty officers of a *hiun-kie*, a military mandarin, came forward to insist that the mules and their riders should all go to the *yamen* of their superior for examination. This was declined, and an answer was given that it was necessary for us first to go to an inn. In half an hour we met again at an inn outside of the north gate of the fort. The mandarin underlings did not again appear.

Friday, November 1st.—Starting before daylight, we left the neighbourhood of the fort, and ascended the pass above us to the Great Wall. The wall is here very dilapidated, and a mere frame of thin spars serves for a gate. A few rods of wall on the east side were ready to sink on occasion of the next rainfall. A decayed tower on one or two of the neighbouring heights indicated how little of the work of Tsin-shi-hwang now remains. The wall maintains a decent appearance only where it has been placed in repair within a few centuries, as on the roads leading from Mongolia to Peking. Yet the Ping-hing-kwan might be well protected, for on the north side of it we came down a valley in the *loess* formation eight or ten miles in length, and in many parts the road is very narrow and flanked by deep fissures. These fissures would form a perfect bar to the progress of invaders if the road were fortified. They are evidently made by water loosening the *loess*, which then falls in avalanches. In one place a broad gorge is crossed by a bridge which rests on a thin wall of friable soil five or six feet thick. Below is an arched water-way for the water of the fissure to escape by. Thirty feet above this arch is the road along the narrow wall. It is strengthened with stones above, but a part is cracked, and unless soon repaired, only three or four feet in the width of the road will be left.

In many parts the road winds round the edge of a precipice at the end of one of the fissures. The action of water perpetually tends to lengthen the fissure. Damp rises from the bottom and rain falls on the top; the whole structure is disturbed, and a new piece of the *loess* falls. Then the road is broken in upon, and the people widen it on the other side by cutting away a new portion of the *loess*. The windings of the road, like those of a river, are in this way constantly growing larger. The sight from the fissure's top will shake weak nerves. You look down sixty, eighty, or a hundred feet of perpendicular depth. The *loess* is usually a fine mould, uniform in texture and very light, but occasionally strata of gravel occur, and also calcareous nodules. The gravel would come by water action during the time of deposition of the *loess*. The *loess* rests on various kinds of rocks, as if blown on them after they had assumed their present position.

We are now on a higher country than yesterday. Our position is at the back of the ridge we crossed at Ping-hing-kwan. No wheat grows here. Oats, *kau-liang*, and black beans are the common produce of the soil. The land-tax is three *fen* per *mow*, or about tenpence an acre.

At mid-day we had to brave the pressure of another crowd, violently anxious to see the strangers feed. It was a market-day. The place was named Tung-ho-nan, "the Eastern Honan" (*honan*, "south of river"). We took advantage of the presence of the crowd to sell a few books.

In the afternoon we came eastward along a beautiful valley to the city of Ling-kiow, which we reached after travelling thirteen miles. The valley was evidently an old lake, the waters of which found their exit at the south-east corner. On each side are *loess* terraces of moderate height, and beyond them rocky hills. It is the valley of the Tang-ho, the same river we crossed at Tang-hien, near Pau-ting-foo. In many parts the valley is left for pasture. We saw feeding there goats, sheep, oxen, donkeys, horses, and pigs, all in harmony.

Saturday, November 2d.—This morning we left at six A.M. the valley of Ling-kiow, where yesterday afternoon we sold a large number of books. Our road lay over the Yun-tsai-ling, "pass of many-coloured clouds." The rock is limestone, which tends to form the most picturesque perpendicular crags and summit pinnacles, chiselled out, as local legend would say, by the hand of some giant or fairy, but in fact by the dissolving power of rain-water, continued through unnumbered years. The limestone is worked two miles away from the road. Though so late in the year, we noticed one blue flower among the abundant grasses.

No small amount of traffic goes over this pass towards Kwang-chang. We were now not far to the north of Tau-ma-kwan, a pass by which the Tang river, whose name remains from the time of the Emperor Yau, B.C. 2500, flows into the great plain of Chihle.

Reached Chau-pai at the breakfast hour. Poverty marks the appearance of the people. Prices are as follows:—Wages, 60 copper cash [1] per day and three meals; cotton cloth, 40 cash per foot; unspun cotton, 250 cash per *catty;* oatmeal, 30 cash per *catty;* wheat flour, 60 cash; suit of clothes, including hat, shoes, and hose, 4000 cash, or one pound of English money nearly. The tax on land produce is 440 cash for oats, 370 for tall millet, 280 for buckwheat. Miscellaneous products are 140. Fuel, mountain brushwood, dry straw, and grass can be had for the gathering. No potatoes or wheat are grown here. There are cabbages and melons. In Peking a labourer gets from one to two pounds a month, if not found in food. In England a labourer possesses many comforts which the Chinese workman cannot afford.

In the afternoon we crossed another mountain pass, Yi-ma-ling, or "horse-stage pass," to Ai-ho, "Artemisia river." The rock was limestone throughout, and there was the same appearance of cathedral-like architecture in the erect precipices, very various in colour and appearance, beside which the road wound. On the western ascent the valley was covered with minute stones for several miles. These

---

[1] At present 1700 cash are exchanged for a tael of silver, and nearly four taels go to an English pound. A *catty* is a pound and one-third in weight.

are all fragments of limestone rock reduced to a small size by water action. In parts large boulders occurred. On the east side of the pass there were traces of iron in red sand and red-coloured limestone. A red hill south of the pass seemed to be the spot where the iron might be found. The road was cut through some strata of mould and gravel which seemed to have been gathered — the mould from *loess* hills not far off, and the gravel from the rocks above the deposit.

The Chinese never fail to erect temples in passes; they are intended to protect travellers from evil influences, robbers, and attacks from wild animals. I entered a temple dedicated to Lau-kiun, founder of Taouism. On the walls were painted twenty-five metamorphoses of this personage, consisting of scenes in his life, of course chiefly imaginary.

Sunday, November 3d.—Came last night to a village where we are perched on one of the undulations of the *loess* formation. In front of us is a little river and a wide reach of cultivated land to the south. It is a branch of the valley of the river called Ku-ma-ho, along which we are now to travel eastward to Tsze-king-kwan. The situation of the village is picturesque. Brooks of pure water irrigate the region for several months in the year. In summer, say the people, these rivulets dry up, and they are great sufferers from drought. They are then obliged to draw water from very wide and deep wells. There is no goitre here, probably because the country is both high and open.

The fields are all ploughed in November to be in readiness for the millet, which is sown in spring. The country is too high for wheat. Winnowing and threshing are proceeding vigorously. The people use a flail whose flying piece, of strong, flat basketwork, is two feet by five inches in size.

Visited a village a mile to the eastward. Went into a temple of Kwan-te, god of war. The pictures on the walls were scenes from the "Romance of the Three Kingdoms," A.D. 200, the time when Kwan-te, god of war, flourished. This hero was strong enough, and had sufficient energy and martial fire, to take a man's head off as he sat on his horse. In one case the body of one of his enemies remained (so the painter represented it) sitting on the horse when the head was on the ground at the feet of Kwan-te's steed. The conventional face of Kwan-te is very red and very decided, honest, and brave. The eyes are long, narrow, and much deflected.

In answer to an inquiry if they smoked opium, the people who pressed into the temple said they did not. They were then reminded that although they did not smoke opium, this temple was a witness that they had a fault of another kind. They forgot God who gave them the ploughing ox, the millet, the land, and the homes and families which made them happy.

Our sleeping and living room at this village was not good. It was used as a barn and a storing house for mules' loads in wet weather. There was a large *kang* at one end which we occupied.

Not finding wheat, flour, or mutton, we regaled ourselves with white rice and sardines which had come in the baggage of some of our party. In these regions oatmeal is the staple of the people, and animal food is a rarity which the poor never see except at a wedding, a funeral, at the New Year, or at the feasts in the fifth and eight months.

Monday, November 4th, 1872.—Leaving Ai-ho in the dark, we continued our home journey partly on the river bed and partly through roads in the *loess* to Kwang-chang. Here I filled a small bottle with a specimen of *loess* to carry home for analysis. Kwang-chang is less important than Ling-chiow, but is in a valley of remarkably fine scenery. Limestone continues to be the prevailing rock.

The road from Yu-chow to Pau-ting passes by this city. Our course lay on the south side through an extensive suburb. Here I noticed a large wooden tablet over the door of a retired mandarin, sixty years of age. It was presented to him by Wo-jen and Kia-cheng, two chief secretaries at court. He had long served the Government in conjunction with these well-known officers of State, and this was the way in which they had shown their friendship and respect. His office was a *tai-chau* of the Han-lin-yuen. In Peking such a testimonial of regard would probably have been placed in the house of the person so honoured, and its position would be in the centre of the visitor's hall, under the roof facing the south. In these parts, as at Siuen-hwa-foo, it is the fashion to place them outside of the house, over the door facing the street—a position preferred in Peking by physicians for exhibiting monumental tablets presented by grateful patients.

A little farther I noticed an advertisement issued by a Buddhist priest, stating that his temple needing repairs, it was his duty to solicit donations. The work of restoration was now complete, and the announcement was hereby made of the re-opening of the temple on certain days, three in number, on which occasion he respectfully invited contributors and others to be present. Those who had not already given were urged to do so on the ground that money should in itself be despised, and that great happiness would be secured by giving, or, as he expressed it, they should give that they might enlarge the field of their happiness, *yi kwang foo tien*. The dedication is called *kai-kwang*, "open light," a phrase which refers to the opening of the eyes of the image.

Outside of the town on the east was a Tung-yo-miau, or "temple to the spirit of the eastern mountain," *i.e.*, Tai-shan in Shantung. Beside it stands a pagoda of five stories.

Passing down the valley, our mules crossed the river Ku-ma-ho, at first by wading; then, when the river became deeper, the mules crossed by bridges. The valley became narrow, and its scenery, as the sun shone through a mist, was very fine. The white spray of the rushing river shone upon by the sunlight was in lovely contrast to the dark waters beneath. The limestone cliffs cast a deep shadow. Above them were the towers of the inner Great Wall appearing at frequent intervals. Beneath flows the river, threading its way through a wide dry strand, overspread with white and blue pebbles of limestone, large and small. Over them, once in every few years, comes down with overwhelming force a torrent from the mountains, which brings a new supply of stones, pebbles, and sand, which disturb all marks, obliterate all paths, and permanently raze the old bed.

We breakfasted at Foo-too-yu. The road from Yu-chow to Pau-ting-foo goes this way to the southward. Our course is east. Thirty towers are seen here, all belonging to the Great Wall. They are on both sides of the river, and would form a convenient refuge for soldiers armed with bow and arrow, but would be of no use in modern warfare. One of my fellow-travellers and I mounted one of these towers by holes in the bricks. They are intended to be ascended by ladders. The tower is built with three arched passages from east to west; there are four arched windows on the east and west sides, and three on the north and south. Upwards of twenty arches, large and small, meet the eye on entering. The structure is square, compact, and strong. Below there are four tiers of hewn granite stones; above large bricks are used. The top is castellated. We ascended and found there a brick platform twenty feet from the ground and surrounded by a castellated parapet. An inscription of the Ming dynasty let into the wall stated that the erection of the tower was completed in the fourth year of Wan-leih, A.D. 1576, and is therefore three centuries old. Any such towers in the Great Wall near Peking may therefore be ascribed to the Ming dynasty with safety. It is not necessary to suppose that these square strong-looking structures have lasted through the summer rains and winter winds and snowstorms of two thousand years. Two great periods of rebuilding and fortifying the more important forts and the more important portions of the wall have occurred, each after a Tartar dynasty. The Sui dynasty, following the Northern Wei, a Turkish race in the sixth century, thought it well to fortify the boundaries of the Empire on its north side. So the Ming also, after expelling the Mongols, determined to produce an impression on the Tartar hordes by the same appearance of an impassable barrier.

These towers are erected at each end of the plank bridge by which the Ku-ma is here crossed, and are also seen crowning the crags east and west as far as the eye can reach.

From Foo-too-yu we proceeded towards "Iron Pass" (Tie-ling), the road over which was repaired thirty years ago. The officer who superintended the work has erected a monument in commemoration of it; its date is 1835. In crossing this pass we also proceeded through a broad *loess* formation. We then came to the banks of the Ku-ma and followed it all the way to Tsze-king-kwan. This river is crossed in several places by bridges so constructed as to be movable at pleasure. Shrubs, twigs, bean stubble, fresh branches, and straw are laid across prostrate trunks of trees, which rest on inclined posts struck as piles into the river bottom. All are removed when the summer rains are approaching, for fear of their being carried away. Land-tax in this neighbourhood is eight or nine *tow* of the produce per *mow;* in bad years it is reduced to three or four *tow*.[1] In the evening we stayed at Ta-yai-yu, "pass of the pagoda cliff." We passed the night in a partly ruined building. The large gaps made by bad weather coming from the north were partially covered by some rush mats. It rained during the night. Venturing out in the dark was found to be dangerous by one of our party, who slipped on some soft mud and kissed his mother earth.

Among our visitors in the evening were some men who had heard of the visit of the Rev. W. C. Burns to a town in this neighbourhood, Pan-pi-tien, several years ago, and had

---

[1] A *tow* is ten pints. This amounts to sixty pints per acre.

seen books which he distributed at that time. This was an interesting reminiscence of a man whose example of devotion and self-denial was of the highest type.

November 5th.—Left late on account of the rain. Here and there we met laden mules. Some carried wine, others cotton, or bags of sugar, or drugs, or pine wood, or cloth. We also saw many herds of sheep and goats feeding. Their bleat often reached the ear from far away, mingling with the jingle of the mules' bells. One pedestrian had gone to Kwang-chang to sell some merchandise, and was now returning with his yoke over his shoulder to his home at Yu-chow. Another having a heavy pack on his shoulder sat on a stone on the roadside immediately in front of another stone, against which he supported the pack while he rested himself.

We now saw the last of the Great Wall. In many places it had dwindled to a mere heap of unhewn stones. But at Tsze-king-kwan we saw it in its best condition. As we approached, it became a very conspicuous object, mounting lofty heights, and presenting everywhere a castellated appearance. It is here built carefully with stone below and bricks above. Tsze-king-kwan is imposing. Inscriptions of the reign of Wan-leih abound. Several times hostile armies have come into Chihle by this route. It is much easier than that of Nan-kow. No vast beds of boulders like those at Ku-yung-kwan have here to be crossed. Great exertions have been made therefore to fortify it. In one inscription over the north gate of the fort it is called *King nan te ye hiung kwan,* "the first strong pass south of the capital." There are more than two hundred families in the fort. The walls and gates are strong and lofty. Customs officers are posted here, who were somewhat troublesome. They demanded transit duty. This we declined, on the ground that we were not merchants, but foreigners travelling with passports and without goods. After loudly vociferating for ten minutes that we must pay, they let us alone.

On the south side of the fortress we found ourselves at the top of a rapidly descending mountain road leading through a most beautiful valley ornamented among other things with persimmon trees. These with their bright red fruit constitute a lovely feature in October both here and in North China generally, especially in hilly regions. The trees are larger, some of them, than the largest apple and pear trees, being thirty or forty feet high. There is a strong astringent element in the fruit when young. When quite soft and ripe, the astringent flavour deserts the pulp but remains in the rind. The persimmon is preserved dry by the Chinese, and in this form lasts till spring. The leaves fall before the fruit, and the trees we saw were at the time nearly bare of them.

We stopped for refreshment at a small inn on the roadside, and enjoyed the view of the valley, richly coloured with autumn leaves, filling the eye with beauty before they fall to the earth and become again a part of that soil from which they were formed.

We descended fast from this spot, and took notice of the rapid change in level from Tsze-king-kwan to the Yu-chow plains. There we were fifteen hundred feet higher than the plain, and yet we were apparently on a level with the Kwang-chang valley. Richthoven went this way to Woo-tai, and doubtless the rapid elevation of level he here witnessed formed a large part of the elevation he assigns to Woo-tai-shan. A little river followed the road for some miles. The valley is bounded by lofty heights, among which many limestone crags are seen deeply indented by the rain-storms of bygone ages. My muleteer pointed to one of these limestone mountains, and with some enthusiasm said, *Che shan shi tsai chang ti you ya*, "This mountain has certainly grown into a very rare and elegant form." But his attention was at once recalled from the poetry of nature to certain perverse exhibitions of temper on the part of one of his animals, which made it necessary for him to crack his loud whip, and urge him on by words which the animal seemed to understand. At the bridges the river is thirty yards wide. Here and there it is diversified by faded green willows. Wheat and cotton now begin to appear. In the upper valley of the Ku-ma these crops are unknown. The field for the botanist seems extensive in the valley which we traversed this afternoon. A great variety of trees and plants grow there. The acacias which overshadowed our inn and the temple near it were very fine specimens of their kind. Over the valley were various other trees shining in their autumn beauty.

The people begin to look better dressed. In some of the mountain districts the clothing of many of them is insufficient. A young man of twenty-nine, whose habiliments were somewhat ragged, told me he had no wife, not being able to pay for one. Many other young men, he said, whom he knew, were in the same position. A boy of fifteen stood behind him also raggedly clothed. This lad, though so poor, had had five years' schooling. Their ordinary food was, they said, millet. They have neither oats nor wheat.

West of the Tsze-king-kwan, "purple twig pass," there are granite mountains as indicated by immense boulders in the river bed. They are rounded by constant attrition, and that very roundness attests their hardness. They present an irritating impediment to the rushing river, causing it to increase its dash and its spray as it roars past them. Remarkable veins of quartz were noticeable in some of these large blocks. Some crossed others at right angles, others at any and all angles. Now we were to enter again a region of softer and more pliable stone.

The Chinese passion for terse sentences arranged in couplets reaches even the mountains. There was there as everywhere a temple to Kwan-te. The words written on the door were *Shan men pu so tai siue feng*, "The temple door needs not to be locked; wait, and the snow will seal it up. In the old monastery why use a lamp? the moon shines into it." At the head of a list of subscribers to the temple funds was the sentence, *Yin kwo puh mei,* "Cause and effect are not concealed from observation." The idea intended to be conveyed in this obscure sentence is that virtue, almsgiving, and love to mankind cannot fail of recognition and reward. Or it may be that this list is intended to commemorate the charitable acts of the persons named.

Buddhism makes much of this doctrine of cause and effect, and asserts confidently that moral retribution attends all actions, good or bad, with the regularity of a fixed law.

Like other things in Buddhism, the doctrine is capable of being utilised in Christian teaching among a people to whom it is familiar. It is an example of the preparation for Christianity which we owe to the doctrinal system both of Buddhism and Confucianism, and in a less degree to Taouism also.

THE END.

www.ingramcontent.com/pod-product-compliance
Lightning Source LLC
Chambersburg PA
CBHW031945230426
43672CB00010B/2054